TENBizPlan

Dynamic Business Planning
for Start-ups

2ND EDITION

RON IMMINK & BRIAN O-KANE

·OAK·TREE·PRESS·

www.oaktreepress.com

Oak Tree Press
19 Rutland Street, Cork, Ireland
www.oaktreepress.com

A catalogue record of this book is
available from the British Library.

ISBN 1 86076 244-1

Acknowledgements

The authors acknowledge the copyright in parts of the content of the
Minister for Enterprise, Trade and Employment, Ireland and the
contribution of Jack Foley to the first edition of **TENBizPlan**.

Disclaimer

The contents of this guide are believed to be correct at the time of
printing but no responsibility can be taken by the authors or
publisher for any errors herein. Readers should take professional
advice before entering into any legally binding commitments or
investing any funds.

CONTENTS

FOREWORD

Economic history teaches us that strong and sustainable economies can only be developed in countries that have vibrant, entrepreneurial and effective small business sectors.

The development of entrepreneurial skills is therefore one of the greatest challenges facing all world governments.

The importance of the small business sector to all economies is evidenced by the fact that nearly one-half of all national and international funding in developed, developing and transitional economies is currently directed at the development of the skills of those working in micro-enterprises (MEs) and small and medium-sized enterprises (SMEs).

For many people with established businesses, self-employment provides an above average income, an opportunity for personal growth and a secure long-term future.

The objectives of this book are two-fold. First, to help you to understand the process you must follow if you want to succeed in business and, second, to ensure that you understand, can identify and avoid the problems that lead to business failure.

I am delighted to recommend it to you.

Dr Alistair Somerville Ford
Chief Executive, Institute of Commercial Management

INTRODUCTION

Welcome to **TENBizPlan**, a dynamic approach to business planning for start-ups that shows you how you can implement world-class best practice in the use of business planning for the establishment, development and management of start-up ventures, in a simple, practical and engaging way so that you can incorporate the lessons of other entrepreneurs into the planning of your own venture.

TENBizPlan has been designed to take you through the whole process of starting a business, from first thoughts about self-employment to the practicalities of start-up, with a specific emphasis on preparation of a detailed, robust and practical business plan. In each chapter, there are exercises designed to make you think about your proposed business. By writing down your answers to these exercises, you will find that you not only clarify your own thoughts but you are directly building up the content of your business plan – an essential document to guide you to sustained success – and providing evidence to support it.

The **TENBizPlan** approach is neither short nor easy. It is a comprehensive programme of knowledge and techniques for those who are serious about their preparation to go into business and about learning how to prepare an effective business plan. It is, in fact, very much like being in business – not for the faint-hearted but exciting and rewarding for those with the commitment to stay the course.

Good luck!

Ron Immink

Brian O'Kane

1

THE TENBIZPLAN
APPROACH

Research and experience both show that an effective business plan is one of the critical factors contributing to successful start-up businesses. The fact that almost 50% of new businesses world-wide fail within three years of start-up, and that 75% of these failures can be shown to be due to lack of planning, emphasises the importance of a structured approach to planning.

The structure for the process of business planning proposed in this guide is one that has been used successfully, with minor variations, in a wide variety of situations, across many industries, in several European countries.

The main reasons for business planning are:

- To establish the fundamental viability of your project
- To define realistic goals for the business and map out the steps and intermediate targets required in achieving them
- To act as a yardstick for measuring progress against the targets
- To communicate your ideas to outsiders, particularly those you want to invest in your business.

In start-ups and very new businesses – to which **TENBizPlan** is addressed – business planning is a process that is carried out to define the goals of the business and the means by which they will be achieved.

The process involves a thorough analysis of the major factors involved in achieving the success of the new business. The output from the process is a formal business plan document that records the final decisions and targets.

THE PROCESS OF BUSINESS PLANNING

The business planning process for start-ups can be as formal or as informal as you like. It may be completed in a weekend or it may take you several months working full-time. What is important is that you consider – and at the end of the process, are able to answer – the following questions, which the **TENBizPlan** approach calls "Key Questions":

- Do I understand the process of business planning?
- Am I the right person to set up and run a business?
- Have I got a feasible idea?
- What formalities must I complete before I start my business?
- What sales do I expect and how will I generate them?
- How, and with what resources, will I meet my planned sales?
- Can I describe the people I will need and how I will organise them?
- How will I fund my business?
- Have I the best plan possible?
- Have I got a business plan document that does justice to my plan?

> **Until you can answer these questions convincingly, your business planning is not complete**

Each chapter in this book has a Key Question. It's asked at the start of the chapter, and again at the end.

The Key Question for this chapter is:

Do I understand the process of business planning?

This is a critical question that underpins the **TENBizPlan** approach, which distinguishes quite clearly between the **process** of business planning and the **output** from that process – the business plan document.

The process of business planning involves research and thinking aimed at identifying:

- What your business will do
- How it will do it
- What resources it needs to do so
- Where those resources will be sourced
- What the likely financial outcome of the business will be
- What milestones and targets will measure its progress
- What evidence underpins all of the above.

Each chapter in this book guides you through information and exercises designed to help you answer these questions.

But the core of the **TENBizPlan** approach is the Key Questions. Let's look at the questions for the chapters that follow.

Am I the right person to set up and run a business?

Some people are born entrepreneurs; others could never face the responsibilities involved. The decision to take on self-employment is not one to be made lightly, because of the risks involved. You need to consider yourself, your family and/or dependants, your personal and financial circumstances before you can decide whether self-employment is the right choice for you. If you lack the combination of personal qualities, skills and experience that are essential for entrepreneurship, you should undertake appropriate training to fill the gaps before starting your new business.

Have I got a feasible idea?

Not simply have you an idea, but have you a *feasible* idea? The marketplace can be cruel, rewarding only a small number of the millions of new products and services that are launched each year. Whether your idea will work in the marketplace is a critical question. Just as important is the research you have done to prove that your idea will work. Until you have established the feasibility of your business idea, you should limit your exposure to risk.

What formalities must I complete before you start my business?

In most countries, businesses are subject to regulation. It is important that you identify and comply with those regulations that apply to your new business.

What sales do I expect and how will I generate them?

Sales are the engine of business growth. Without sales, you have nothing. So the level of sales that you plan for your business is critical. Equally critical is a clear explanation of what you plan to do to create these sales – since they will not happen of their own accord.

How, and with what resources, will I meet my planned sales?

Generating sales is not the end of the story. Once a customer has placed an order, they expect that order to be fulfilled – promptly, efficiently, with a product or service that meets their needs, at a price they can afford. Are you ready to do this?

Can I describe the people I will need and how I will organise them?

People are critical to any business. How many people, with what skills and experience and how they are organised for maximum efficiency and effectiveness are all important questions.

How will I fund my business?

The 64-million-dollar question, literally. Many entrepreneurs start here and then try to build their business according to the funds they can raise. A better approach is to plan your business and then to seek funding based on a clear, logical and robust plan that sets out what funding is needed, what it will be used for and what risk and return can be expected.

Have I the best plan possible?

If you haven't, perhaps you should look at it again. A weak business plan can cripple – or kill – your new business.

Have I got a business plan document that does justice to my plan?

As outlined earlier, your business plan document serves many purposes. It needs to address a number of audiences and capture the essence of your business – in as few pages as possible.

When you can answer all these questions convincingly, with clear evidence underpinning your answers, you have completed the process of business planning. At the point, you can focus on the output – the business plan document.

It's important to understand that business planning is not a variation of fortune-telling but a skill like any other management function. It is a dynamic on-going process that helps the business to make sense of emerging trends and to react faster than the competition. Business planning involves identifying the factors that will make the business successful, and then following through with plans and action to make sure these factors happen. It is a dynamic and on-going process that has to be incorporated into the everyday management of the business.

> *Are you in earnest? Seize this very minute: What you can do, or dream, you can do. Begin it and the work will be completed.*
> JOHANN WOLFGANG VON GOETHE

THE OUTPUT FROM THE PROCESS

The output of the business planning process is a business plan, a document that summarises these points about your business:

- Where it has come from
- Where it is now
- Where it is going in the future
- How it intends to get there
- What resources it needs to fulfil its plans
- What makes it likely to succeed
- What threats or disadvantages must be overcome on the way.

Just as each business is unique, its business plan is also unique. However, bankers and investors have come to expect a broadly standard format that presents information in an easily-digested logical sequence.

The format that **TENBizPlan** uses can be summarised as:

- **Executive Summary:** A single page that encourages further reading
- **Introduction:** Basic information about the business and the purpose of the plan
- **Promoter(s):** Who you (and your team) are and your qualifications for starting and running the business

A simple format that can be adapted to most businesses' needs

- **Project Overview:** A description of the business, its mission statement, trends in its industry, targets, employment (actual and potential) and the legal status of the business
- **Marketing:** A summary of your marketing plan, backed up by a market overview, details of your customers, competition, products/services, price, distribution and promotion strategies and a sales forecast
- **Process & Resources:** Your products/services in more detail, how they are made/delivered, how you will ensure quality, what staff you will need and how they will be organised
- **Finance & Funding:** A summary of your financial projections, with your funding requirement (and your own contribution) highlighted

- **Appendices:** Including financial projections – profit and loss account, balance sheet and cashflow – and any other relevant information.

This structure for the business plan document is shown in more detail in **Appendix A** and is provided in a Microsoft Word template format on the **TENBizPlan** website (**http://www.tenbizplan.com**).

No matter how poor a writer you consider yourself to be, if you can't put your business proposition clearly and persuasively in a written business plan document, it suggests that you have more thinking to do.

It doesn't mean that your project won't work. On the contrary, your business may have the potential to be a resounding success — but you need to be able to communicate it!

THE TENBizPLAN APPROACH

TENBizPlan provides the know-how needed to complete a business plan to the highest standards:

- Leading you, step-by-step, through all the knowledge you need to complete a business plan
- Providing interesting and challenging exercises, as well as templates to help you to construct and organise your business plan document
- Showing you – simply and intuitively – how to extract the numbers at each stage so that, by the time you have finished your research, your financial projections are prepared and ready for you to use.

You should work through each of the chapters in sequence, completing the exercises as you go. Each chapter is focused on one of the Key Questions. Make sure that you can answer the Key Question before moving ahead to start the next chapter.

The **TENBizPlan** approach uses exercises, which are designed to encourage you to explore your environment, gather information and draw conclusions from it. Each chapter contains a number of exercises that lead you through the process of business planning, all the while helping you towards the preparation of your business plan document. Document all your answers to the exercises. They form an essential part of your evidence.

From time to time, you may need to return to an earlier exercise to correct your analysis, based on new information that has now come to light. This is natural, since business planning is an iterative, not a linear, process.

TENBizPlan identifies three elements in the output from the business planning process:

- Text
- Evidence
- Numbers.

Text

The text elements of the business plan are important in attracting – and keeping – the reader's attention. This is so whether the reader is a potential investor, a banker, a supplier or key member of staff.

Some of the exercises within this book directly input as draft text into the text sections of your business plan document. These exercises are all clearly marked like so:

In this way, you can prepare a first draft of your business plan document, as you work through this book and the process of business planning.

The structure used by **TENBizPlan** for the business plan document, outlined in the previous section, is shown in more detail in **Appendix A** and is provided in a Microsoft Word template format on the **TENBizPlan** website (**http://www.tenbizplan.com**).

Evidence

Most of the exercises in this book help you to provide evidence that supports the targets, strategies, decisions and resulting text and financial projections that make up your business plan.

Some of this evidence is your own answers to the exercises in this book, other evidence comes from market research and external sources.

All of it builds up into a "Book of Evidence" that supports your business plan document and provides immediate answers to queries raised by readers of your plan.

Each evidence-collecting exercise is clearly marked like so:

Numbers

Business planning requires that the business' activities and expected results are not only described in words but are also translated into financial projections to show the viability of the proposed venture.

For this, you can use dedicated financial projection software, spreadsheets that you develop yourself, or paper-based models.

However you prepare your financial projections, it is important that you fully understand and explore the financial implications of your business plan. Unless you do this, you have not completed the process of business planning. Simply hiring someone, however qualified or experienced, to tack on financial projections is not the answer – it is essential that you understand the financial implications of the business decisions and actions you plan to take.

Exercises that develop information for inclusion in your financial projections are within the Guides, which are all clearly marked like so:

In this way, you can prepare a first draft of your financial projections, as you work through this book and the process of business planning.

In **Chapter 9**, you will subject your financial projections to the kind of rigorous analysis that investors and bankers use, making certain that you have explored fully the potential of your new business.

This is the heart of the **TENBizPlan** approach – a systematic review of the financial projections, so that you can explore the consequences of decisions made during the planning process. Just as airlines use flight simulators to train pilots and test new technology, you can use this approach as a business simulator to test your strategies in a safe environment – a model of your business – before putting them into practice.

This exploration is the real core of the business planning process. It empowers entrepreneurs to:

- Examine systematically every detail of the business, the cost structure of each product, the make-up of every overhead expense, etc. to produce a composite plan of small improvements that in aggregate may dramatically improve profitability and/or cashflow

- Identify an emerging trend (advantageous or threatening) and quickly quantify the impact on the business, as well as testing the steps needed to offset the effects

- Take a broad view of the business and explore larger issues involving capital investment, employment and volume issues.

Clearly, this key element of the process of business planning is greatly facilitated by suitable software, whether dedicated financial projection software or spreadsheets you have designed yourself. However, the approach itself is independent of any software – you don't need to learn a new package or new skills in order to implement the **TENBizPlan** approach. Instead, you use the approach with whatever tools you are comfortable with. And if you want to use software, the **TENBizPlan** website (**http://www.tenbizplan.com**) provides some recommendations.

The beauty of the **TENBizPlan** approach is that long before you enter the Execution stage, where the planning is tested under fire in the real business world, you can reduce the risk of start-up failure. And that's what business planning is all about.

In summary, the **TENBizPlan** approach to business planning is:

- Develop the knowledge and complete the research to prepare financial projections and a business plan document

- Complete a dynamic analysis to explore all aspects of your forecast to produce the best possible plan

- Back-up your finished plan with research and evidence

- Continue to use the approach to develop your skills as you manage your business through its start-up and initial growth phase.

The TENBizPlan Approach to Business Planning

Text

There is no draft text for input into your business plan document created as part of the process of business planning in this chapter.

Evidence

There is no evidence created as part of the process of business planning in this chapter.

Numbers

There are no numbers created for input into your financial projections as part of the process of business planning in this chapter.

Key Question

The Key Question for this chapter is:

Do I understand the process of business planning?

To answer the question, you need to:

- Understand the distinction between the process of business planning and its output, the business plan document
- The structure of a standard business plan document
- The **TENBizPlan** approach to business planning.

2

PERSONAL

ASSESSMENT

The Key Question for this chapter is:

Am I the right person to set up and run a business?

Launching your own business is like writing your own personal declaration
of independence from the corporate beehive, where you sell bits of your life in
forty-hour (or longer) chunks in return for your paycheck.
Going into business for yourself, becoming an entrepreneur,
is the modern-day equivalent of pioneering on the old frontier.

PAULA NELSON

Before you begin reading this chapter, turn to **Appendix A**, which shows the structure of a typical business plan. Notice that the first two sections of the business plan – the Executive Summary and the Introduction – cannot be written until the rest of the plan has been written.

So the first "real" section of the business plan is the one called "**The Promoter(s)**" – for a good reason: Behind every new venture is a promoter – the entrepreneur (or, in some cases, entrepreneurs). The success or failure of the new business depends on the drive, personality, experience and skills, network, personal circumstances and, last but definitely not least, the commitment of the promoter(s).

Bankers, financiers and those involved in enterprise support all over the world now support the view – well-documented by research – that the individual or individuals behind the business are the main asset of a business, more important than all the money or property invested in the business venture. And therefore, because the business is so dependent on them, the promoter(s) could also be the main liability of the business.

As a result, in analysing a business proposal, the first thing a financier does is to examine the people behind the idea. Sometimes, the analysis stops right there, because the financier does not trust the people, or does not have any confidence in their abilities, or simply does not believe what they say.

And, even if you are in the lucky position of not needing external funding to support your start-up, you still need to take an objective look at your suitability to run a business before you commit your time and resources.

Output from this chapter

This chapter will take you through the process of personal assessment, so that you are fully aware of your skills, abilities and experience and their value to your new business. It will also make you aware, perhaps, of some weaknesses – don't be concerned: Identifying weaknesses is the first step towards overcoming them.

By the end of this chapter, you will be able to write a first draft of the section in your business plan entitled "**The Promoter(s)**" – the section about yourself and your business partners – which will include for you and your business partners:

- Your name and contact details
- Your educational background, insofar as it is relevant to the business you plan to start
- A summary of your skills and experience and how they benefit the business

- Any other information that will help a reader of the business plan understand why you will make a success of the business.

You will probably refine this draft as you work through the other chapters in this book.

Links to other chapters

By the end of this chapter, you will be aware of the links to other stages in the **TENBizPlan** process of business planning, especially to:

- **Marketing & Sales (Chapter 5):** Throughout this guide, you will see the key role of marketing being emphasised, over and over again, because of its importance. How you market your business will reflect how you see yourself – cool and street-wise, business-like, or elegant and sophisticated. If you don't know yourself, you won't know how to market your business in a way that you will be comfortable with – and good at

- **People (Chapter 7):** If you are to manage people in your business, you need to be able to manage yourself, you need to know yourself. Your management style will reflect your personal style. And your skills and experience will dictate the kind of people you need to hire to help run your business, and thus your staffing costs

- **Finance & Funding (Chapter 8):** These will be impacted by your staffing costs (from **Chapter 7, People**). More importantly, if you are looking to raise finance from other people to start your business, you must be willing to risk some of your own money, however, little you may have. Therefore, you will need to identify how much money you are willing and able to invest in your own business.

All of the links will inform your first draft of the section, "**The Promoter(s)**", as well as influencing each other. So, later in the guide, you will have an opportunity to revise and redraft – for now, just read on.

> Entrepreneurs are risk-takers, willing to roll the dice with their money or their reputations on the line in support of an idea or enterprise. They willingly assume responsibility for the success or failure of a venture and are answerable for all its facets. The buck not only stops at their desk, it starts there too.
> VICTOR KIAM

WHAT MAKES AN ENTREPRENEUR?

Entrepreneurship is the dynamic process of creating wealth. It is undertaken by people who assume a risk in terms of money, energy, time and/or career commitment in order to create value by providing some product or service.

Research suggests people become entrepreneurs for one or more of four reasons:

- A dramatic change in their personal situation (unemployment, divorce)
- The availability of resources (idea, money)
- Possession of certain entrepreneurial skills
- The example of another successful entrepreneur.

Which of these apply to you?

A lot of time and money has been spent in universities and institutes all over the world to discover what makes the ideal or typical entrepreneur. However, researchers generally agree that there is no such thing. An international hi-tech venture needs a different kind of entrepreneur, with different skills and experience, from a local window-cleaning business. An entrepreneur active in the retail sector needs different traits from an entrepreneur in music publishing. There is no typical entrepreneur.

What the research shows are generic characteristics, which entrepreneurs have in a balance that varies from individual to individual but which exist in the entrepreneur to a greater degree than in the rest of the population.

Entrepreneurs are:

- **Well-rounded:** The person who can make the product, market it and count the money
- **Able to bounce back:** The person who can cope with mistakes and have the confidence to try again

Which of these apply to you?

- **Innovative:** Not an "inventor" in the traditional sense but a person who is able to carve out a new niche in the market, often a niche invisible to others
- **Results-orientated:** To make the business successful requires a drive that only comes from setting goals and targets and getting pleasure from achieving them

- **Professional risk-takers:** To succeed means taking measured risks. Often the successful entrepreneur uses a step-by-step approach to risk-taking, at each stage exposing themselves to only a measured amount of personal risk and moving from one stage to the next only as each decision is proved
- **Totally committed:** Hard work, energy and single-mindedness are essential elements in the entrepreneurial profile.

Note that the entrepreneurial characteristics required to launch a business successfully are often not those required for growth and, even more frequently, not those required to manage the business once it grows to any size. The role of the individual needs to change with the business as it develops and grows. In particular, the management skills of the entrepreneur – in managing staff, managing his/her own time, and in strategic planning – become more important as the business grows.

Research also highlights "success factors", which include:

- **Hard work:** Entrepreneurs work 65 hours on average every week in the year
- **Perseverance:** Rome was not built in a day, your business will not succeed overnight

Which of these apply to you?

- **Motivation:** The driving force behind your business
- **Social skills:** The ability to deal with people from all walks of life in a wide variety of circumstances
- **Leadership:** The ability to persuade people to follow your direction
- **Good management:** Not only in starting the business, but also in running it on an ongoing basis
- **Integrity:** Honesty to yourself and the people you work with
- **Good health:** Essential, since running a business is physically and mentally demanding
- **Common-sense:** Not as common as you might think
- **Luck:** Making your own luck helps
- **Support of family:** Are they fully behind you? Can they cope with the changes that self-employment will bring?
- **Clear initial goals:** Knowing what you want to achieve – and how to achieve it
- **Creativity:** Coming up with the ideas
- **Ability to accept uncertainty:** Being prepared to take risks.

SELF-ASSESSMENT

From research into traits of successful entrepreneurs and the success factors that they share, it is clear that there are a number of elements to be considered in conducting a self-assessment. The key elements are:

- Drive
- Personality
- Values
- Skills and experience
- Networks
- Personal circumstances
- Commitment.

Drive

The drive or motivation of the entrepreneur is one of the critical factors that determine how a new business will develop.

Entrepreneurship asks for a lot of commitment. It is both physically and mentally very demanding. Research shows that:

- The average working week for an entrepreneur is 65 hours

- Their income is unlikely to increase above normal salary levels

- Most entrepreneurs do not earn anything in the first 18 months.

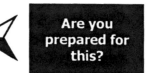

Are you prepared for this?

In that context, it is important to establish why you want to become self-employed. The "why?" has strong links to your view of life, the things that are important to you and your view of where you want to be in five years' or ten years' time. So, you need to ask yourself – and answer as honestly as you can – the questions in **Exercise 2.1**.

Exercise 2.1: Drive

What do you want out of life?
Where do you want to be in five years' time?
Where do you want to be in 10 years' time?
Does all this fit with self-employment as an option?

The questions in **Exercise 2.1** may appear very simple but they are often hard to answer. They cannot easily be answered in five minutes or 10, or an hour – or even in a day. Take plenty of time to think them through – take as long as you need. What you are trying to establish (and what any financial backer will try to establish) is whether your drive – the fuel for the engine that will power your venture – will be sufficient to go all the way, or whether it will run out just when the road gets difficult. These questions are essential in establishing whether entrepreneurship is what you really want.

The bottom line is whether you have enough drive to commit yourself to all the hard work, effort, blood, sweat and tears to make the business work, not just for today, but for tomorrow and the next five or 10 years. Only you can answer the question in **Exercise 2.2**.

Exercise 2.2: Why do I Want to be Self-Employed?

Check your motivation now! Write down the reasons why you want to become self-employed.

If you become discouraged later, whether during the planning process or when your business is operational, use your answer to this exercise to remind yourself of why you chose to become self-employed. Having this use in mind will focus your thinking and writing.

At this stage you should ask yourself, "What style of business do I want?". To be successful, the style of your business must fit with your motivation and personality. For example, the table below shows three styles of business, the expectation of the kind of business that the style arouses and the business attitude that goes with the style. Which style is closest to your own? Or have you a different style?

Business style	Business expectation	Business attitude
Craftsman	Lifestyle	Emotion
Trader	Build quickly and sell	Pragmatism
Dynasty	Long-term development over several generations	Ambition
		Sacrifice of short-term gains for the long-term

Each style sets different parameters for a new business and it's useful to bear them in mind as you develop your plans.

Personality

As a practical starting point in assessing your own personality, answer the questions in **Exercise 2.3**. Then ask two other people that you know well and trust to give their opinions.

> Persistency is what makes the impossible possible;
> the possible likely; and the likely definite.
> ROBERT HALF

> From as early as I can remember, my father would say to me,
> "The most important thing in life is to love what you're doing,
> because that's the only way you'll ever be really good at it".
> DONALD TRUMP

EXERCISE 2.3: PERSONALITY

Answer the questions yourself first. Then ask two other people who know you well to give their opinions. Stress that it is important that they give you honest answers (even if you don't like what they say!).

	Your own opinion	**Opinion 1**	**Opinion 2**
Can you "stick" with something for a long period of time?	☐ Yes ☐ No	☐ Yes ☐ No	☐ Yes ☐ No
Can you work alone?	☐ Yes ☐ No	☐ Yes ☐ No	☐ Yes ☐ No
Are you flexible?	☐ Yes ☐ No	☐ Yes ☐ No	☐ Yes ☐ No
Are you curious?	☐ Yes ☐ No	☐ Yes ☐ No	☐ Yes ☐ No
Can you take decisions?	☐ Yes ☐ No	☐ Yes ☐ No	☐ Yes ☐ No
Can you think on your feet?	☐ Yes ☐ No	☐ Yes ☐ No	☐ Yes ☐ No
Are you self-assured?	☐ Yes ☐ No	☐ Yes ☐ No	☐ Yes ☐ No
Do you like to take the initiative?	☐ Yes ☐ No	☐ Yes ☐ No	☐ Yes ☐ No
Are you an active person?	☐ Yes ☐ No	☐ Yes ☐ No	☐ Yes ☐ No
Are you enthusiastic?	☐ Yes ☐ No	☐ Yes ☐ No	☐ Yes ☐ No
Are you creative?	☐ Yes ☐ No	☐ Yes ☐ No	☐ Yes ☐ No
Are you patient?	☐ Yes ☐ No	☐ Yes ☐ No	☐ Yes ☐ No
Are you honest?	☐ Yes ☐ No	☐ Yes ☐ No	☐ Yes ☐ No
Can you work under pressure?	☐ Yes ☐ No	☐ Yes ☐ No	☐ Yes ☐ No
Can you set goals and priorities?	☐ Yes ☐ No	☐ Yes ☐ No	☐ Yes ☐ No
Are you a good listener?	☐ Yes ☐ No	☐ Yes ☐ No	☐ Yes ☐ No
Are you a good communicator?	☐ Yes ☐ No	☐ Yes ☐ No	☐ Yes ☐ No
Do you like to take responsibility?	☐ Yes ☐ No	☐ Yes ☐ No	☐ Yes ☐ No
Do you like new ideas?	☐ Yes ☐ No	☐ Yes ☐ No	☐ Yes ☐ No
Are you prepared to ask for help or advice when you need it?	☐ Yes ☐ No	☐ Yes ☐ No	☐ Yes ☐ No
Do you believe in yourself and in your own abilities?	☐ Yes ☐ No	☐ Yes ☐ No	☐ Yes ☐ No
Do you get along with people?	☐ Yes ☐ No	☐ Yes ☐ No	☐ Yes ☐ No
Do you have a positive outlook?	☐ Yes ☐ No	☐ Yes ☐ No	☐ Yes ☐ No
Do you hate losing?	☐ Yes ☐ No	☐ Yes ☐ No	☐ Yes ☐ No

Don't be too concerned if you answer "No" to a question (or one of your opinion-givers answers "No" for you). Instead, reflect on why you (or they) said "No" and consider what you can do to change. Obviously, if you have a lot of "No" answers, it may simply be that your personality is not suited to running a business.

Other factors that you have to take into consideration with regard to yourself and your personality are very basic things such as health and age. It should be obvious that if you already have a lot of problems with your health, it is going to be difficult to maintain the energy and time commitment needed for a successful business.

The same applies to age – as people get older, they have less energy. Age is something that financiers look at from two points of view:

- If you are young, you may not have the experience needed for your business
- If you are old, there are fewer working years to pay off a debt in case of failure.

These factors alone can make the difference between viability and bankability. Viability determines whether your business will succeed; bankability determines whether you will get the funding you need/want. Sometimes good businesses don't succeed simply because they are not bankable – they may only need small changes to get the funding they require and to go on to become roaring successes.

Values

Whether you are conscious of them or not, your life (and everyone else's) is run according to a set of personal values. Instinctively, we seek out like-minded people to share our life with and to work with; we seek out situations that fit with our values and avoid those that do not fit with our values. When we find ourselves in situations that conflict with our values, we feel uncomfortable, guilty, remorseful – all negative emotions.

Your own value system is an important element in this exercise of self-assessment, since it is a key determinant of the shape and direction of your proposed business. Identifying your value system and documenting it is a useful task at this stage in preparing to launch your own business. Use **Exercise 2.4** to help you.

EXERCISE 2.4: YOUR VALUE SYSTEM

Identify your personal value system by answering these questions:

What is important to you?

What do you believe in?

What do you stand for?

What aims in life do you have?

How do you treat other people – especially in circumstances where you do not need to care about their reactions?

What do ethics mean to you in your daily life?

What do ethics mean to you in your business life?

If you didn't have to earn a living, what would you do with your life?

How do you define success?

What do you think of people who have not achieved success:

◊ By your definition of success?

◊ By the marketplace/society's definition of success?

How would you like to be remembered?

Why are values important? Return to the beginning of the chapter. Remember that you, the promoter, are the key to the business. The business therefore must reflect your way of thinking, your way of life, your values. If you are uncomfortable with the way you do business, or with the people or circumstances with which you have to deal, you will not be successful at your business. Therefore you must make sure that your business is true to yourself, your beliefs, your ethics, and your principles. And the only way to do that is to know yourself – the purpose of this section of the guide.

Experience and skills

This element of self-assessment comes down to the question: "What do you bring to a business venture?".

What is there in your education, training, experiences and hobbies that will be beneficial to a new venture? Use the questions in **Exercise 2.5** to help you to assess yourself.

This time around, answer the questions in relation to business in general. Later, you may want to return to **Exercise 2.5** after you have defined your business idea in **Exercise 3. 22**.

Then later still, in **Chapter 7, People**, you will be asked to repeat this exercise, focusing on the needs of your new business, which you will have defined by that stage. Then you will be able to relate your experience and skills directly to your business.

EXERCISE 2.5: SELF-ASSESSMENT OF EXPERIENCE AND SKILLS

What experience do you have of:	From work	From outside work
◊ Idea development?		
◊ Marketing?		
◊ Process?		
◊ People?		
◊ Finance?		
◊ Business management?		

How does this experience benefit a business?
What education do you bring to a business?
How does this education benefit a business?
What skills do you bring to a business?
How do these skills benefit a business?
What are you good at?
What are you weak at?

Take all the answers you have given and draft a *curriculum vitae* or resumé for yourself. Include it in your working papers.

Networks

"It is not what you know, it is who you know", says the proverb. Like all proverbs, it contains a lot of truth in very few words. A network of connections is an especially powerful tool for entrepreneurs starting a new business. Research among high achievers show that one of the reasons for their success is the fact that they cultivate (that is, develop **and** use) a strong network of personal contacts.

You already know how useful it is to have a personal introduction to someone you have not met before, or to have a contact or interest in common with someone you are meeting for the first time. Both these help to build trust – the core of every business and personal relationship.

By being very deliberate in the way that you use your network of personal contacts, you can develop your business at a much quicker pace. You know people, who know other people, who know other people ... and before you know it, you have personal introductions to clients, investors, and suppliers and are starting from a relationship that is already established.

The academic researcher Marconi suggests that everyone knows about 250 people. You should use those 250 people and let them work for your company (remember that all the 250 people know 250 other people). This concept underpins network-marketing businesses (see the section on *Start-up Alternatives* in **Chapter 3**).

Another soundbite from academic research into networking suggests that, with no more that six links, anyone in the world can make contact with anyone else, however far away or inaccessible they may appear – again, you know someone, who knows someone, who knows someone....

What you should do now is make a list of everyone who might be able to help with your new business. Use the structure suggested in **Exercise 2.6**. Think about where your sales will come from ..., where you might need an introduction ..., who knows whom ..., etc.

> Always tell yourself:
> The difference between running a business and ruining a business is "i".
> FRANK TYGER

EXERCISE 2.6: NETWORK PROFILE AND ANALYSIS

Develop a profile of your own current network along the following lines.

Contact organisation	Contact individual	Level of contact: Operational Managerial CEO	Quality of contact: Strong Average Weak	Nature of contact: Direct Indirect/ via intermediary
ACME Corporation	Joe Smith	Manager, Purchasing	Average – meet socially about once a month	Direct

Analyse your network to identify:

◊ Strong points in your network
◊ Contacts lacking in your network
◊ Obstacles within your network

How can the quality of your network be improved?

◊ By you personally
◊ By the contribution of others

For each contact, ask yourself:

◊ In what area would this contact be useful? (for example, help in recommending product to potential buyers, etc)
◊ How does this contact link with others?
◊ What is the best way to approach this contact – directly or through another mutual contact?

Personal circumstances

Your personal circumstances will have a huge bearing on your new business. You need to look not only at how you fit into your personal environment but also at how your activities will impact on others in that environment.

First, assess your:

- Family situation
- Financial situation.

Your Family Situation

The average working week for a self-employed person is 65 hours. In almost half of those businesses, the spouse or partner of the entrepreneur is involved for another 21 hours (a total of 86 hours per week on average).

If you have a spouse or partner, you should be aware that their support is a critical factor in the success or failure of a start-up business, because of the need for this level of direct commitment by the other person to the business. Your ideas about self-employment might not necessarily fit with the ideas of your spouse/partner. As you will need all the support you can get, it is important to involve your partner in the decision to start a business. That means that your partner too has to ask whether he or she can commit to the business. If your partner cannot give you the support you will need, it is time to think again and to reconsider your idea.

This does not mean putting off forever your ambition to be self-employed. Perhaps it is your timing that's wrong – if you are in your late twenties, just promoted to your first managerial position, with a wife or partner who is at home minding small children, and large borrowings on a new house, this might not be the best time to take on the burden of a new business, but the situation might change in a few years' time.

Your relationship with your family is going to change because of your new business. In particular, you must think of those who depend on you – your children, your parents who may be infirm or seriously ill, or other family members for whom your time or input is important. You need to think about how you will balance business and family responsibilities.

You will no longer have a regular income. Some months, you may have no pay-check at all. Can your family survive on what your spouse/partner earns? For how long?

You will be working long hours, through weekends and at times when other people are off. Your working hours will be irregular – nothing to do for periods and then several urgent jobs all to be done at once. You will be under pressure, since you will no longer have a boss to take the final responsibility for everything – you will now be the boss.

You will have more at risk than just your money – your reputation, savings, borrowings, and even your self-esteem are also at risk.

While you consider this, answer the questions in **Exercise 2.7**.

EXERCISE 2.7: PERSONAL CIRCUMSTANCES

Answer the questions yourself first. Ask your spouse/partner and other members of your family to answer the questions – from their own point of view. It is important that they give honest answers (even if you don't like what they say!).

	You	Your Spouse/ Partner	Your dependant family
Are you healthy?	☐ Yes ☐ No	☐ Yes ☐ No	☐ Yes ☐ No
Are you willing:			
◊ To work hard?	☐ Yes ☐ No	☐ Yes ☐ No	☐ Yes ☐ No
◊ To deal with long hours?	☐ Yes ☐ No	☐ Yes ☐ No	☐ Yes ☐ No
◊ To wait for your business to take-off (up to three years)?	☐ Yes ☐ No	☐ Yes ☐ No	☐ Yes ☐ No
Can you cope with stress?			
◊ Deadlines	☐ Yes ☐ No	☐ Yes ☐ No	☐ Yes ☐ No
◊ Difficult clients	☐ Yes ☐ No	☐ Yes ☐ No	☐ Yes ☐ No
◊ Commitments	☐ Yes ☐ No	☐ Yes ☐ No	☐ Yes ☐ No
◊ Pressure	☐ Yes ☐ No	☐ Yes ☐ No	☐ Yes ☐ No
◊ Money trouble	☐ Yes ☐ No	☐ Yes ☐ No	☐ Yes ☐ No
How much time can you give to the business per week?	_____	_____	_____
Is this enough?	☐ Yes ☐ No	☐ Yes ☐ No	☐ Yes ☐ No
Do you accept that your relationship with your partner/spouse may change because of:			
◊ Less time together?	☐ Yes ☐ No	☐ Yes ☐ No	☐ Yes ☐ No
◊ Pressure?	☐ Yes ☐ No	☐ Yes ☐ No	☐ Yes ☐ No
◊ Irregular hours?	☐ Yes ☐ No	☐ Yes ☐ No	☐ Yes ☐ No

	You	Your Spouse/ Partner	Your dependant family
Do you accept that there will be changes in your social life?	☐ Yes ☐ No	☐ Yes ☐ No	☐ Yes ☐ No
Can you cope with financial insecurity?			
◊ Unpaid bills	☐ Yes ☐ No	☐ Yes ☐ No	☐ Yes ☐ No
◊ Shortage of cash	☐ Yes ☐ No	☐ Yes ☐ No	☐ Yes ☐ No
◊ Being in debt	☐ Yes ☐ No	☐ Yes ☐ No	☐ Yes ☐ No
Can you cope with:			
◊ Reduced income?	☐ Yes ☐ No	☐ Yes ☐ No	☐ Yes ☐ No
◊ Irregular income?	☐ Yes ☐ No	☐ Yes ☐ No	☐ Yes ☐ No
◊ Unexpected setbacks?	☐ Yes ☐ No	☐ Yes ☐ No	☐ Yes ☐ No
◊ Pressure/criticism from your friends/relatives?	☐ Yes ☐ No	☐ Yes ☐ No	☐ Yes ☐ No
Do you accept the risks involved?			
◊ Money	☐ Yes ☐ No	☐ Yes ☐ No	☐ Yes ☐ No
◊ Time	☐ Yes ☐ No	☐ Yes ☐ No	☐ Yes ☐ No
Do you accept the impact that self-employment will have on your family life?	☐ Yes ☐ No	☐ Yes ☐ No	☐ Yes ☐ No
How will self-employment change:			
◊ Your own life?	_____	_____	_____
◊ Your spouse/partner's life?	_____	_____	_____
◊ Your family's life?	_____	_____	_____
List the good things and bad things about being self-employed.	_____	_____	_____
	_____	_____	_____
	_____	_____	_____
	_____	_____	_____

Now discuss the situations in **Exercise 2.8** with your family. It will help you – and them – understand what lies ahead and how you will react to the choices that may need to be made.

EXERCISE 2.8: SITUATIONS TO DISCUSS WITH YOUR FAMILY

The children need new shoes. The business needs a new piece of machinery that costs €100. There is only €100 in the bank. Which comes first?

Don't skip the questions, lest you hear answers you won't like.

These are REAL issues.

A big order comes in (Congratulations!). For the next two weeks, you need to work at least 14 hours every day (including weekends) in order to meet the order. It is also your turn to look after the kids. What are you going to do?

You promised your spouse/partner a night out. That night a client insists on meeting you and there is a prospect of a large order. Which comes first?

You have booked a holiday and the whole family is really looking forward to it. Suddenly, the person who was supposed to look after the business while you are away cancels. You cannot find another replacement on such short notice. What happens?

A deadline needs to be met. You get ill. Who will take over the running of the business while you are out sick?

The business is not going as well as expected. Your business needs an extra loan to survive. Your partner/spouse wants you to quit. What happens?

Your business has a cash flow problem. As a result, you have not been able to take out a salary for the past two months and some of your household bills (telephone, gas, and electricity) are running behind. How long will that be acceptable to your partner/spouse?

Your Financial Situation

Don't forget that you need to earn a salary from your new business. Perhaps you have savings that mean you can avoid drawing out a salary initially, but someday that will change and your business must be able to afford to pay you for your efforts.

Use **Exercise 2.9** to calculate your minimum salary – be sensible about what you need – and make sure you include it in your financial projections.

EXERCISE 2.9: CALCULATING YOUR PERSONAL EXPENSES

	€
Estimate your personal expenses per year:	
Rent/mortgage	
Gas/water/electricity	
Telephone	
Insurance (health/home, etc.)	
Car (insurance, tax, depreciation)	
Repayments	
Other expenses	
Subtotal A	
Household expenses	
Allowances for:	
> Food	
> Clothing/footwear	
> Education	
> Holidays	
> Repair/maintenance	
> Renewal of household appliances	
> Savings	
Subtotal B	
Total A+B	
Deduct:	
Other earnings	
Government benefits	
Rent subsidies	
Total deductions C	
Total needed per year (A+B-C)	

Be sensible when calculating your personal expenses.

Don't inflate your income needs with unnecessary luxuries — but don't cut your cloth too tight either!

What you have calculated in **Exercise 2.9** is the money you need over a year to get by and pay all the bills. This personal expenditure figure is the **minimum** salary that you should include in your financial projections, when you come to the appropriate point (**Chapter 7, People**). Anything less and you won't be able to concentrate on your business because of money problems at home – and you'll be fooling yourself about the profitability of your business too. You may need to review this calculation, as you work through later chapters.

At this stage, and bearing your family circumstances in mind, you have to re-consider whether you can cope with irregular and reduced income and financial insecurity.

How will self-employment affect you and your family? This is a very important issue because money, or the lack of it, can have a huge impact on your self-esteem and stress levels, not just on the your obvious ability to pay mortgage, education for the kids, social life, clothing, food, etc., etc.

Another element to consider here is your own financial resources and how much you are willing (or able) to invest in your new business.

In **Chapter 8, Finance & Funding,** we will consider Promoter(s)' equity and loans, the two main source of capital for the start-up contributed by the entrepreneur. For now, you should think through the questions in **Exercise 2.10**, which will form an introduction to the later chapter.

EXERCISE 2.10: PERSONAL CAPITAL

How much money do you have saved?   € _____
What other valuable assets do you have?
Could these be sold to help finance your start-up?   ☐ Yes ☐ No
If not, why not?
If yes, how much would they realise?   € _____
What commitments or responsibilities do you have to meet from
these financial resources (excluding salary needs in **Exercise 2.9**)?€ _____
Therefore, how much free capital do you have available for
investment in the new business?   € _____

The capital that you have decided is available for investment in the new business is the **maximum** amount that you can allocate to a business.

As you work through the guide, you may want to return and review this figure. For example, once you have defined your business and the equipment, etc that it needs, you may find that you may have some of these items already – and can add them to your investment. Again, if you have difficulty raising all the funding you need to start your business, you may need to rethink how much you commit to your business and may consider selling other assets. The exercises in **Chapter 8, Finance & Funding** will help you when you reach this point.

Now answer the questions in **Exercise 2.11**.

> The seven deadly sins ...
> Food, clothing, firing, rent, taxes, respectability and children.
> Nothing can lift those seven millstones from a man's neck but money;
> and the spirit cannot soar until the millstones are lifted.
> GEORGE BERNARD SHAW

Exercise 2.11: Personal Circumstances Summary

What personal motivation do you bring to the business?
What skills do you bring to the business?
What experience do you bring to the business?
What training/education do you bring to the business?

What supports do you bring to the business?
◊   Network of useful contacts   ☐ Yes ☐ No
◊   Support of your partner/spouse   ☐ Yes ☐ No
◊   Support of your family and friends   ☐ Yes ☐ No
◊   Finance € _____   ☐ Yes ☐ No
◊   Other (list)

What personal characteristics do you bring to the business?
◊   Health   Good/OK/Bad
◊   Endurance   Good/OK/Bad
◊   Flexibility   Good/OK/Bad
◊   Creativity   Good/OK/Bad
◊   Honesty   Good/OK/Bad
◊   Confidence   Good/OK/Bad
◊   Ability to handle stress   Good/OK/Bad
◊   Other (list)   Good/OK/Bad

What time commitments do you bring to the business?
◊   Social activities   _____ hrs/week
◊   Family   _____ hrs/week
◊   Hobbies   _____ hrs/week
◊   Other (list)   _____ hrs/week
Total time commitment outside business   _____ hrs/week
Could this be reduced to allow time for the business?   ☐ Yes ☐ No
By how much?   _____ hrs/week

What personal capital available for investment
   do you bring to the business?   € _____
Overall, are your personal circumstances a good fit
   for self-employment?   ☐ Yes ☐ No

Commitment

Your commitment – total and utter commitment – to your new business must be taken for granted before you start, otherwise there is no point going ahead.

The point has been repeatedly made that self-employment is stressful and hard work – it is, but it's also a great deal of fun – if you are suited to it.

Use the questions in **Exercise 2.12** to assess the level of your commitment. Get at least two other people to give their opinions on your level of commitment by answering the questions as well. You might not like their answers but they will help you to see yourself as others see you – and perhaps as you really are.

Return to the questions several times during the course of your planning and re-assess yourself.

EXERCISE 2.12: COMMITMENT

Answer the questions yourself first. Then ask your spouse and other members of your family or your friends to answer the questions. Stress that it is important that they give honest answers (even if you don't like what they say!).

	Your own Opinion	Other Opinion 1	Other Opinion 2
Do you think that your "drive" to become self-employed is strong enough?	☐ Yes ☐ No	☐ Yes ☐ No	☐ Yes ☐ No
Do you have the disposition, skills, experience and self-knowledge for self-employment?			
◊ Disposition	☐ Yes ☐ No	☐ Yes ☐ No	☐ Yes ☐ No
◊ Skills	☐ Yes ☐ No	☐ Yes ☐ No	☐ Yes ☐ No
◊ Experience	☐ Yes ☐ No	☐ Yes ☐ No	☐ Yes ☐ No
◊ Self-knowledge	☐ Yes ☐ No	☐ Yes ☐ No	☐ Yes ☐ No
Do you still want to become self-employed?	☐ Yes ☐ No		

If you answered "No" to the question "Do you still want to become self-employed?" in **Exercise 2.12**, don't give up.

In many cases, answering "No" shows that you have carefully and sensibly considered the risks involved in starting your own business. This may not be the right time to start – perhaps you lack experience, or capital, or you have other commitments that would prevent you from taking on a new business venture wholeheartedly. If that's the case, accept the "No" and plan to try again at a later, and more suitable, time.

Then continue on with the programme and learn all you can, to prepare yourself for when you are free to take the plunge.

Involve your Business Partner(s)

This section, "Self-assessment", has been addressed to you as an entrepreneur working on his/her own. But that may not be the case: You may be working with a business partner or partners, or as a member of a team. If you are, you should make sure that everyone on your team – all the key players, at least – reads through this section and completes the exercises.

The Promoter(s)

The paragraph or two that you write below in **Exercise 2.13** will form the basis of the section, "**The Promoter(s)**" in your business plan. You may want to revise this draft as you work through later chapters of this guide.

EXERCISE 2.13: THE PROMOTER(S)

Describe yourself, your education, experience and skills relevant to the business:

Why do you want to be self-employed?

THE TENBIZPLAN APPROACH TO BUSINESS PLANNING

Text

In this chapter, you have created draft text for input into your business plan document in relation to:

* The Promoter(s) – **Exercise 2.13**.

Evidence

File copies of all of the exercises that you have completed in **Chapter 2**, for ease of reference later. They will be a crucial part of your evidence supporting your business plan.

Where you have identified other information that would be good evidence for your business plan, file it in the appropriate section of your working papers also.

Numbers

There are no numbers created for input into your financial projections as part of the process of business planning in this chapter.

You have identified the minimum salary that you require to meet your personal expenses in **Exercise 2.9** and the personal capital that you have available in **Exercise 2.10**. These will be input into your financial projections at a later stage.

Key Question

The key question for this chapter is:

 **Am I the right person to set up and run a business?**

To answer the Key Question, you will need to consider your:

- Drive
- Personality
- Values
- Skills and experience
- Network
- Personal circumstances
- Commitment – the most important of all.

3

IDEA ASSESSMENT

The key question for this chapter is:

Have I a feasible business idea?

Often, business ideas grow out of personal observations of the market. It is unusual for a new product to emerge where no need has been expressed. Most ideas are responsive.

Most entrepreneurs have started to research their idea long before they come to the formal planning stage. Often, the idea has grown out of a long period of personal interest and the "research" is based on:

- Personal experience
- Talking to friends
- Talking to suppliers.

A problem sometimes encountered in this phase of the business planning process is that the idea for the business – the product or service that it will supply – is already fixed in the mind of the entrepreneur, who has not taken the time to consider properly all the options that are available. As a result, any market research that is done (and some entrepreneurs do not even bother with market research, preferring to rush into the market blindly) is too narrowly focused and thus valuable insights are lost.

Before you start to plan your market research (an essential part of business planning), you should devote some time to:

- Expanding your idea to its limits
- Identifying other opportunities linked to your idea.

This chapter, which inputs into the section of your business plan called **"Project Overview"**, will take you back to basics before you consider more detailed planning stages. The aim of the chapter is to make sure that you have the "right" idea before moving forward with your detailed business planning.

The idea must be right in terms of:

- Your own experience and skills: Can you execute it?
- The market: Does the market want it?
- Timing: Are you, the market and any necessary technology ready?

Output from this chapter

This chapter will take you through the process of idea assessment, so that you are fully aware of the benefits and downsides of your business idea from having spent time thinking about it and from having done market research. You will be convinced by your business idea, because you will have done your research, which will make it easier for you to convince others.

By the end of this chapter, you will be able to write a draft of the second section of your business plan – the section **"Project Overview"** – the section about your idea. This draft will describe your business idea (including the product or service to be supplied).

Links to other chapters

By the end of this chapter, you will also be aware of the links from idea assessment to other stages in the business planning process, especially to:

- **Personal Assessment (Chapter 2):** Your own personal circumstances will have an impact on the business idea you develop and how you progress it
- **Marketing & Sales (Chapter 5):** The way in which you market your product or service will depend on the product or service itself – and *vice versa*. So there's a clear loop – not just a link – between Idea Assessment and Marketing and you can expect to move back and forward between these two chapters quite a lot as you work your way through this guide

- **Process (Chapter 6):** What you supply affects, and is affected by, how you propose to supply it
- **People (Chapter 7):** The type of product or service that you supply will determine the skills of the people that you will need to hire – or perhaps the lack of availability of the necessary skills will force you to amend your product.

> I was figuring on starting some kind of business, but most every business is already engaged more than's necessary; and then, I ain't got no business ability. What I want is something that don't call for no kind of ability whatsoever and no kind of exertion to speak of, and ain't out of town, and pays good, and has a future.
>
> ANON

DEFINING YOUR IDEA

Let's start by defining the idea that you propose to build your new business around. Most entrepreneurs will already have some idea of what they want to do, even at this early stage. If you have an idea, you can use this chapter to qualify and refine it.

If you don't have a business idea yet, consider commercialising one of your hobbies, or developing one part of the business you are already working in as an employee. Alternatively, read the section, *Identifying future trends* later in this chapter as a starting point for ideas and then come back to this section. But do define some business idea. Without a firm idea, one that you are interested in and feel capable of exploiting, you will not get the full value from this chapter or even from the theory elements of later chapters of this guide.

To start with, answer the questions in **Exercise 3.1**, which will help you define your idea. As you work through this chapter of the guide, you will redefine (and refine) your idea several times, so don't be too concerned about getting it perfect first time. This is the first of three occasions in this chapter when you will define your business, refining more and more each time. Use **Exercise 3.1** to get your first outline definition.

EXERCISE 3.1: IDEA DEFINITION – I

What kind of business are you thinking about?

◊   Manufacturing?   ☐ Yes ☐ No
◊   Retail?   ☐ Yes ☐ No
◊   Wholesale/distribution?   ☐ Yes ☐ No
◊   Import /export?   ☐ Yes ☐ No
◊   Service?   ☐ Yes ☐ No
◊   Some combination of these?

Describe your business idea:

START-UP ALTERNATIVES

Most people who have developed a business idea think immediately about starting a new business in order to develop their idea. However, it's not always necessary to start from scratch. Sometimes, someone else will have done the groundwork for you. So, before doing anything else, it is useful to consider alternatives such as franchising, buying a company, network marketing, etc.

Even if you have an idea, it may be worth considering buying an existing business, which has the manufacturing, sales and other necessary expertise and resources in place.

Or, if you see yourself as more an inventor than a businessperson (look back at **Chapter 2, Personal Assessment**), perhaps you should consider licensing your idea to another company to manufacture and sell, to leave you free to invent other new ideas. If it's appropriate, read the section on *Technological development* **in Chapter 6** – in particular, the sub-sections on intellectual property and technology transfer.

Buying an existing business

Buying an existing business is a sensible alternative to starting a business from scratch. The main advantage is that you acquire a business with existing products, markets, customers, staff, etc and do not have to build the whole venture up yourself. The disadvantage is that you have to commit a considerable investment to acquire the business and may have to add to this investment in order to develop the business further. You also need to know why the business is being sold – it may be that the business is in trouble or is about to face major competition.

Buying an existing business needs a methodical approach. Insist on both historical figures (preferably three years or more) and future projections. Have the information checked over by a person you trust or hire an expert. Do your own SWOT analysis, get feedback from clients, suppliers and competitors. Particular areas to look into are:

- Financial data
- Management and key personnel
- Recent investments (or lack of)
- Product development/improvements (or lack of)

- Innovation (or lack of)
- Use of modern technology (or lack of)
- Hidden liabilities
- Verification of assets.

You need to know how much more money you will have to put into the business, on top of the purchase price, and how risky is this investment. How long will it take to recover your investment?

When you think you are ready to buy a specific business, write down your answers to the questions in **Exercise 3.2**. Only buy when you are sure that the business is right for you. Above all, make sure that you take professional advice before committing to buying.

And remember, buying the business is only the beginning. You still need to work through the rest of this guide to develop a business plan for your "new" business – while you run it on a day-to-day basis.

EXERCISE 3.2: BUYING A BUSINESS

Why is the business for sale?
What are its primary activities?
How is it organised?
What is its position in the market-place?
What are its future prospects?
Is there a current Business Plan? What does it tell me?
Does the culture of the company fit my style of working and managing?
How dependent is the company on the current owner or managers?
How dependent is the company on key staff?
What are my overall conclusions?

Buying into a franchise

Across the world, there are over 3,000 franchised businesses, covering almost every industry. Some are international brands like McDonald's; others are national brands; a few are smaller, local opportunities.

When you buy a franchise, you are buying the right to use a specific trademark or business concept, which has been tested in practice. The chief benefit is that you are able to capitalise on the business format, trade name, and support system provided by the franchisor.

You pay an initial upfront fee for the rights to open your franchise. This fee may include items such as training costs, start-up promotional costs, stock, equipment/fixtures (you may be required to purchase or lease specific equipment and fixtures from the franchisor), and any other costs that are necessary to start your business. Usually, the franchisor helps you during start-up, with selection of premises and equipment, a business plan, raising finance, and publicity. In return, the franchisor supplies a detailed operational manual, which sets out exactly how you should run the franchise.

You also have to pay ongoing fees to maintain the rights to your franchise. Most franchisors charge a royalty fee – typically a percentage of your gross sales, ranging from 1% to as much as 15%. It is also usual for franchisees to pay into a co-operative national advertising and promotional fund that benefits all franchises through increased exposure to the common trade name.

The advantages of buying a franchise are:

- Franchises traditionally have a much lower failure rate than other start-up businesses, since most of the problems have been discovered and solved **Franchises have advantages**

- You get a complete package, including trademarks, easy access to an established product, proven marketing method, equipment, stock, etc.

- You have the buying power of the entire network, which can help you against larger competitors

- Many franchisors provide financial and accounting systems, on-going training and support, research and development, sales and marketing assistance, planning and forecasting, stock management, etc.

- Some franchisors help with site selection, making sure that your business is located in an area where it can thrive

- You benefit from national or regional advertising and promotional campaigns by the franchisor.

But, as in most things in life, there are disadvantages, too. These can include:

- The essence of a franchise — buying and operating a proven concept — can make it seem like you're more of a manager than a entrepreneur

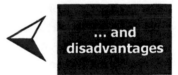

- It can take a good deal of cash to open and operate a franchise. Upfront costs can be significant, and ongoing royalty fees may impact on your cash flow

- Just as a franchisor's reputation can benefit you, the franchisor's problems are also your problems

- Your franchise agreement is a binding contract, and may be quite restrictive.

Although you own the business, its operation is governed by the terms of the franchise agreement. Therefore, you should have your lawyer and/or accountant review the franchise agreement before signing anything.

Before you decide on a franchise, talk to other franchisees. Ask about their experiences. Would they do it again? What would they do differently? Listen carefully to their answers.

When you think you are ready to buy into a specific franchise, write down your answers to the questions in **Exercise 3.3**. Only buy when you are sure that the franchise is right for you. Above all, make sure that you take professional advice before committing to signing up.

EXERCISE 3.3: BUYING INTO A FRANCHISE

Does the franchisor have a track record of success?   ☐ Yes ☐ No
What will the franchise cost me to buy?   Once my current income? ☐
                                                 Twice my current income? ☐
                                                                    More? ☐
What annual income will the franchise give me? Once my current income? ☐
                                                 Twice my current income? ☐
                                                                    More? ☐
Will the franchisor give me an exclusive territory for the period
of the franchise?
                                                                 ☐ Yes ☐ No

Will the franchisor assist me with:
◊   A management training programme?   ☐ Yes ☐ No
◊   An employee training programme?   ☐ Yes ☐ No
◊   A PR and advertising programme?   ☐ Yes ☐ No
◊   Raising equity capital/borrowing money?   ☐ Yes ☐ No
◊   Merchandising ideas?   ☐ Yes ☐ No
◊   Finding a suitable location?   ☐ Yes ☐ No
How long has the franchisor been operating?   Less than 3 years? ☐
                                                     More than 3 years? ☐
Has the franchisor a reputation for fair dealing with its franchisees?
                                                                 ☐ Yes ☐ No
Has the franchisor enough finance to carry out its plans?   ☐ Yes ☐ No
What happens when I want to leave/give up?
Can I sell the business to anyone I like?   ☐ Yes ☐ No
Has the franchiser shown me any certified figures indicating
net profits of one or more franchisees, which I have personally
checked with them?   ☐ Yes ☐ No
Has the franchisor investigated me carefully enough to be sure
that I can successfully operate at a profit to both of us?   ☐ Yes ☐ No
Is my lawyer completely happy with the franchise contract?   ☐ Yes ☐ No
What are my overall conclusions?

Network marketing

As with franchising, everyone is familiar with network marketing, even though they may not know it by that name. Examples of network marketing businesses are:

- Tupperware – Household storage items
- Avon – Cosmetics
- Amway – Household products.

Network marketing skips the wholesalers and retailers in the normal distribution chain and delivers a product directly from the producer to the customer. This means quick delivery, good service and that the product is sold by people who know the product since they use it themselves.

Because there are no intermediaries between producer and customer, a large margin is available to pay those who replace the distribution chain. Network marketeers (usually called "distributors") earn this margin by selling direct to customers and also from a royalty on sales made by other distributors whom they have introduced.

The process is based on the idea that more gets sold by a lot of people each selling a little than by a small number of highly-effective salespeople on their own.

Because all distributors are self-employed and self-motivated, only the successful survive. Within the network, back-up is available to provide the members of the network with training, workshops, information materials, manuals, etc.

Unfairly, network marketing has a poor reputation – in part caused by its similarity in a number of respects to the now universally outlawed "pyramid selling". Network marketing, according to one researcher, is not a "get rich quick" scheme – he says it is a "get rich scheme for those prepared to perform consistent, persistent, productive, income-producing activities".

Even though it can be done part-time while you work at another job or in the home (and this is one of its key attractions), network marketing needs a lot of time and commitment not only in selling but also in learning about the products, in training in how to do the presentations, in developing and maintaining a network, delivering the products, book-keeping and administration, etc. Therefore, it's just as important to write a business plan for a network marketing business as for any other business idea.

When you think you are ready to join a network marketing scheme, write down your answers to the questions in **Exercise 3.4**. Only join when you are sure that the scheme is right for you. Above all, make sure that you take professional advice before committing to joining.

EXERCISE 3.4: NETWORK MARKETING

E

Can I do it part-time?	☐ Yes ☐ No
How good are the products?	Very good? ☐
	Good? ☐
	Just OK? ☐
What customer guarantees does the company give?	No quibble? ☐
	Money back? ☐
	None? ☐
What is the company's track record, history, management, financial standing, etc?	Very good? ☐
	Good? ☐
	Just OK? ☐
What investment must I make at the start?	£ _____
How much do I have to sell to break-even?	£ _____
How much time do I need to invest?	_____
Am I prepared to do sales presentations for people I know and recruit them for the network?	☐ Yes ☐ No
Do I have a well-established network of personal contacts that I can use to develop my network marketing business?	☐ Yes ☐ No
Have I discussed the scheme with existing distributors?	☐ Yes ☐ No
Do I believe the income figures they quote?	☐ Yes ☐ No
What are my overall conclusions?	

Never acquire a business you don't know how to run.
ROBERT W JOHNSON

Other alternatives

Other alternatives to the traditional start-up include:

- **Inheriting a business from a relative:** Nice, but you still have to run it afterwards
- **Management or employee buy-outs:** Where a group of employees buys the business they work in from the owners
- **Intrapreneurship:** Setting up a business within an existing business, which is becoming more and more in fashion
- **Hybrid entrepreneurs:** Setting up and running a business part-time, while remaining employed by another business
- **Co-operative:** Setting up a business with a group of people.

In every case, there is a need for planning. However you arrive at your chosen business, if it is to be successful, you should work through this guide and develop your business plan.

Developing Your Idea

Go back to **Exercise 3.1**, where you first defined your business idea in writing. Look again at what you wrote. Try to expand on the definition. Generalise. Are you selling music or relaxation? Are you selling cars, or are you **selling transport or safety**? Are you selling furniture or **selling comfort**? Are you selling insurance or security?

For example, look at Amazon.com, which began life in 1994 as an on-line bookstore, selling books over the Internet. If the founder, Jeff Bezos, had defined his business idea as selling books, Amazon.com would not have developed to its present situation of selling music, videos and toys – anything that can be catalogued and sold on-line.

These simple questions have implications for how you define your business. Developing your idea to its fullest potential involves creative thinking. This section provides an overview of some of the most common creative thinking techniques. They will help you to identify new ideas, to develop your existing idea and to create new opportunities.

Thinking

We all think in two stages:

- The first stage is to look, simplify what we see, recognise and name what we see, then filter it through our experience and knowledge

- In the second stage, we judge and conclude.

Unfortunately, we spend most of our time thinking in the second stage. With creative thinking, most of the time is spent in the first stage of thinking.

Look below. What do you see?

●

Your answer is probably: "A black dot".

Yes, there is a black dot, but there is also more text, white space at the end of the page, etc – all on the same page. By jumping straight into second stage thinking, you missed all the surroundings.

You did not take time to sit back, relax and look a little bit longer. You rushed for the obvious answer. But, by taking time to step back, you will see more and, by seeing more, you will also see better possibilities. That is the idea behind creative thinking.

As an entrepreneur, it is important to spend time looking at your idea and trying to come up with new possibilities, extra features, alternatives, etc. This will not only give you an even better understanding of your idea, it will improve it and will make you more competitive. This kind of thinking should be an ongoing process to keep your business competitive.

In the process of creative thinking, you are your own worst enemy. Most people have a strong tendency to curb their imagination and to block new ideas. This comes from their upbringing, their education, their experience, their beliefs, their circumstances and their personality – all of which condition people to accept the world as it is. All information and ideas that they encounter are filtered by those factors. Most people are examples of the concept that change always meets resistance. As an entrepreneur, you must be different.

Returning to the black dot and our tendency to jump to conclusions too quickly, you need to change the way you think. You need to be able to "see it strange" in order to get new insights that will allow you to broaden your perspective. Below you will find some techniques that will help you to be more creative in your thinking.

Technique 1: Brainstorming

Get a group together (four people is the minimum, preferably more). Define your idea for a product/service to them and discuss it. Redefine the product/service.

Do a practice run to warm up the mind. Take this challenge: *How many uses can you find for a paperclip?* Then start brainstorming:

- Aim to generate as many ideas as possible
- All ideas are acceptable
- The crazier the idea the better.

Make sure you nominate one of the group to record ideas (it needn't prevent them contributing), otherwise they may be lost. Select the craziest idea and brainstorm that idea for a while.

Then apply the same technique to your own business idea. When you have finished brainstorming, take a break before starting to evaluate your ideas critically. Extract the most useful ideas for follow-up. Use **Exercise 3.5** to help you.

EXERCISE 3.5: BRAINSTORMING

Your business idea (starting point):
Useful ideas from the session:

Technique 2: Attribute listing

This technique is best used when you are thinking of adapting or developing an existing product or service.

Take your idea for a product/service and list its attributes: For example, shape, size, design, materials, colour, functions and cost. Then take each attribute and try to find as many alternatives to it as possible. Use **Exercise 3.6** to help you.

EXERCISE 3.6: ATTRIBUTE LISTING

What are the attributes of your proposed product/service?
What are the alternatives?

| | Alternatives | | | | |
Attributes	1	2	3	4	5

Useful ideas from attribute listing:
◊
◊

Technique 3: Who, what, where, when, why, how
Tease out different perspectives on your idea for a product or service, using the six prompts – Who, What, Where, When, Why, How.

EXERCISE 3.7: WHO, WHAT, WHERE, WHEN, WHY, HOW

Select (after formulating as many questions as possible), the five most promising questions:
1.
2.
3.
4.
5.

Putting creative thinking into practice
There are many different ways of stimulating thinking. Here are some more ideas:

• Meditation
• Breathing techniques
• General relaxation
• Doing things outside your normal routine.

In general, you should allow your subconscious to do its work and be open to the ideas that will bubble to the surface. Do not dismiss them. Write them down. Keep a notebook near your bed, to capture ideas as they occur to you at night. In combination with some of the techniques described, you will be amazed with the ideas you will gather.

EXERCISE 3.8: SUMMARY OF IDEAS

List the most useful ideas that emerged from the creative thinking exercises and use them to develop your business idea further:

1.

2.

3.

4.

5.

6.

7.

8.

> The majority of business people are incapable of having an original idea because they cannot free themselves from the restraints of logic.
> **DAVID OGILVY**

> We haven't the money, so we have to think.
> **LORD BEAVERBROOK**

> If you can dream it, you can do it.
> **WALT DISNEY**

IDENTIFYING FUTURE TRENDS

If you want to be in business for a long time, you need to develop a vision of the future and the place of your business in that future. You need not only to be aware of the trends in your market area (technology, competition, trade regulations, etc.) but also have a sense of the general direction in which the world is developing. Consider these current trends in developed societies:

- To protect themselves from crime and hostility, people are retreating into the safe environment of the home

- People want to do exciting things but want to be safe – emotional escape in a risk-free fantasy world. Consider changes in food (exotic meals), shopping (retail therapy), interactive movies and games, etc

- Luxuries are no longer big purchases but include "rewards" like handmade chocolates, week-end breaks and expensive restaurant meals Spending patterns are becoming less predictable

- Technology allows products to be focused on very specific needs

- People are less concerned about job security and more willing to change jobs several times during their careers to pursue new opportunities

- Consumers are more health-conscious and critical about the behaviour of companies and the quality of products and services

- People have higher expectations of life and want to achieve more

- Individualism is being taken to an extreme

- There is a fusion of cultures

- Businesses are becoming more and more knowledge-based, instead of being production-based

- Time is a major factor in most people's lives. They feel a need to cram activities into the day (reading, movie, theatre, socialising, being a good parent or partner, do a course, make a career, etc.) Therefore people are more and more conscious of trying to make the time (or of their lack of time) to do all the things they want to do. A major currency in the future will be time instead of money

- Older people stay healthier much longer and age does not dictate the pace of life anymore. Old people act young

- Society and business is more and more influenced by women.

Read science fiction. Much of what was written as science fiction 20 or 30 years ago is now part of our everyday lives.

Train yourself to watch trends. Look for:

- Changes in food, new products, trendy restaurants
- The introduction of new products (failures and successes)
- Changes in family structure
- Changes in demographics
- Changes in work environment
- Changes in environmental behaviour
- Whether there is optimism or pessimism in relation to the economy
- New cultures
- New words (Internet Nanny, search engine, dinky)
- Rapid changes in technology
- Science fiction becoming real.

EXERCISE 3.9: NEW PRODUCTS

List five completely new products introduced into your country in the last year:

1.
2.
3.
4.
5.

> Business, more than any other occupation, is a continual dealing with the future:
> it is a continual calculation, an instinctive exercise in foresight.
> HENRY R LUCE

EXERCISE 3.10: NEW WORDS

List five new words introduced into your language in the last year:

1.
2.
3.
4.
5.

Watch for the balancing impact of the Action = Reaction principle.

Action		Reaction
• Rapid change of technology, increasing role of computers	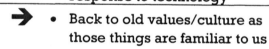	• Back to nature (in the widest sense of the word) in response to technology
• Globalisation of markets and multi-cultural influences due to all information available		• Back to old values/culture as those things are familiar to us
• Information overload/stress due to excess information • Dealing with complex new technology and society • Constant change		• Back into our homes to protect us from the outside (hostile) world • Escapism in movies, adventure trips, computer games, etc. • To balance stress, "perks" to cheer us up (massage, fancy dinner, clothes)
• Easy access of information and technology		• Filters on information (for example, the Internet Nanny) • Simplifying information

EXERCISE 3.11: IMPACT OF DEVELOPMENTS

Consider the impact on your country, your region and your business idea of the developments below and write them down:

	Country	**Region**	**Business idea**

The use of drugs for specific purposes
    (memory enhancers, warfare, work)

Development of genetic engineering

The role of computers, and telecommunications in our society

The ability to connect with anyone in the world

Merging of biology, cybernetics, nano-technology, computers, genetics, telecommunication into new products

The impact of the Internet on almost every aspect of our lives, in both personal and business contexts

The mix of technology and ancient wisdom/different cultures

Virtual reality.

EXERCISE 3.12: PREDICTING THE FUTURE

Write down your answers to the following questions:

What will your country or region look like in 2010 – or even in 2025?

Where will your business fit?

What should you be doing to prepare?

> The future: A great land; a man cannot go around it in one day; he cannot measure it with a bound; he cannot bind its harvest into a single sheaf; it is wider than vision and has no end.
> DONALD G MITCHELL

Go back to the section ***Developing your idea*** earlier in this chapter, and use some of the techniques described to develop your idea further. Use **Exercise 3.13** to redefine your idea afterwards.

EXERCISE 3.13: IDEA DEFINITION – II

Refer back to your Idea Definition in **Exercise 3.1** and your thinking over the past few exercises.

Summarise your idea/product/service.

Why is it a good idea?

On what assumptions is that opinion based?

Can you prove that those assumptions are correct?

List four reasons why the idea may not work:

List four reasons why it will work:

Where does it fit in the future?

The process you have been through, using creative thinking and future trends to develop your idea, should be an ongoing process within your business.

However, it has been essentially an internally-focused assessment. Now it is time to expose your idea for a product/service to the marketplace, through some market research.

However, unless you can define your idea clearly – in terms of what it is, what it will cost and what you can sell it for – your market research may not be worthwhile. Return to **Exercise 3.13** and review your idea before proceeding.

> You see how things are, and you ask "Why?"
> But I dream of things that do not yet exist, and I ask "Why not?".
> GEORGE BERNARD SHAW

MARKET RESEARCH

So far, you have developed your business idea in a vacuum, with no inhibitions or barriers. But you will be competing within the market-place and in a competitive environment, so you need to ask yourself a few basic questions:

- What types of customer will be interested in your product or service?
- Why?
- What is different about this idea from others already in the market-place?
- Why are those differences important?

You need to do some market research, which should inform your marketing approach. Marketing is about keeping your customers central in your thinking, behaviour and planning. To do that, you need a combination of information, vision and creativity. Your market research will help you to:

- **Inform:** Consumer behaviour, market trends, developments abroad
- **Evaluate:** Are goals achievable?
- **Experiment:** Testing markets or products.

Why market research?

Market research is the core of your business and business plan. It is important that you:

- Are aware of market developments
- Find out for yourself whether you can approach people at all levels
- Find out whether you can sell (if not, you will have to find someone to do it for you)
- Find out whether there is a market for your product/service, how big it is, how it can be reached, etc.

What you must do now is focused on feasibility. As the businessman remarked, "There may be a gap in the market, but is there a market in the gap?" That's what you need to find out now – whether there is a market in the gap that is big enough to sustain you. If there is, great – you can proceed further with your planning; if not, it's back to the drawing board!

Making your market research practical

Market research is often considered by entrepreneurs to be too theoretical to be bothered with. That's both dangerous and wrong: Dangerous because without market research you may start a business for which there is no demand; wrong because market research can be very practical.

Practical research includes things as simple as:

- Counting the cars on your competitors' parking lot (to tell you how many customers they get and how well-off they are)
- Counting the people passing by the premises you are planning to rent (big stores sometimes do this for months before deciding on a location for a new shop)
- Counting the waste bags outside the backdoor of a restaurant (to give you some idea of the volume of their business)
- Checking the number of trucks delivering supplies to competitors (on the basis that purchases gives you an insight into their sales)
- Counting the numbers of customers walking into a competitors' office/shop
- Knocking on every door in a housing estate in which you are planning to open an outlet (to ask whether there is a demand, at what price, etc.)
- Collecting all your competitors' brochures and price lists (to find out what they are offering and at what prices)
- Checking where your competitors advertise and how big an advertisement they take
- Surfing the Internet (to identify global trends that might have a local impact soon).

Note that market research should be an ongoing process. It should not stop after the business has started but should become an integral part of your business.

Small opportunities are often the origins of great enterprises.
DEMOSTHENES

Sources of information

When you are looking for information as part of your desk research, there is an almost endless list of sources of information, including:

- Your network
- Your local library
- Government Publications Office
- Business magazines and trade journals – including international editions, if you can get them
- Newspapers – national and local – and international, if you can get them
- Banks
- Professional associations and trade bodies
- Telephone directories
- Trade exhibitions and conferences
- Competitors' catalogues, brochures and price lists
- Professional advisers (accountants, solicitors, consultants)
- Friends
- Chambers of Commerce
- Customers (existing or potential)
- Local authorities
- Internet web-sites
- Other entrepreneurs.

The world's largest information resource – the Internet – is only available by computer. Beyond all the hype, Internet access is a valuable tool for many small businesses. The wealth of information on the Internet is literally unimaginable and the ease of access is improving as new software becomes available. Using search engines (Lycos, Yahoo, etc.) is a cost-effective and fast way of finding your way to the information you need. Use the Internet as part of your information collection process. Other sites with useful information for entrepreneurs are included on the **TENBizPlan** web-site (**http://www.tenbizplan.com**).

Many sources will give you information free of charge, or at very little cost. Recognise their help where you can – even with just a "Thank You". You'll be amazed at how much it will be appreciated – and how much you will benefit when you go back for more information.

EXERCISE 3.14: YOUR NETWORK AS A SOURCE OF INFORMATION

Review the network you developed in **Exercise 2.6**. Make a list of people you know who might be able to help you with your market research or whose opinion you trust. Ask their opinion about your idea. Ask them to be critical and honest.

EXERCISE 3.15: BUSINESS MEDIA AS A SOURCE OF INFORMATION

List the business magazines and trade journals that you have access to. If you already know the magazines well, rate them for their likely usefulness.

Magazine	Source	Usefulness
The Economist	Library	Good regional and business surveys

Twenty-four out of twenty-five products do not survive the test of the marketplace.
DAVID OGILVY

EXERCISE 3.16: PROFESSIONAL/TRADE ASSOCIATIONS AS A SOURCE OF INFORMATION

List the professional associations and trade bodies that might be of assistance to you in your market research.

Association	Information it can provide	Contact details

Remember:

- Seek information from a variety of sources, not just from the "experts"
- Get feedback from a variety of sources
- Let people play "the devil's advocate" and argue against you
- Don't be afraid to ask "stupid" questions – You will get some very clever answers
- Look for yourself – Don't assume anything.

> The way to do research is to attack the facts at the point of greatest astonishment.
> CELIA GREEN

Doing your own market research

Your market research should be structured to make sure you collect all the information you need. The structure depends on your product/service, your budget and the time you have available but it ought to cover:

- **Issue definition:** What do you want to find out?
- **Desk research:** Consulting directories, magazines and newspapers and the Internet
- **Pre-study field research:** A first test to see whether you are on the right track
- **Concept questionnaire:** Your initial questions
- **Testing the questionnaire:** Make sure that the questions can be understood and will give you useful answers
- **Field research:** Asking the questions
- **Data processing:** Processing the results
- **Reporting:** The final stage.

Research techniques

The starting point of all research is to define the issue: What do you want to know? Write it down in **Exercise 3.17**.

EXERCISE 3.17: ISSUE DEFINITION

I want my market research to tell me:

There are many ways of researching your idea, including:

- **Qualitative/quantitative:** Quantitative involves researching figures and percentages; qualitative means researching opinions, reasons why, etc.
- **Consumer/distribution/industrial:** You can research the end user of your product, how the product is brought to the end user, or how the product is made
- **Questionnaires/observation:** You can ask people personally, by mail, by phone, or observe their behaviour (which may be different from what they tell you)
- **Ad hoc/on-going:** You can do once-off research, or research over a longer period of time
- **Group/single:** You can interview a group of people or every person in your sample individually
- **Open/half-open/closed questions:** You can ask open questions (no control over the answer), half-open questions (give different options), or closed questions (yes or no).

EXERCISE 3.18: RESEARCH TECHNIQUES

Which research techniques will you use?

☐ Qualitative	☐ Quantitative	
☐ Consumer	☐ Distribution	☐ Industrial
☐ Questionnaires	☐ Observation	
☐ Ad hoc	☐ On-going	
☐ Group	☐ Single	
☐ Open	☐ Half-open	☐ Closed questions

After you have completed the desk research (and only then), start designing a questionnaire for the target customer groups you have identified. This will need some research in the target groups itself (location, availability, language, level of questioning, perceptions, etc.). Choose your research techniques from the following:

- Group discussion
- Questionnaire by direct mail
- Direct questioning
- Questioning by phone.

Based on the techniques (don't just choose one) you have chosen, design a questionnaire. Go back to basics. Ask yourself: Who? What? Why? When? Where? How?

EXERCISE 3.19: RESEARCH QUESTIONS

Make a list of questions you want to ask in your research.
Record them in your working papers.

Select only the most relevant questions. Depending on the approach you plan to take, you may need to take the length of the questionnaire into consideration. If the questionnaire is too long, people won't want to answer it – especially in the case of direct mail or questioning over the phone.

Then test the questionnaire with a small group of people to make sure that it is clear and user-friendly. If you get a poor response here, redesign your questionnaire and test it again.

When the questionnaire is complete, you are ready to do the field research. If your aim is to get quantitative information, the number of people questioned should be sufficient to be statistically valid (minimum between 500 and 1,000). Depending on the number of people who respond to your questionnaire (not everyone will agree to complete it and some may not complete it fully/correctly), you will need to approach many more people than the 500 or 1,000 needed for statistical validity.

Remember that the more time spent on market research before you start your business, the more it will benefit you in future stages. What you are doing here is, in effect, laying the basis for your business plan.

Before you finalise your market research, use the checklist in **Exercise 3.20** to make that you have not overlooked anything of importance.

EXERCISE 3.20: MARKET RESEARCH CHECKLIST   **E**

Does your market research cover:

Market size?	☐ Yes ☐ No
Market structure?	☐ Yes ☐ No
Market trends?	☐ Yes ☐ No
Market potential?	☐ Yes ☐ No
Market share?	☐ Yes ☐ No
Competitor activity?	☐ Yes ☐ No
Competitor prices?	☐ Yes ☐ No
Competitor products/services?	☐ Yes ☐ No
User attitudes/behaviour?	☐ Yes ☐ No
Government factors?	☐ Yes ☐ No
Economic factors?	☐ Yes ☐ No
Demographic factors?	☐ Yes ☐ No

Future trends:

◊ Economic?	☐ Yes ☐ No
◊ Technological?	☐ Yes ☐ No
◊ Environmental?	☐ Yes ☐ No
◊ Cultural?	☐ Yes ☐ No
◊ In your industry?	☐ Yes ☐ No

Now you need to analyse the information generated by your market research. Analyse the results of your research, identifying each result as an opportunity or threat in **Exercise 3.21**.

Use the summary from **Exercise 3.21** as the starting point for the Marketing phase of the business planning process – see **Chapter 5, Marketing & Sales**. By that stage, you will be looking for much greater detail.

> *Better to return and make a net,*
> *than to go down to the stream and merely wish for fish.*
> CHINESE PROVERB

EXERCISE 3.21: ANALYSIS & SUMMARY OF MARKET RESEARCH RESULTS

                                                          Opportunities   Threats

List the results of your market research here, identifying
whether they represent opportunities or threats to the business

◊

◊

◊

Now summarise your market research as follows:

◊ Market description

◊ Target customers

◊ Trends

◊ Conclusion

◊ APPENDIX: Market research questionnaire; detailed responses, etc.

Three-quarters of all entrepreneurs start up without doing any market testing to
establish whether there is demand for their product/service.

Only three in ten carry out market research to determine whether a market exists
for their business in the first place.

Fewer still – one in five – draw up a detailed customer profile to build up
knowledge about their prospective customers and their buying habits.

Knowing who your customers are and why they will buy from you, rather than
from your competitors, should be a crucial part in deciding how a business will
fit into the market and whether it is likely to succeed.

Those that do not assess their long-term market potential and overall competitive
stance may risk early closure or failure.

BARCLAYS BANK

Network development

Write down the names down of the people you talked to during your market research and add them to your personal network (**Exercise 2.6**).

Now redefine your business idea in **Exercise 3.22**.

EXERCISE 3.22: IDEA DEFINITION – III

Does your market research allow you to:

Describe your idea/product/service clearly?

Identify the key materials, experience, skills, equipment that you will need to produce and deliver your product/service?

Identify your customers and competition?

Assess the scale of the project?

Assess the likely selling price(s), margin(s) and sales quantity(ies) for your product/service?

Decide whether the idea is a good fit with your personal circumstances and resources?

You may find it useful, now that you have defined your business idea for the third time, to go back to **Exercise 2.5** and re-examine how your experience and skills contribute to your business.

As you work through the other parts of this guide, you will revisit this definition of your business idea and amend it further, based on the new information you learn.

But before you move on, just apply a quick reality check – is your business idea feasible in your personal circumstances?

Your market research should have given you some sense of the likely scale of your project – in terms of turnover, capital investment, staffing, costings, etc. Is it realistic for you to follow through with the project? Will your resources – financial, managerial, etc – allow you to do so?

For example, you discover through your research that your project needs an investment of £1 million, but your personal capital amounts only to £50,000 and you have no track record in the industry. Realistically, even if the project succeeds, you won't be in the driving seat since you have no leverage. On the other hand, if the project needs £200,000 and you have £50,000 already and you have a decade's good experience in the industry, and can build a team of experienced professionals quickly, then you have a much better chance of success.

If your project is not right, see where you can fix it. If it can't be fixed, drop it, and look for another project.

THE TENBIZPLAN APPROACH TO BUSINESS PLANNING

Text

In this chapter, you have created no draft text for input into your business plan document.

Evidence

File copies of all of the exercises that you have completed in **Chapter 3**, for ease of reference later. They will be a crucial part of your evidence supporting your business plan.

Where you have identified other information that would be good evidence for your business plan, file it in the appropriate section of your working papers also.

Numbers

There are no numbers created for input into your financial projections as part of the process of business planning in this chapter.

Key Question

The key question for this chapter is:

Have I a feasible business idea?

To answer the question, you will need to consider:

- Your idea – **Exercise 3.22**
- Future trends
- Your market research.

FORMALITIES

The key question for this chapter is:

> **What formalities must I complete before I start my business?**

This is a critical stage for start-ups, so it's appropriate to pause and reflect for a moment.

    You have completed a detailed personal assessment and have identified and developed your business idea. You are anxious to make progress towards starting your business, yet this is when you should take a little time out to deal with the formalities lest they trip you up later.

> It is more important to know where you are going than to get there quickly.
> Do not mistake activity for achievement.
> MABEL NEWCOMBER

Output from this chapter

By the end of this chapter, you will have:

- Decided on your business' legal structure, tax status and other necessary formalities.

Links to other chapters

The links between this chapter and the other elements of business include:

- **Personal Assessment (Chapter 2):** Your personality will influence your choice of legal structure for your business – for example, you may prefer to run your business as a co-operative rather than being the "boss" in a company

- **Idea Assessment (Chapter 3):** Again, your social awareness will influence the type of idea you develop and help you to determine the best legal structure in which to develop it

- **Marketing & Sales (Chapter 5):** The image you want to present of your business will influence its legal structure, the name that you choose for it and the bank with which you hold your accounts, since your customers' perception of all these will be important to you

- **Finance & Funding (Chapter 8):** The type of funds you want to raise will influence your legal structure – and *vice versa*.

LEGAL STRUCTURE

When starting in business, subject to the differences in business law between countries, you have a choice of five main types of business entity through which to conduct your enterprise. They are:

- Sole trader
- Partnership
- Unlimited company
- Limited company
- Co-operative.

Seven things will decide which structure you choose:

- **The kind of business you are starting:** Some professional services firms, for instance, can only be formed as sole traders or partnerships
- **The expectations of those with whom you plan to do business:** Many business people expect to deal with limited companies and are wary of trading with other forms of business entity
- **Your attitude to risk:** In particular, your attitude to risking those of your assets that you are not planning to commit to the business. A limited liability company limits the risk of losing all your personal capital if your enterprise is not successful
- **How you wish to organise your tax affairs:** Certain kinds of favourable tax treatment are only available to limited liability companies
- **Your financial needs:** Fund-raising is easier in a corporate structure
- **The image you want to project:** Corporate structures often appear grander than non-corporate entities
- **National and local business laws:** These may only permit a certain structure for your business – for example, partnerships for professional services firms.

You are taking a risk in starting an enterprise. You are risking your money, time and reputation. You are entitled to protect those of your assets that you do not wish to commit to your enterprise. For this reason, you are strongly advised to form a limited liability company. However, because of the tax and other implications of doing so, you should take professional help and advice before making your decision.

At this point, you should check with your local company/business registration authority for details of relevant local legislation.

Sole trader

In most countries, you automatically become a sole trader by starting up a business. Setting up as a sole trader usually needs little by way of legal formality.

An advantage of being a sole trader is that apart from normal tax returns, which every business must make, a sole trader usually is not subject to the same public disclosure of financial performance as limited liability companies. The downside of being a sole trader is that you have no protection if your business fails. All your assets become available to pay off your creditors.

Partnership

A partnership is an agreement between two or more people to go into business together. It may be no more formal than a handshake or may run to a multi-page legal document.

Whichever route you take, build the following points into your planning:

In a partnership, each partner is liable for all the liabilities of the business. If the business fails, and your partner (or partners) abandons you, you could be left to pay for everything out of your own pocket. Before entering a partnership, decide whether you trust your partner(s)-to-be with everything you own — because that's what you will be doing

If you write down nothing else, write down and have all the partners sign a partnership agreement setting out how the business is to be financed, how profits and losses are to be shared, and what will happen if one of the partners decides to leave. These are important points. Failure to agree on them at an early stage can lead to difficulty later.

> One of the most fruitful sources of ruin to men of the world is the recklessness or want of principle of partners, and it is one of the perils to which every man exposes himself who enters into business with another.
> SIR R MALINS

An unlimited company

An unlimited company is much the same as a limited liability company. The principal difference is that the company's Memorandum of Association (part of the company's constitution) states that the liability of members is unlimited.

Again, like sole traders and partnerships, an unlimited company exposes your total assets in the event of the failure of the company. This form of company is more suitable for clubs and associations than for trading businesses.

A limited liability company

A limited liability company is a legal entity separate from its shareholders. The shareholders are only liable, in the event of the business becoming unable to pay its debts, for any amount outstanding on their subscribed shareholdings. This means that, if the share capital is fully paid up (as it usually is), the shareholders' have no further liability – though they may lose their entire share capital.

Some limited companies are limited by guarantee – the guarantee being the amount that the members agree to pay in the event of the company going into liquidation. Like unlimited companies, this form of company is more suitable for clubs and associations than for trading businesses.

The advantages of a limited company over a sole trader or partnership are:

- **Limited liability status:** This protects those of your assets that you have not committed to the business

- **Scope for tax planning:** Tax legislation and incentives are usually directed at limited liability companies rather than sole traders.

Limited liability companies have advantages

The disadvantages of a limited liability company include:

- The cost of formation expenses
- The requirement for an annual audit (in some countries, limited liability companies with turnover below a specified threshold are exempt from the requirement to have their financial statements audited each year)

... and disadvantages

- The public disclosure of company financial and ownership information

- The need for accounts to comply with companies legislation and relevant auditing and accounting standards
- The fact that business losses may not be set against personal income
- The possibility of further taxation on capital gains if appreciating assets are withdrawn from the business.

A co-operative

A worker co-operative is where a team comes together to form and run a business according to a set of values that include self-help, self-responsibility, democracy, equality, equity and solidarity. The business is jointly owned and democratically controlled, unlike other more hierarchical business structures. Co-operative members believe in the ethical values of honesty, openness, social responsibility and caring for others.

The Co-operative Principles, which provide guidelines setting out how the business should conduct itself, are:

- **Voluntary and open membership:** Co-operatives do not permit gender, social, racial, political or religious discrimination and are open to all willing to accept the responsibilities of membership
- **Democratic member control:** Co-operatives are democratically controlled by their members, who actively participate in setting policies and in decision-making
- **Member economic participation:** Members contribute equitably to the capital of their business. Surpluses are used to develop the business, benefiting members in proportion to their transactions with the co-operative and supporting activities approved by the membership
- **Autonomy and independence:** In all contracts with external bodies, co-operatives ensure that members retain democratic control and their co-operative autonomy
- **Education, training and information:** Co-operatives provide education and training for their members and employees to ensure their effective contribution
- **Co-operation among co-operatives:** Co-operatives work together through local, regional, national and international structures
- **Concern for community:** Co-operatives work for sustainable development through policies approved by their members.

Local legislation will determine the legal structure of a co-operative, although in many countries co-operatives can be formed as limited liability companies.

EXERCISE 4.1: LEGAL STRUCTURE

You will need to state your business' legal structure in your business plan and explain if it differs from what would be expected. In most cases, the choice will be between being a sole trader or forming a limited liability company.

Which legal structure is most suitable for your business?   Sole trader? ☐

Limited liability company? ☐

Why?

BUSINESS NAMES

The name of a business is one of its most important assets, even though it does not appear in the balance sheet with the other assets. Choose the name of your business carefully. The right name will be:

- Unique
- Easy to remember, pronounce and spell
- Informative
- Image-creating.

You cannot use the name of an existing business, or one that will be confused with the name of an existing business.

A limited company that wishes to trade under a name other than the company's registered name (for example as *West European Forest Advisory Services*, even though the company is registered as *John Smith Limited*), usually must register the business name.

However, note that registration of a business name does not:

- Give protection against duplication of the name (since others may be entitled to use it, though you can prevent them from "passing off" – pretending to be you)
- Imply that the name will prove acceptable as a company name (it may already be registered, or become registered later, as a company name)
- Authorise the use of the name, if its use could be prohibited for other reasons — for example, because the name proposed is the trademark of another person.

Because of this last point, it is important not to spend any money on stationery, signs etc. until your company or business name is officially registered.

Internet names

Because of abuse of the facility to register Internet "domain" names, you may now be required to provide evidence that you have some entitlement to a domain name that you wish to register. A company registration or a registered business name may help provide this evidence.

EXERCISE 4.2: BUSINESS NAME

What do you plan to call your business?

Why?

Are there other businesses with similar names?   ☐ Yes ☐ No

How will you distinguish your business from these?

Have you checked the availability of your preferred business name:

◊   In your own country?   ☐ Yes ☐ No

◊   In other countries where you plan to operate?   ☐ Yes ☐ No

◊   As an Internet domain name?   ☐ Yes ☐ No

TAXATION

Although taxation legislation varies from country to country, in general businesses are subject to the following types of taxes, however they may be described:

- **Income tax:** Sole traders and partnerships on their profits
- **Corporation tax:** Limited liability companies on their profits
- **Value added tax (VAT)/Sales tax:** All businesses on sales
- **Social insurance:** All businesses with employees (including owner/directors)
- **Capital gains tax:** All businesses on capital gains made on the purchase and resale of non-trading assets.

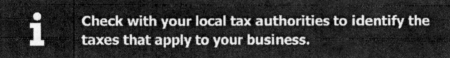

i Check with your local tax authorities to identify the taxes that apply to your business.

Registration for tax

It is usually your obligation to notify the taxation authorities, through your local tax office, of the establishment of your business and to provide them with the information they require to register your business for the relevant taxes.

Record-keeping

Taxation authorities usually have certain requirements regarding record-keeping and accounts that you must comply with. Your accountant or local tax office will provide you with all the information you need.

Returns

For most taxes, you are required to supply the taxation authorities with specific information on, or by, specific dates. These are called "returns" and there are usually penalties for late submission or not submitting returns at all. Again, your accountant or local tax office will provide you with all the information you need.

Information and assistance

Information and assistance on tax regulations, etc. is available from your local tax office, or from an accountant.

EXERCISE 4.3: TAXATION

E
N

Have you contacted your local tax office and obtained all the
information you need?   ☐ Yes ☐ No
Have you identified the taxes that will apply to your business? ☐ Yes ☐ No
Have you registered for these?   ☐ Yes ☐ No
If "No", when must you do so?
List the rates of taxation that will apply to your business:
◊   VAT/Sales tax
◊   Corporation/Income tax
◊   Other ....
List the dates when you must make returns of information and payments to the tax authorities.

Having established your responsibilities under local tax legislation, you must make sure that someone competent is charged with ensuring compliance with these on an on-going basis. Allow for this important role when you come to plan your administrative process and staffing in **Chapters 6** and **7**.

> There's nothing so hard to understand as the income tax.
> ALBERT EINSTEIN

BANK ACCOUNTS

At least one bank **account** is essential for any business, however small. Don't be tempted to run your business through your own personal bank account "until it gets off the ground". That is a recipe for disaster. Open a separate bank account for your business as soon as you begin to trade.

Check with the bank of your choice about the procedure for opening an account.

Take professional advice from an accountant on the type, or types, of account that your business needs.

EXERCISE 4.4: BANK DETAILS

Have you opened a bank account(s) for your business?   ☐ Yes ☐ No
List the interest rate that will apply to your borrowings.
List the dates when interest will be charged or credited to your bank account.

Licensing

Despite a global move towards de-regulation, many industries and types of business are subject to a great deal of regulation by government, both central and local. In many cases, licences are required to carry on certain trades or activities.

> **i** Check with your local professional adviser, from a business lawyer, or from a local business support/advisory body about the regulations that may apply to your business and take appropriate steps to ensure compliance with these.

Since the detail of international business regulation is beyond the scope of this guide, you must take local professional advice. Look at the section on *Professional Advisers* in **Chapter 7** to help you choose an appropriately qualified and experienced adviser to assist you in this task.

Use **Exercise 4.5** to help you on licensing.

Exercise 4.5: Licensing   **E**

Have you contacted an appropriately qualified and experienced adviser and obtained all the information on local business regulations that you need?   ☐ Yes ☐ No

Have you identified the regulations that will apply to your business?

☐ Yes ☐ No

Have you taken the necessary steps to ensure compliance with these?

☐ Yes ☐ No

If "No", when must you do so?

Have you obtained all the licences necessary to start your business?

☐ Yes ☐ No

INSURANCE

Business is full of risks. However, many business risks can be foreseen and action taken to avoid, or at least reduce, loss. A programme of risk identification and management can pay dividends, but the most common way of reducing the risk of loss is through insurance.

Insurance can be divided into two types:

- Business-related
- People-related.

Business insurance

The main kinds of business insurance are:

- **Fire:** To cover rebuilding costs, etc following a fire
- **Burglary/theft:** To replace stolen or damaged assets
- **All risks:** Coverage against loss of assets, however caused
- **Public liability:** Coverage against claims by members of the public
- **Product liability:** Coverage against loss arising from defective or dangerous products
- **Employer's liability:** Coverage against claims from staff
- **Motor insurance:** Coverage against driving accidents.

The availability, extent of cover and price of these various forms of insurance will depend on local legislation and market conditions.

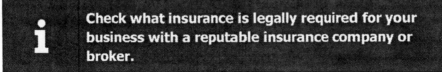

Check what insurance is legally required for your business with a reputable insurance company or broker.

Most insurance companies offer the types of insurance listed above (or some combination of them) in a single "Office" or "Business" policy, which is more cost-effective for a small business than separate policies for each.

Other areas for which you might consider the protection of insurance include:

- Legal fees protection
- Credit insurance
- Bad debt insurance
- Data/computer
- Travel
- Goods in transit
- Patents
- Business interruption.

Since insurance companies rate risks differently, it is worth talking to an insurance broker, whose role is to find you the widest coverage at the lowest price.

Ask whether you can reduce the premiums by paying an excess (just like motor insurance). Ask also whether the premiums can be paid in instalments throughout the year rather than all at the start.

People-related insurance

If the business is dependent on yourself, or one or two key staff, it is also a good idea to take out "keyman insurance" on these people. Then, if these key staff die or are unable to work, the insurance company will pay a lump sum to the business to help it overcome the difficulty posed by their absence.

You may also want to look at life assurance (to provide "death-in-service" benefits), critical illness, permanent health insurance or medical expenses insurance for your staff. Here cost, and whether staff value the insurance, will be major factors.

Your own insurance

What insurance you take out on yourself depends on the risk you are willing to take, your budget and your family situation. You may already have some insurance in place, in which case taking out more through the business would be duplication.

Look at the key risks:

- **You could get sick and not be able to work** – You need insurance to provide a replacement income (permanent health insurance)
- **You could get sick or die and have no one to take over the running of the business for you** – You need a replacement income plus enough extra to pay someone else to run your business (permanent health/critical illness/life assurance).

Talk to a life assurance broker about coverage against these risks. Talk to him/her also about pensions. A pension can be a tax-effective way of transferring cash from your business to yourself.

Use **Exercise 4.6** to calculate your business' insurance premiums. You will not input these into your financial projections until **Chapter 6**, when we will input all overheads together, since it may not be possible to determine some of your premiums until your business processes have been defined in **Chapter 6**.

EXERCISE 4.6: INSURANCE

Calculate your business' insurance premiums.

	Annual Premium €	Month payable
Business insurance		
Fire		
Burglary/theft		
All risks		
Public liability		
Product liability		
Employer's liability		
Motor insurance		
Other		
Total business insurance		
People insurance		
Health		
Disability		
Life assurance		
Pension		
Other		
Total people insurance		
Total insurance		

THE TENBIZPLAN APPROACH TO BUSINESS PLANNING

Text

In this chapter, you have created draft text for input into your business plan document in relation to:

* The legal status of your business – **Exercise 4.1**.

Evidence

File copies of all of the exercises that you have completed in **Chapter 4**, for ease of reference later. They will be a crucial part of your evidence supporting your business plan.

In this chapter, you will also have identified other information that will be good evidence for your business plan – for example, information regarding, or copies of, licences that your new business may require. File these safely as part of your working papers also.

Numbers

The numbers created for input into your financial projections as part of the process of business planning in this chapter are:

* Tax rates – **Exercise 4.3**
* Bank interest rates – **Exercise 4.4**.

You have also begun to identify the insurance costs that your business will bear (**Exercise 4.6**). We will not input these into your financial projections until **Chapter 6**, **Process & Resources**, when we consider overhead expenses as a whole.

Key Question

The key question for this chapter is:

> **What formalities must I complete before I start my business?**

To answer the question, you will need to consider the following aspects of your business:

- Name
- Legal and taxation status
- Banking arrangements
- Licensing and regulatory requirements
- Insurance cover.

5

MARKETING & SALES

The key question for this chapter is:

What sales do I expect and how will I generate them?

In **Chapter 3, Idea Assessment**, you defined your idea for a product or service for your business and you carried out some market research.

This chapter takes you to the core of your business. It asks a simple question that will determine whether your business is going to be a success – How much are you going to sell and how will these sales be generated? It's a question that is much of interest to an established business as it is to a start-up – except that a start-up has no track record of previous sales to learn from.

We will work through a number of important topics before considering sales forecasts for your business plan. It's unlikely that you have enough information from your market research alone to substantiate any sensible sales forecasts at this early stage. That's not surprising, since you are still at an early stage of the business planning process.

But the sales forecast is pivotal. The heart of the business planning process involves substantiating your estimates, by gathering evidence that supports them. This evidence is found by doing further market research. You will research your customers, competitors and marketing mix and, from these, you will develop a detailed marketing and sales plan.

Many small businesses claim that they cannot afford a marketing department. But, whether you intend to have a formal marketing department or not, as an entrepreneur you will have to face marketing decisions about:

- The product itself
- Price
- Customer service levels
- Physical distribution
- Advertising
- Sales
- The sales force
- Information about markets.

Marketing department or not ... you must decide these

Whether you formalise this decision-making in a marketing department is irrelevant – the decisions must still be made. This chapter will show you how.

Output from this chapter

The main aim of this chapter is to help you to develop:

- A mission statement
- A marketing strategy
- Sales forecasts
- Draft text for input into the **"Marketing"** section of your business plan.

Link to other chapters

Your marketing strategy will determine your sales forecast and your profit. This is because marketing shapes all the other parts of your business as your marketing approach determines the processes, your staffing, etc.

As you work through this chapter, you will touch on many other topics – this is a long and important chapter in the guide.

And, you will find that marketing has an impact on – and is impacted by – decisions you make in other stages of the business planning process. Specifically:

- **Personal assessment (Chapter 2):** Your personal values will decide the values of your business, which in turn will impact on your mission statement and your marketing approach
- **Idea assessment (Chapter 3):** Your preliminary market research will have told you that your business idea is feasible. More detailed research in this

chapter may change that view or cause you to change your product/service in some way to meet the needs of the market more closely

- **Process & Resources (Chapter 6):** As you research your business idea, you may discover opportunities or problems for your process
- **People (Chapter 7):** Your marketing approach has a direct impact on your staffing and the way your business is organised. Your choice of channels of distribution is the main deciding factor here.

> The responsiveness of a firm to the customer is directly proportional to the distance on the organisation chart from the consumer to the chairman of the board.
> VIRGINIA KNAUER

CUSTOMERS

Your market research should have defined the customers that the business is going to target. If not, go back to the section on *Market research* in **Chapter 3** and use the techniques shown there to do more research on your potential customers.

In **Exercise 5.1**, you will expand your preliminary definition of customers into a more detailed profile that will direct the promotion and selling plans you develop in this chapter.

If you can answer the questions in **Exercise 5.1**, you will know that you have a good understanding of your potential customers. Note that, if your product/services are very different from each other, you may need to define separate customer/target groups for each, repeating **Exercise 5.1** as often as necessary.

EXERCISE 5.1: YOUR CUSTOMERS

Your customers/target groups:
Who are they?
Which are the most promising?
Where are they located?
How do they spend their time?
How do they spend their money?
Where do they spend their money?
How are they organised?
Where do they socialise?
What issues are important to them?
What do they read?
What do they watch on TV?
What do they listen to on radio?
Who forms their opinions?
Where do they buy products/services similar to yours?

Defining your customer/target groups is not an abstract exercise. There is a clear interaction between your customers and the definition of your product/service. **Exercise 5.2** identifies this interaction. Again, you may need to repeat this exercise for each customer/target group and product/service combination.

It is important to find out what elements in your service or product are most important to them. A customer who intends to buy a PC for home use may be more concerned about the PC's price than its specification, whereas the same person buying for his employer's business may be more concerned with reliability than price. If you do not understand your customers' buying motives at this level, you may promote the wrong aspects of your product/service and not achieve the sales that you deserve.

To understand fully your customers' needs, make sure to clarify exactly what the customer means by probing until you are clear what the real needs are. You must see things through the customers' eyes. For example, if customers say they want "Total quality", ask "What do you mean by that?". When they answer "Quick response", you ask "What do you mean by quick response?". After asking "What do you mean?" a few times, you will define the real need accurately.

In answering **Exercise 5.2** below, it is critical that you answer from a full knowledge of your customers' wants – not your perception of their wants.

EXERCISE 5.2: INTERACTION BETWEEN CUSTOMERS AND IDEA DEFINITION

What are the five elements of your product/service that are most important to your customers:

1.

2.

3.

4.

5.

How do you know that these are the five most important elements?

What implications do these elements have for your product/service?

As business becomes more sophisticated, it is proving more and more difficult to generalise about customers and their needs. Indeed, marketing practice is focusing more and more on one-to-one marketing, wherever possible, building long-term relationships with individual customers.

Trends show that customers are:

- Driven by value, as distinct from price
- Highly individualised (one-to-one marketing)
- Very sophisticated in recognising marketing and sales techniques (and avoiding those they do not wish to respond to)
- Using access to information to make better informed buying decisions
- Aware of global competition.

As well as identifying the exact needs and wants of your customers, it is also important to identify how the customer makes a buying decision. Use **Exercise 5.3** to help you identify this process. Again, you may need to repeat this exercise for different customer/target groups.

EXERCISE 5.3: CUSTOMERS' BUYING DECISIONS

How much information does the customer collect before buying?
How much time is spent on selecting the right item to buy?
Is it a once-off buy or a regular purchase?
Who is involved in making the buying decision?
◊ Customer only?
◊ Customer and spouse/partner or customer and business colleagues?
◊ Customer and family?
◊ Customer and outsiders?
Is buying based on an impulse?
How quickly do customers want delivery of the product/service after making the purchase?
Does the product need service or maintenance?
If so, can this be sold to the customer at the time of buying the product?
How long will the customer use the product?
What implications does this buying process have for your product/service?

Customer service

Businesses spend a lot of money on attracting new customers. But it is cheaper to keep your existing customers than to find new ones.

Loyal customers:

- Spend more money with you than other customers
- Bring in new customers (word-of-mouth recommendations)
- Cost less than acquiring new customers.

Use **Exercise 5.4** to calculate the lifetime value of one of your customers.

Exercise 5.4: Calculating the Lifetime Value of a Customer

E

Average sale value per customer	€ _____
multiplied by	
Number of sales per year per customer	_____
Total sales value per year per customer	€ _____
multiplied by	
Number of years customer buys from you	_____
Gross lifetime sales value per customer	€ _____

Plus, if every satisfied customer tells one or two other people and they become customers, look how fast your sales will grow!

What steps will you take to keep your customers loyal to your business:

◊ Regular visits?   ☐ Yes ☐ No

◊ Regular telephone contact?   ☐ Yes ☐ No

◊ Regular direct mail contact?   ☐ Yes ☐ No

◊ Regular evaluation of your business' performance
  in meeting their needs?   ☐ Yes ☐ No

◊ Interviews with customers whose business you
  have lost to find out why this happened?   ☐ Yes ☐ No

One way of creating and keeping loyal customers is through customer service – not just any old customer service but through superb world-class customer service.

World-class? Why not? Where's the competition? When did you last get service from any business that was so good that you would recommend someone else to use them? When did you last get service so good that you noticed?

The fact that you have only a small business makes no difference – in fact, it makes it easier for you to be close to the customer.

Customer service involves:

- Doing what you promised the customer
- Willingness to help
- Providing prompt service
- Well-trained staff
- Individual attention
- Little things which make the difference.

Research studies show that businesses that provide top class customer service experience:

- Improvements in morale (reducing staff costs)
- Lower staff turnover (reducing recruitment costs)
- Longer customer retention (up to 50% longer)
- More repeat business (20-40% lower selling costs)
- More referrals (20-40% lower promotional costs)
- Higher prices (7-12% higher)
- Increased margins (7-17% more profit).

Calculate the difference that even some of these – let alone all of them! – would make to your profits.

Then decide how you are going to put customer service into action in your business. Use **Exercise 5.5** to record your ideas.

> If we are not customer-driven, our cars won't be either.
> DONALD PETERSEN, CEO Ford

Exercise 5.5: Customer Service

I plan to implement world-class customer service in my business by:

All these exercises will inform your marketing strategy. Next you should summarise what you know about your customers, for inclusion in the text section of your business plan. Use **Exercise 5.6**.

Exercise 5.6: Customers – Summary

My customers ....

> The four advantages of loyal customers: They buy more; they're cheaper to service; they bring new customers; and they don't rely on price.
> MURRAY RAPHAEL

COMPETITION

A competitor is a business that provides:

- Similar products/services to yours ("direct" competition)
- Alternatives to your products/services ("indirect" competition).

In either case, a competitor has the potential to take away sales that could be yours. This is why it is important to understand who your competitors are, how they operate, and why they are successful.

Use **Exercise 5.7** to identify and assess your competitors.

Approach this from two points of view:

- **Product/service alternatives:** Your customers can buy one of your competitors' product/service instead of yours

- **Alternatives based on the customer's budget:** Your customer can decide to spend his money on something entirely different – for example, on a holiday or on clothes.

This second point introduces the concept of indirect competitors, those who compete with you, not with similar or alternative products/services, but simply for the same share of the customer's budget. They are just as much part of your competition as your direct competitors.

Exercise 5.7: Competitors

	Direct	Indirect
What are the alternatives to your products/services?		
Who makes/sells these alternatives?		
Among these, who are your main competitors?		
What range of products/services do they have?		
What kind of choices do they offer customers?		
How broad is their range?		
What are their target groups?		
What are their future prospects?		
What are they good at and what are they not so good at?		
What implications do your competitors have for your products/services?		

Next, you should look at your closest direct competition. **Exercise 5.8** will help you.

> There is no finish line.
> NIKE CORPORATION MOTTO

> Competition is the keen edge of business, always shaving away at costs.
> HENRY FORD

EXERCISE 5.8: PRODUCT/SERVICE COMPARISON WITH DIRECT COMPETITORS

Take the five features of your product/service that your customers identify as being most important to them and rate these features against each of your five closest direct competitors' product/service.

   Repeat for each competitor.

		Name of Competitor:	
Feature	**Better**	**Same**	**Not as good**
◊			
◊			
◊			
◊			
◊			

Repeat the exercise for each feature.

		Feature:	
Competitor	**Better**	**Same**	**Not as good**
◊			
◊			
◊			
◊			
◊			

What implications does this analysis have for your product/service?
Where can you compete most strongly?

> Competition makes life turbulent and uncertain;
> competition almost always eats into profits.
> Worse, you can lose at competition.
> CHARLES MANN

You need to establish a competitive advantage over your competitors – price, quality, service or some other area of importance to your customers.

Review your competitors on a regular basis. Check whether you need to act to keep your competitive advantage. If you do, you can:

Deter:

- Create barriers through contracts, licensing, trade agreements or agents.
- Exploit advantages of contacts (see network), location, economy of scale, flexibility
- Seek alliances

Attack:

- Head on through price, promotion, technology or marketing.

Defend:

- Defend through customer database and network.

Respect your competition. They can help you broaden the market for your products/services.

Next you should summarise what you know about your competition, for inclusion in the text section of your business plan. Use **Exercise 5.9**.

EXERCISE 5.9: COMPETITION – SUMMARY

My competition ....

DEVELOPING A STRATEGY

Developing a strategy is as simple (or as complicated) as answering:

- Where are we now?

- Where do we want to go?

- How and when will we get there?

The first question – **Where are we now?** – is answered by the market research you did in **Chapter 3, Idea assessment**, and by your business' value statement. Look at your market research in the context of a SWOT (Strengths, Weaknesses, Opportunities and Threats) analysis. Use **Exercise 5.10**.

EXERCISE 5.10: SWOT ANALYSIS

Review your market research from **Chapter 3** and categorise each finding as a:
◊ Strength
◊ Weakness
◊ Opportunity
◊ Threat

Summarise the trends in relation to your business:
◊ Use of technology:
◊ Customer needs:
◊ Competition:

Your value statement

Your business' value statement expresses its values and guiding principles. These are not abstract concepts, but practical realities, rooted in your own personal value system (see **Exercise 2.4**), that determine the way your business will be managed and operated.

For example, if your business develops computer games software, its **value** statement will determine its position on issues such as:

- **Extreme violence in the games it develops:** Is violence acceptable at all? And, if so, what level of violence?

- **Determining suitability of its games for young children:** Will you adopt industry standards for suitability of content? Or work to higher standards?

- **Epilepsy as result of playing computer games:** Will you avoid features that may cause epilepsy – even in a tiny percentage of users? Or will you ignore the research?

Use the following exercises to consider your business' values.

If "values" are difficult for you to pin down, consider starting by developing a "Passion" statement instead. Write down what it is that you – and by extension, your business – are passionate about. What makes a difference? This will give you a good insight into your values.

EXERCISE 5.11: VALUES

Rank the following in their order of importance to you **in a business context**:
(1= not important, 10 = very important):

◊ Personal development
◊ Maximum profit
◊ Creating employment
◊ Sustainable development
◊ Satisfying customers
◊ Beating the competition
◊ Raising your children
◊ The environment
◊ Developing good relationships
◊ Developing new products.

Based on your answers above, how would you deal with the following scenarios:
You discover that a supplier has been under-billing you for the last 8 months. Will you inform your supplier, knowing that as a result you will have to pay him the difference?

☐ Yes ☐ No

Your company has an important deadline to meet. One of the key people on the project must work overtime, but will miss a child's birthday as a result. Who would you regard as the "better" employee:

◊ The employee who declines to work overtime and instead attends the birthday party
◊ The employee who willingly agrees to work overtime.

You find that your packaging might cause an allergic reaction to a very small group of users. Redesign of the packaging will put a strain on your profit margins. Will you redesign the packaging? ☐ Yes ☐ No

What do your answers tell you about your business values?

An excellent, if long, example of a value statement was prepared by RW Johnson, of Johnson & Johnson, in 1943 and is shown in **Figure 5A**.

FIGURE 5A: JOHNSON & JOHNSON CREDO

Our Credo

We believe that our first responsibility is to the doctors, nurses, hospitals, mothers and all others who use our products. Our products must always be of the highest quality. We must constantly strive to reduce the cost of these products. Our orders must be promptly and accurately filled. Our dealers must make a fair profit.

Our second responsibility is to those who work with us – the men and women in our plants and offices. They must have a sense of security in their jobs. Wages must be fair and adequate, management just, hours reasonable, and working conditions clean and orderly. Employees should have an organised system for suggestions and complaints. Supervisors and department heads must be qualified and fair-minded. There must be an opportunity for advancement for those qualified and each person must be considered an individual standing on his own dignity and merit.

Our third responsibility is to our management. Our executives must be persons of talent, education, experience and ability. They must be persons of common-sense and full understanding.

Our fourth responsibility is to the communities in which we live. We must be a good citizen – support good works and charity, and bear our fair share of taxes. We must maintain in good order the property we are privileged to use. We must participate in promotion of civic improvement, health, education and good government, and acquaint the community with our activities.

Our fifth and last responsibility is to our shareholders. Business must make a sound profit. Reserves must be created, research must be carried on, adventurous programs developed, and mistakes paid for. Adverse times must be provided for, adequate taxes paid, new machines purchased, new plants built, new products launched, and new sales plans developed. We must experiment with new ideas. When these things have been done, the stockholders should receive a fair return. We are determined, with the help of God's grace, to fulfil these obligations to the best of our ability.

Not every value statement is – or need be – as long as the Johnson & Johnson Credo. But each one needs to cover the essential points, as seen by the business' owners. What is important to you. Write your value statement in **Exercise 5.12**.

EXERCISE 5.12: VALUE STATEMENT

Write a value statement for your business that explains the values that you will aspire to in your dealings with:

◊ Customers
◊ Staff
◊ Suppliers
◊ Public/Community in general
◊ Shareholders.

The second question in deciding your direction – **Where do we want to go?** – is determined by the targets you set for your business and is explained in your business' vision statement. Use **Exercise 5.13** to consider the market positioning you want for your business. You may need to return to this exercise after you have worked through some of the later sections of this chapter.

EXERCISE 5.13: MARKET POSITIONING

Which markets will you focus on?
◊   Focus: On what?
◊   Product/market combinations: What fits what?
◊   Growth, decline, stabilisation: How is your market developing generally?
◊   Life cycle of the product: What stage is your product at?
◊   New markets: Where? At what cost?
◊   New products: How?
◊   National or international: What are your ambitions?
◊   Broad market or niche market: Where are you aiming?
◊   Innovation: What part will it play?
◊   Mission Statement: What is your business' Mission Statement? How does this determine your strategy?
◊   What position do you want to take in those markets?
◊   Market share: What market share do you want to achieve?
◊   Image: How much do you want to distinguish yourself from your competitors?

What resources do you need to achieve that position?
What timeframe have you set to achieve that position?

Once you have established the positioning you want, you need to set yourself targets. Use **Exercise 5.14** to do this.

> Obstacles are things a person sees when he takes his eyes off his goal.
> E JOSEPH COSSMAN

EXERCISE 5.14: TARGETS

What do you want to achieve with your business?

What are your targets:
◊ For year 1?
◊ For year 5?
◊ For year 10?

How are you going to achieve the targets:
◊ For year 1?
◊ For year 5?
◊ For year 10?

In answering the questions in **Exercise 5.14**, you probably found that you could be very specific about the first year targets, but that five-year and 10-year targets are necessarily more aspirational.

Every year, you should set yourself targets for the next year, keeping in mind your 10-year plan, which sets out the direction of your business. Compare it to a road map. The 10-year plan is the destination; the one-year plans are the turns (right, left, straight, short cut, scenic route, stop-over, break for coffee, etc.). The direction you have decided needs to be checked on a regular basis to see whether your plans need adjustment.

Your vision statement

The vision statement explains the business as it expects to be in 10-15 years' time. This is how you communicate your targets. They may be ambitious, but all good targets are. They must be achievable, but not too easily. They must set a broad description that challenges everyone working within the business. And, finally, they must be measurable.

For example, your vision statement might be:

• "To be one of the 10 largest accountancy practices in the country by the year 2010"

- "To own and operate a chain of 20 profitable computer re-selling stores in more than 10 key cities by 2010".

Before developing a vision statement for your business, you should re-read the section on *Identifying future trends* in **Chapter 3**. Look back at **Exercises 3.11** and **3.12**. Remind yourself of your predictions of the future. Where does your business fit? What is your ambition for your business in 10 or 15 years?

EXERCISE 5.15: VISION STATEMENT

Now write a vision statement for your business.

Your mission statement

The final question – How and when will we get there? – is answered by your business' mission statement. This sets out the reason why the business exists – what it aims to achieve, why it does what it does. It defines what the business does. The challenge is to define what the business does sufficiently narrowly to provide a focus and yet, at the same time, in sufficiently broad terms to allow the business to grow. It should capture the essence of your idea and how it distinguishes you from your competitors.

For example, your mission statement might be:

- "We will provide general accountancy and financial-based advisory services to clients in knowledge-based industries, such as software and telecommunications. Our service will be characterised by a high level of use and awareness of modern accounting and information technology".

Start developing the statement for your own business by answering this question: What is the purpose of your company?

Mission statement: A talisman, to be hung on the wall, to ward off evil spirits.
EILEEN SHAPIRO, *Fad-surfing in the Boardroom*

Exercise 5.16: Mission Statement

Now write a mission statement for your business:

_____

Developing value, vision and mission statements is not easy, but it is important because they define the core of the business and strongly influence its ethics and direction. Obtain the annual reports of some international companies and read their statements to help you define your own.

What if you find it difficult to write these statements? That's not surprising – they are hard to write, since they demand that you have a very clear and concise picture of your business and where you want to take it.

Instead, leave whatever rough drafts you have written and return to them when you have worked through the remaining chapters of this guide. Think of them as an introduction to your plan that cannot be written until the plan itself is finalised. When you have finished your plan, you will find it easier to write your statements.

In the meantime, try **Exercise 5.17**.

_____

Exercise 5.17: 30-Second Spot

Write down what you would say in answer to someone who asked you "What do you want your business to be known for?", when you know that you have no more than 30-seconds of their attention (Vision).

Write down what you would say in answer to someone who asked you "What does your business do?", when you know that you have no more than 30-seconds of their attention (Mission).

Once you have developed the statements, you will have a communication tool to explain the philosophy of the business in relation to:

- The environment
- The way in which you do business
- Staff, customers and suppliers
- The community within which your business is based.

The statements can be used both internally (your staff and suppliers) and externally (your customers and the community you are working within).

Your company's statements must be shared and explained to all your staff. It's not a secret. It's the way you do business. If your staff don't know what it is, how can they work for you?

Trends show that customers are starting to take value statements seriously and expect businesses to develop a social conscience. Make sure that your statements are in line with what your customers expect.

> A good way to outline a strategy is to ask yourself:
> "How and where am I going to commit my resources?".
> Your answer constitutes your strategy.
> R HENRY MIGNON

IMAGE

The image that your business presents to your customer can be critical to your success. Image consists of many things, some of which are called "corporate identity" and include the styles you adopt for letterheads, brochures, uniforms, etc.

What sort of image do you want your business to convey to your customers? For example, you may want your business/office/shop to appear:

- Practical, simple and objective
- Exclusive, high value and durable
- Modern, new and trend-setting
- Personal, multi-faceted and result-oriented.

EXERCISE 5.18: IMAGE – 7 KEY WORDS

Define the image you want your business to project in seven key words:

If you have difficulties in defining the image that you want to project, try to imagine three colours that fit the image. Is your business blue, brown and grey or yellow, orange and blue? Or think about music. Is your business Rolling Stones or Pavarotti?

Once you have chosen an image, make sure it is expressed in all aspects of your business. Think about your image in every area of your business. Use **Exercise 5.19** to help.

EXERCISE 5.19: IMAGE

Which of these areas is important for your business' image:

◊ Interior?   □ Yes □ No
◊ Accommodation?   □ Yes □ No
◊ Pricing?   □ Yes □ No
◊ Name?   □ Yes □ No
◊ Business stationery?   □ Yes □ No
◊ Brochures?   □ Yes □ No
◊ Packaging?   □ Yes □ No
◊ Quality?   □ Yes □ No
◊ Business plan?   □ Yes □ No
◊ Advertising?   □ Yes □ No
◊ Correspondence?   □ Yes □ No
◊ E-mail?   □ Yes □ No
◊ Service?   □ Yes □ No
◊ Telephone answering?   □ Yes □ No
◊ Presentation?   □ Yes □ No
◊ Promotion?   □ Yes □ No
◊ Selling?   □ Yes □ No
◊ Employees?   □ Yes □ No
◊ Web-site?   □ Yes □ No
◊ Relations with neighbours and community?   □ Yes □ No

Wherever you answer "Yes", explain below how you intend to implement image in that area.

Once you have chosen the image you want to present to your customers, you should remain committed to it for the long term. See it as an investment in the future of your business.

Image needs to be maintained and should be checked on a regular basis with the reputation the company actually has. What perception do you want to project (= image)? And what is the image of your company with your customers (= reputation)?

Reputation depends on:

- Customer service
- Quality
- Consistency in your marketing approach
- Product development

and is informed by:

- Your ongoing market research
- Feedback from customers.

Reputation is more important than image.

Use your logo

If your business has a strong visual appeal, design a logo. Use it as widely as you can. Use it on:

- Envelopes
- T-shirts
- Posters
- Pens
- Van signs
- Lighters/matchboxes
- Floppy discs
- Umbrellas.

EXERCISE 5.20: IMAGE – SUMMARY

E

What image do you want to present?

Why?

How does this link back to your customers/target group?

How do you plan to achieve this image?

THE MARKETING MIX

To market your product/service, you need to use a mix of techniques and tools to get the best effect. To work out your marketing mix, you should use the 4Ps, which stand for: Product, Price, Place and Promotion.

As an example of the marketing mix at work, take perfume.

Broken down to its essentials, perfume is nothing more than water with a smell. But the price customers pay for perfume is many times the value of water with a smell. Why? Because the marketing mix has been so well-crafted that the customers' image of perfume is that of an exclusive, special, luxurious, sensual product – far removed from our crude description of it as "water with a smell". The image in customers' minds is created with the building blocks of the marketing mix: Price, Product, Place and Promotion.

Let's see how:

- **Product:** The product is essentially water with a smell. However, customers see something more than this, because perfume is sold in a sophisticated and well-designed bottle, with expensive-looking packaging. Because it looks expensive, customers begin to think that it is expensive

- **Price:** The cost price (excluding packaging) of perfume is perhaps less than €1 per bottle. If it is sold for many times that, the customers' perception again changes. If it is expensive, it must be special

- **Place:** Perfume is not sold at every local shop but is only available from expensive-looking retail shops that already have an up-market image. This makes the product exclusive (or appear so). And again the customers' perception of the product changes – if the product appears exclusive, it must be so.

- **Promotion:** Perfume is not sold by local leaflet drops or mass mailings, but is promoted by elegant life-style advertisements on national television and in glossy up-market magazines. Again, this changes customers' perception of the product.

By using the right combinations of the different elements in the marketing mix, you can determine how customers perceive your product/service.

With this example in mind, let's look at the individual elements of the marketing mix.

PRODUCT

This section will help you take the definition of your product/service a stage further by considering:

- The product/service itself
- The packaging of the service/product
- The choices you give customers (assortment)
- The life cycle of the product
- After-sales service.

Product

For most customers, a product is not only the product itself (the core), but also the services and intangibles that surround it (the product surround). For example, a restaurant sells food (core) and quick service and atmosphere (surround); a clothes shop sells clothing and appearance or personal image; a flower shop sells plants and flowers and ambience in the house.

This distinction between product core and product surround explains why there are so many different types of restaurant. Otherwise, the only people who would eat in restaurants would be those who cannot cook or those who are away from home and their own cooking facilities. But people eat in restaurants for other reasons: To celebrate, to "see and be seen", or to experience different kinds of food. And different restaurants cater for different markets: The local café for working-men, the fast-food outlet for young people, the fancy restaurant for up-market diners. In each case, it is usually the product surround, not the core, which determines the market for the restaurant and whether it is successful in attracting customers.

The link between the product core and the product surround is shown in **Figure 5B**. The product is defined in the inner circle as being made up of:

- **Function:** What does it do?
- **Packaging:** How is it presented?
- **Design:** Is it modern or old-fashioned?
- **Features:** What features does it offer?
- **Price:** How much?
- **Integrity:** Does it do what it promises?

This is the basic product. It's what makes the customer buy a car rather than a bicycle. But it's only a small part of what makes the customer buy one make of car rather than another.

Why **do** people buy different brands of cars? Transport is a well-known technology. All cars meet basic standards of moving people and the baggage from point A to B. Why choose one brand over another? Because people buy the surround – the image of driving one brand over another; the features one offers which may never be used, the perception of quality – rather than the core.

FIGURE 5B: PRODUCT CORE AND SURROUND

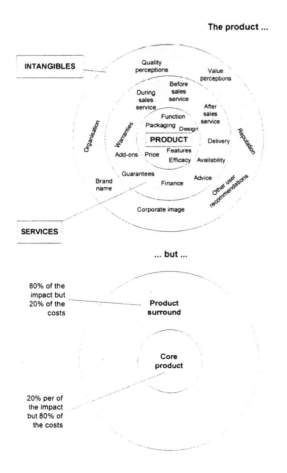

In addition to the basic product, the customer also expects services. These can include:

- **Before-sales service:** Brochures, information on product use, etc
- **During-sales service:** More information, costs comparisons, advice on use
- **After-sales service:** Dealing with problems, breakdowns, etc
- **Guarantees:** Promises to fix the product if anything goes wrong
- **Warranties:** Fixing what's gone wrong, when it does
- **Delivery:** May be important for bulky items
- **Availability:** Customers hate waiting once they have decided to buy something
- **Add-ons:** Extra features to improve performance, ease-of-use, etc
- **Finance:** To help them afford the purchase.

Think back on recent significant purchase that you made. How did these elements impact on your buying decision? These are factors that distinguish between different models of the same product – or, sometimes, different sellers of the same product.

And then there are the intangible elements, which are equally important:

- Quality perceptions
- Value perceptions
- Reputation
- Brand name
- Corporate image
- Other users' recommendations.

So the straightforward question of "Do I want to buy this product/ service?" suddenly becomes very complex. This is what makes marketing so challenging.

Packaging

Packaging has many different functions, including:

- Protection against damage during storage and transport
- Differentiating the product from competitors' products
- Creating an emotional appeal to potential customers.

Exercise 5.21 sets out some questions you should ask about your product's packaging.

EXERCISE 5.21: PRODUCT PACKAGING

How are you going to package your product?
How are you going to distinguish it from similar products?
How are you going to make it recognisable?
How are you going to make different versions of your product recognisable?
How will your packaging communicate the product's quality?

Packaging applies just as much to services as to tangible products, except that it no longer refers to physical packaging – boxes, bottles, wrapping, etc. So how do you package a service?

Packaging services is more difficult than packaging products but is more critical as packaging is one of the few tangible displays of an intangible service and an easy way for customers to assess its quality.

Packaging of services is closely linked with Promotion (see later in this chapter), as that is one of the few ways you can communicate your service. Services therefore should put also more emphasis on image and reputation-building to alleviate the intangible character of the service itself.

Think of the items in your service that a customer can actually hold and touch – for example, brochures, letterheads, correspondence, the equipment you use, your furniture, etc. The customer will use all these aspects to get a feeling for the quality of your service.

Consider other ways in which you can communicate your service, such as the way your staff answer the phone, your web-site, the dress code of your employees, the way you sell and advertise, your language and more basically the way you present yourself.

If you want to buy in the service of a business consultant, what are the things you look at to make a judgement whether you want to do business with that consultant? Now look at your business from the perspective of your clients. What do you see?

If you intend selling a service, go back to **Exercise 5.21** and complete it for your service.

Range

Most customers want a choice. What you have to offer consists of a range or selection of products/services that complement each other and make it attractive for the customer to come and buy.

First you must decide how broad you want your product range to be. Will you sell only computers? Or will you also sell printers, scanners, cables, etc? Or will you broaden the range even further to include a complete range of office equipment, furniture, stationery, etc? Each of these choices will determine the type of customer that will visit your premises. In fact, your decision on the breadth of the range of products/services that you carry should be determined by your customer analysis (**Exercise 5.1**) – what do your customers want?

Next, you must decide how many varieties of product will you offer. Will you sell only one manufacturer's computers? Will you sell only that manufacturer's desk-top range – or will you sell portable and hand-held computers also?

Will you offer an installation service for customers who are not familiar with computers? Will you provide training in using computers? Will you provide finance and leasing of computers (through a local bank perhaps or from your own resources)?

EXERCISE 5.22: RANGE

What choices will you offer?

Breadth (different products):

◊

◊

Depth (different specifications/options):

◊

◊

Product life cycle

Nothing lasts forever – not even your product or service. The competition, or changing technology, will catch up sooner or later and make it obsolete. This is called the product life cycle.

The life cycle of a product or service can be divided into five stages:

- Introduction
- Growth
- Maturity
- Saturation
- Decline.

Figure 5C shows these stages graphically.

FIGURE 5C: PRODUCT LIFE CYCLE

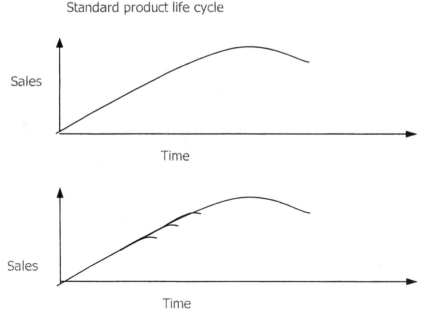

Standard product life cycle

Product life cycle with innovations boosting product and preventing slippage into decline stage

The speed of developments in technology and force of global competition has reduced the life cycles of most products considerably. For example, PCs are now considered to have a life cycle of only three months, in which the development costs of the new model need to be earned back. This puts immense pressure on sales volumes and margins.

You need to plan ahead and develop your own mix of products/services in the different development stages to prevent business failure at a later date. Perhaps it sounds a little extreme to be planning for the impact of the product life cycle when you have yet to start trading, but that's the time to do it.

In **Chapter 6, Process & Resources**, we will consider product development more closely. For now, you should be looking at developments that can be incorporated into your product/service over time to keep it new, fresh and exciting. Therefore, you will not wait until all possible development of your product is complete. Instead you will release a "Version 1" of your product. Version 2 will add new features – some planned from the beginning, some added in response to the market – and sell perhaps at a higher price. Version 3 will be better again – and so on.

Note that the same life cycle principle also applies to services.

Be aware that you should have a policy for product development – and replacement. We will return to this in **Chapter 6, Process & Resources**.

After-sales service

After-sales service – support for the user after they have bought – is an integral part of your product. Ask yourself the questions in **Exercise 5.23**.

EXERCISE 5.23: AFTER-SALES SERVICE

What does your after-sales service consist of?
Is it needed for your product, or it is just a comfort to customers?
Can you use your after-sales service as a distinctive feature?   ☐ Yes ☐ No
If "Yes", how?
If "No", why not?
Do you plan to charge for after-sales service (or some parts of it)?
If "Yes", how much and how?
If "No", why not?

However you organise your after-sales service, you should use it as an opportunity to get feedback from your customers. True, much of the feedback will be in the form of complaints – if the product worked, the customers would not need after-sales service – but use the complaints to find out more about your customers and their needs.

Complaints are an opportunity for you to:

- **Deepen your relationship with customers:** Customers who are well-treated when they complain and have their complaint solved, often tell lots of other people about your business and project it in a positive light
- **Improve your product:** From complaints, you may see opportunities to add new features or reach new customer/target groups
- **Distinguish yourself from competitors:** Most businesses provide very poor after-sales service (in fact, most provide very poor service at all times!). This provides an opportunity for you.

Links to the marketing mix

All the decisions you make about your product/service have a direct impact on the other Ps of the mix – Price, Place and Promotion. To make sure that they all fit together, go back to the last time you defined your product/service (**Exercise 3.22**) and give a detailed description of the product/service from nothing to the actual sales and after-sales. Use **Exercise 5.24** to help you.

EXERCISE 5.24: PRODUCT/SERVICE – SUMMARY

Describe briefly the product(s)/service(s) you want to launch:

For each product/service, describe its core:

For each product/service, describe its surround:

For each product/service, what extras do you offer compared to the competition?

For each product/service, write down why it appeals to customers. Substantiate this from your market research.

PLACE

Place can mean two things in marketing:

- Location
- Channels of distribution.

In many cases, Place means the location where your business will be established. But, in some cases, a customer will never come near your place of business – for example, if you run a window cleaning or mail order business. And in other cases, the means of getting your product/service to the customer is more important than the location of your business – in such cases, we use the P for place as meaning the channels of distribution.

Location

While location can be important for all types of business, it is most important for retail businesses, where place can be the most important part of the marketing mix. If you are planning a retail business, you should complete **Exercise 5.25**.

EXERCISE 5.25: RETAIL LOCATION

What will the customer see and experience when he or she visits your business?
How easy is it to find you?
Where are you situated (shopping area, a hotel or restaurant district, an office centre, in the centre or in the outskirts of town, etc.)?
What does the area look like?
What draws customers to your location?
Do you provide a location map for your customers? Do you need to?
Why did you choose this location?

Channels of distribution

Just as you need to understand your customers and your competition, you need to understand the channels of distribution that you will be using for your product/service. The channels determine how your product/service reaches the customer. Each channel has implications – for example:

- Long channels are slower and more expensive than short channels
- Long channels spread risk over a greater number of intermediaries
- Short channels provide greater interaction with customers.

Figure 5D shows some typical channels of distribution between the originating producer and the customer – from left to right:

- **Direct to customer:** Customer orders from producer and receives delivery direct (or collects)—for example, producers who sell direct to the public from their factory
- **Via retailer:** The producer sells to a retail shop, from which the customer buys
- **Via wholesaler and retailer:** The producer sells in bulk to a wholesaler, who sells on in smaller quantities to a retail shop, from which the customer buys
- **Via agent, wholesaler and retailer:** The producer sells in bulk to an agent, who sells on to a wholesaler, who in turn sells on in smaller quantities to a retail shop, from which the customer buys. Sometimes the agent only solicits orders from wholesalers and does not take physical delivery of the products himself
- **Via post office:** Direct mail, where the product is advertised and the customers buy by post – once the "forgotten channel" but coming back into its own as e-commerce develops.

Each of these channels has advantages and disadvantages. Usually, the fewer stages, the lower the distribution cost – which is why lots of businesses try to cut out the middleman. On the other hand, the middleman provides a useful service – holding stock, sourcing customers, advising on market conditions – and cannot always be dispensed with.

You need to balance distribution costs with promotion costs. Very often, sales channels with low distribution costs have high promotion costs.

You must decide which channel is appropriate for your product/service. And, remember, it is possible to use more than one channel, particularly if you are aiming at separate target groups of customers.

FIGURE 5D: CHANNELS OF DISTRIBUTION

```
ORIGINATING PRODUCER



                                          Agent



              Wholesaler       Wholesaler


Retailer      Retailer         Retailer        Post office



                    CUSTOMER
```

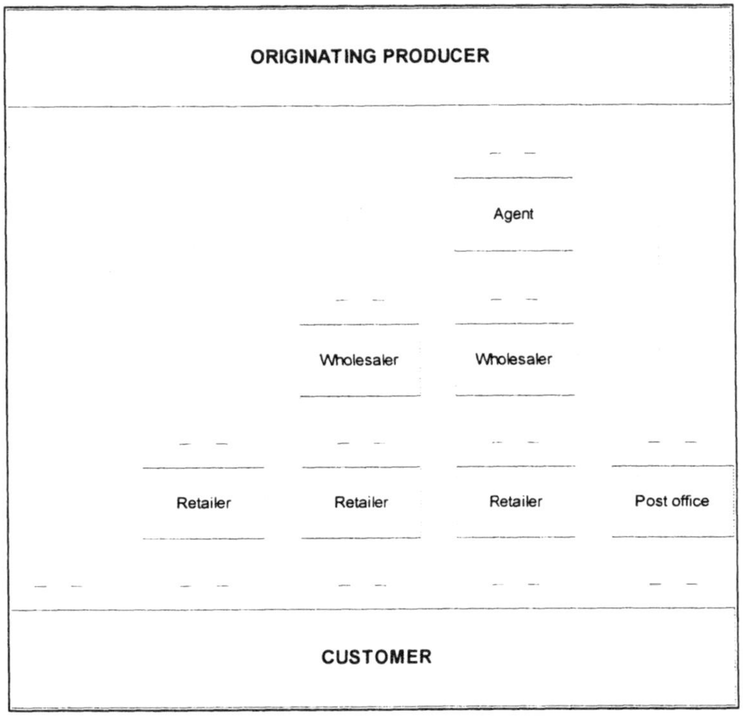

Use **Exercise 5.26** to decide which channel(s) of distribution you will use for your products/services.

EXERCISE 5.26: CHANNELS OF DISTRIBUTION

For my products/services, the following channels are suitable:

_____

Once you have identified the channel(s) appropriate to your business, you must determine where your business fits within the channel. Use **Exercise 5.27** to help.

_____

EXERCISE 5.27: POSITION WITHIN CHANNELS OF DISTRIBUTION

Are you a:

◊ Producer?   ☐ Yes ☐ No
◊ Agent?   ☐ Yes ☐ No
◊ Wholesaler?   ☐ Yes ☐ No
◊ Retailer?   ☐ Yes ☐ No

What are the advantages of this position within the channel of distribution?
What are the disadvantages of this position?
What implications does your position within the channel have for your product/service?

_____

Each industry is different and fortunes have been made (and lost) on changes to the channels of distribution. Look at how Dell and Gateway have changed the way people buy computers. Look at Amazon.com and how it has changed the way people buy books (and now CDs and videos).

It is a fact that technology – including, increasingly, e-commerce – is eroding the traditional channels of distribution. In thinking about channels of distribution, you should also think about alternatives to the traditional channels above.

Distribution systems

You already know which channel(s) of distribution are typically used for your type of product/service. Now answer the questions in **Exercise 5.28** to decide on the most suitable distribution system for your specific situation.

If you want an exclusive image for your product, you will restrict the number of places where your customers can buy it – and therefore your distribution system will reflect this. If your product/service needs to be widely available, then your distribution will be more intensive and will require a different system – as well as projecting another image of the product/service. In the middle ground is selective distribution, with many but not too many outlets.

Apart from the intensity of your distribution, you also have to decide in what type of outlet you want to sell your product/service.

Channel pricing

Your choice of distribution system has a direct effect on your margin. Every element in the channel will get a portion of the final price. The decision you must make is whether the added value of certain type of distribution systems outweighs the costs involved. For example, distribution can buy you access to existing and new customer groups, access to an established image, assistance in selling products, cheaper promotion, etc.

Direct marketing through mail order, direct sales and the Internet will save you the discounts payable in traditional channels but requires a higher investment in marketing and promotion.

Note that you should distinguish discounts on the retail price given within your channel of distribution – "trade" or "channel" pricing -- from price reductions given to special customers as part of your pricing policy, which we will call "special offers" (see the next section in this chapter).

Use **Exercise 5.29** to help you decide your channel pricing policy.

EXERCISE 5.28: DISTRIBUTION SYSTEM

E

Are you selling fresh products? ☐ Yes ☐ No

Is your product/service:

◊ An impulse buy (very short decision-making cycle)? ☐ Yes ☐ No
◊ A convenience buy (short decision-making)? ☐ Yes ☐ No
◊ A considered buy (longer decision-making cycle)? ☐ Yes ☐ No
◊ A business purchase (formal – and sometimes complex –
  decision-making cycle)? ☐ Yes ☐ No

Is timing of delivery crucial or are clients prepared to wait for delivery?

Timing crucial ☐
Prepared to wait ☐

Does the product/service need explanation or installation? Explanation ☐
Installation ☐

Do you want it to be available:

◊ Exclusively? ☐ Yes ☐ No
◊ Selectively? ☐ Yes ☐ No
◊ Anywhere possible? ☐ Yes ☐ No

What outlets will you use for your product/service?

What outlets do customers associate with your product?

Does the image of the outlet(s) chosen reflect your image? ☐ Yes ☐ No
Does it complement your product or service? ☐ Yes ☐ No
Does it fit with your values? ☐ Yes ☐ No

Can you sell it through:

◊ Catalogues? ☐ Yes ☐ No
◊ Internet? ☐ Yes ☐ No
◊ TV shopping channels? ☐ Yes ☐ No

Can you deliver directly to the customer? ☐ Yes ☐ No
Will you give people a choice in delivery? ☐ Yes ☐ No
Have you considered network marketing? ☐ Yes ☐ No

If "Yes", how will you organise network marketing for your product/service?

If "No", why not?

How does your main competitor organise its distribution?

Exercise 5.29: Channel Pricing Policy

What type of channel discounts are different channels looking for?
What is the added value of the different distribution approaches?
What channel prices are you going to offer?
What flexibility will you offer in this channel pricing policy?

Summarise your decisions on Place in **Exercise 5.30**.

Exercise 5.30: Place – Summary

Where are you going to work from (location)?
What distribution channels are you going to use?
How many outlets will sell your product?
In what type of outlets are you going to sell your product?
Have you a (written) policy on pricing for all intermediaries in your chosen channel(s) of distribution?

Link to the marketing mix

Place has an impact on all the other Ps of the marketing mix. As you work through the Ps, look back on earlier sections and make sure that your decisions are consistent. If necessary, review your decisions and consider them again in the light of new information.

PRICE

As part of your marketing mix, you must decide on Price and establish your pricing policy. This is one of the hardest things to do in business.

There are two basic approaches to pricing:

- **Customer-driven:** The price is set around what customers are willing to pay, based on market research
- **Cost-driven pricing:** The price is determined by the cost of the product/service plus a premium for profit.

You will not always be able to use both approaches. In some cases, where your product/service is very similar to existing products/services, your pricing will be constrained by competitors. In other cases, you may have no competitors at all and be able to charge what you like.

Obviously, the marketing approach needed for each of the two different pricing approaches is different. The cost-plus approach is common in State and other monopoly situations and in certain contracting projects. The customer-driven pricing approach is the most likely situation that you will encounter.

Price is important because:

- The price you charge will determine your sales volume and margins and, in the end, your own salary
- Price is also closely associated with the quality and credibility of your product or service
- Once you have established your price, it is very difficult to increase it without losing customers.

Pricing is also a strategic tool in penetrating your markets. Are you going to sell your product/service cheaper than the maximum price you could charge in order to establish a market share? Or, are you going to sell it for a higher price to establish a perception of prestige and allow for a focused approach toward a limited number of customers. Recognise that the price you charge sends a message to the market.

To establish your price, it is important to know what your customers are used to paying, and what they are prepared to pay. Use **Exercise 5.31** to determine this. Do this for each product.

You need to be well informed about competitors' prices. Sometimes prices are prescribed or recommended by industry organisations or professional associations. You can always deviate from established prices by means of special offers, discounts, reductions in rates, etc.

But be careful when researching price. You need to listen **very** carefully to what people say and how they say it. If your pricing is way off line, people will tell you quickly. But, if it's a little dear, and they don't want to suggest that they can't afford it, they may say the price is fine. You will only find out that it's not when you can't sell the product/service. You must also bear in mind that anyone who intends buying a product or service is unlikely to tell you if it is too cheap. Tread carefully!

EXERCISE 5.31: PRICE – SUMMARY

Work through this exercise for each product and be prepared to revise it – if necessary, several times – as you learn more about your market.

What are customers accustomed to paying already?   € _____
What are your competitors' prices (on average)?   € _____
What is your price?   € _____
What do you want your price to say about your product/service?
Will you give special offers?   ☐ Yes ☐ No
If "Yes", what will they be and on what conditions?
If "No", how will you deal with requests for special offers?

> *Price: Value plus a reasonable sum for the wear and tear on conscience in demanding it.*
> AMBROSE BIERCE

Pricing services

When you sell a product, you have something tangible to show the customer. With services, you have nothing to show until you have done the work – and sometimes not even then.

If you offer a service, when you agree a price it is a good idea to write down exactly what your customer can expect – for example:

- Details of your service
- The time to complete the service
- The time when the service will start
- The price
- The agreed method (and time) of payment
- Whether the cost of materials is included
- Whether other expenses (travel to the customer's location, for example) are included.

All of this will help make the service "real" in the eyes of the customer.

Price erosion

The concept of price "erosion" is used to illustrate how the price the customer pays gets whittled down through the various channels until the originators of the product or service receive their share.

Look back at **Figure 5D**, which shows some of the standard channels of distribution. Each channel creates a different price structure, as costs are deducted by each intermediary within the channel from the price the customer pays.

Many entrepreneurs start their business because they have seen a product for sale with a retail price of €100, which they "know" they can make for €20. Thinking that they can dramatically undercut the existing manufacturers, they launch into business without further thought. But, when the €100 retail price is broken down, it may look like this:

> *The real issue is value, not price.*
> ROBERT T LINDGREN

	€
Retail price	100
VAT/Sales tax	20
	80
Retailer's share	40
	40
Wholesaler's share	20
Manufacturer's selling price	20

The entrepreneur must be able to make the product for €20 – and make a profit in doing so – because the existing manufacturers work within this pricing structure. This highlights the importance of understanding how channel discounts determine your pricing.

Credit terms

Different industries and different channels have their own norms for credit terms. Typically, retail sales are paid for at the time of purchase. Business-to-business sales usually receive credit of 30 to 60 days.

The importance of credit terms lies in their impact on cash flow. If you get paid 30 days after the sale, this is not as good for cashflow as being paid on the day of the sale, but better than waiting 60 days for payment. Credit terms are a major determinant of cashflow.

Because of their impact on cashflow, it is essential that you provide evidence to support the credit terms that you use in your financial projections. If the standard policy on credit terms in your industry is payment within 30 days, but the practice is nearer 60 days (or worse, 90 days), you should base your financial projections on the longer period.

Credit: The only enduring testimonial to man's confidence in man.
JAMES BLISH

EXERCISE 5.32: CREDIT TERMS

Will you offer credit?   ☐ Yes ☐ No

If "Yes", to whom and on what basis?

If "No", why not? Is this standard in your industry?

Summarise the impact of your credit terms in the table:

What percentage of your sales do you estimate will be paid:	%
Within 0 to 30 days?	
Within 31 to 60 days?	
Within 61 to 90 days?	
Within 91 to 120 days?	
In more than 120 days?	

Note: The credit terms recorded in the table above will usually be longer than the credit terms you offer your customers, reflecting the reality of delays in payment, etc.

Links to the marketing mix

Again, Price cannot be decided independently of the other elements of the marketing mix. Look back at your earlier decisions on Product and Place and make sure that they are consistent with your decisions on Price.

PROMOTION

Promotion is the vehicle that is used to communicate both your business and specific products/services.

Promotion involves two elements:

- Coherent communication with your market
- Support for your sales effort.

There are hundreds of ways of promoting your business and the products/services you offer. The main methods of promotion include:

- Advertising
- Direct mail
- Internet
- Personal selling
- Public relations
- Trade shows and exhibitions.

Before you make a decision on the promotion mix, you need to decide what you want your promotional activity to achieve and the audience you are aiming it at (**Exercise 5.1**). Unless you do this, you will be pressured into activity that does not generate the results you want.

Promotional activity can achieve a number of different things, sometimes altogether, sometimes one at a time. Promotion can be used for:

- **Sales:** Generate actual orders – direct mail is suited to this
- **Awareness:** Make customers aware of your existence – advertising is good for this
- **Image:** Create the right perception in customers of your products/services – public relations is good at this
- **Information:** Communicate information (perhaps technical specifications) to your customers – advertising or trade shows are good at this.

Use **Exercise 5.33** as a starting point.

EXERCISE 5.33: PROMOTION TARGETS

What do you want to achieve with your promotional activity:

◊ Sales?   □ Yes □ No
◊ Awareness?   □ Yes □ No
◊ Image?   □ Yes □ No
◊ Information?   □ Yes □ No

Set quantifiable targets for each of these (for example, to increase sales volume by 10% or increase awareness by 40% in a specific sector of the market).

                                                              Target

◊ Sales
◊ Awareness
◊ Image
◊ Information

How will you measure achievement of these targets?
Who is the promotional activity targeted at?
What is the time frame for the promotional activity?
What is your initial budget for the promotional activity?

Advertising

It is a mistake to think that marketing begins and ends with advertising. Advertising is just a part of the promotion policy, and it is therefore only one of the means of promotion. However, effective advertising can have enormous impact on your business.

The key steps in advertising are:

• Use your chosen image as the basis for your advertising

• Look for an aspect of the image that can be represented graphically

• Always emphasise the benefits for the customer

• Remain credible and trustworthy

• Gain attention with a headline and give sufficient information

• Raise interest with a special offer

• Motivate your public to come and buy

- Stimulate action by including something that has to be returned, an invitation, an opening, special sales days, discount coupon valid until ...

Advertising is a way of communicating your product/service. Based on your market research, you know your target groups and how to reach them. The next step is to decide what you want your advertising to achieve.

Go back to your market research. Remind yourself of your customers' buying motives. Then decide which of your product's/service's features meet these motives and should be emphasised in your advertising.

Next begin to consider where you might advertise. You want to use an advertising vehicle (newspaper, magazine, radio, TV) that reaches your target group as economically as possible. Therefore, advertising in a national Sunday paper or on prime-time TV (even if you could afford either!) makes no sense if your market is made up of customers in your own locality. But there are now lots of local papers and radio stations, which might suit your needs much better. Review the analysis of your customers in **Exercise 5.1**, to make sure of the best fit.

Take control!

Ask for a "media pack". This will tell you not only the rates, but who the readers/listeners/viewers are, how many they are, what income groups they are in, etc. You need this information in order to decide whether a particular magazine, newspaper or radio station is suitable as a means of reaching your customers. Use the Advertising Control Sheet in **Figure 5E** to help you place your advertising.

> You can't advertise today and quit. You're not talking to a mass meeting. You're talking to a parade.
> BRUCE BARTON

> The most important word in the vocabulary of advertising is TEST. If you pre-test your product with consumers, and pre-test your advertising, you will do well in the marketplace.
> DAVID OGILVY

FIGURE 5E: ADVERTISING CONTROL SHEET

Use a copy of this Advertising Control Sheet for each ad you place

Advertising objective	What do you expect to achieve with this ad? More sales? Better name recognition?
Advertisement	Identify the ad (give it a name or reference).
Media selected	Identify the media – newspaper, magazine, radio – to be used. Identify the specific paper or station.
Advertising size/duration	How big an ad? How long should it run for?
Timing	When should it run?
Location	Where should it run? (in what part of the newspaper or magazine?)
Whose responsibility?	Who makes the decision and bears the consequences?
Budget cost	€
Actual cost	€
Criteria by which success will be judged	Identify these **AT THE TIME THE AD IS PLACED**.
Evaluation	If you don't do this, how will you know whether to repeat the ad?

Don't be pressurised into advertising, either in the wrong place or at the wrong time. Most ad salespeople are paid commission on sales – often this is their only income. They want you to buy NOW! and will give you "special discounts" – but only if you decide today. Don't do it until you are ready.

Don't be fooled by price either. Yes, one magazine costs €500 for a half-page against €300 for a full page somewhere else – but it goes to 20,000 of your core customers whereas the other really doesn't cover your market at all. Which is better value?

When you have placed your ads, you must measure the response. Unless you do this, you will never know whether your advertising works.

If it is appropriate, place a coupon (order form) or response mechanism ("Call us now for special offer details") on your advertisement. Record the number of responses you get from each ad. When people phone or call to place an order, ask them where they heard about you. This builds up invaluable information and will save you from advertising in the wrong places in future.

There is a famous advertising story of a survey, which showed that consumption of a certain brand of beer was lower among people who remembered its advertising than among those who did not. The brewery's advertising was "un-selling" their beer!

Writing advertisements

Writing advertisements is an art. It looks simple but it is, in fact, very hard. Keep the following words by David Ogilvy, founder of Ogilvy & Mather, one of the world's largest advertising agencies, in mind.

> "I do not regard advertising as entertainment or as an art form, but as a medium of information. When I write an advertisement, I don't want you to tell me you find it 'creative'. I want you to find it so interesting that *you buy the product*."

The secret is to keep it simple. Be direct. Explain what you are selling, its benefits to the customer, and where they can get it.

You need lots of information to plan an advertising campaign. Use **Exercise 5.34** to help you what you need.

> Doing business without advertising is like winking at a girl across a darkened room: You know what you are doing but no one else does.
>
> ANON

EXERCISE 5.34: ADVERTISING

Identify five potentially suitable advertising vehicles (newspapers, magazines, radio, etc) and obtain copies of their media packs. Analyse these for the following information:

Media	Circulation (total)	Circulation in your market	Big ad		Small ad	
			Size	Cost €	Size	Cost €
Local newspaper	20,000	15,000	Full page	500	1/16 page	40

You are now in a position to determine your advertising budget for the year. Look back at **Exercise 5.33** to determine the balance of spending between the different promotion objectives – indeed to decide whether advertising is an appropriate promotion tool for your customers/target groups. Then use the Advertising Control Sheet (**Figure 5E**) to plan the individual advertisements. Summarise your planned advertising spend in **Exercise 5.35**.

> Advertising: The education of the public as to who you are, where you are, and what you have to offer in way of skill, talent or commodity.
> FRANK McKINNEY HUBBARD

Exercise 5.35: Advertising Budget

Summarise your planned advertising spend (from the individual Advertising Control Sheets):

Objective	Advertisement	Budget	Timing Months 1 - 12
Total			

The total of this exercise will feed forward into Exercise 5.47, your Promotion Summary.

Direct mail

Direct mail is a highly effective way of approaching new and existing customers. The main benefits are that it is:

- Personal
- Extremely selective
- Easily and immediately measured
- Easy to test
- Controllable.

If it is done properly, direct mail can help you to communicate with your customers on a very personal basis. You can make one approach a day or 1,000 approaches a day. In many ways, it is the ultimate one-to-one marketing.

But check local regulations, which may prevent you from using direct mail or may reduce it effectiveness by imposing restrictions.

To make your direct mail personal, you need to know as much as possible about the people who are going to receive the mailing. The quality of information you have on your target audience, combined with an up-to-date database is crucial and is 60% of the work. Start with your own network (see **Exercise 2.6**) and test the water.

Consider the carrier that you use for your approach:

- Post
- Fax
- E-mail
- Web-site
- CD
- Interactive TV
- Catalogue
- Mix of the above.

Some carriers work better for specific audiences than others. Knowing your customers, make sure you choose the right one.

It is said that 30% of the success of direct mail lies in making the right offer. Use the AIDA formula to structure your message:

- **Attention:** Grab the **Attention** of the person who opens the letter (make sure they open the letter!) as quickly as possible by a good opening sentence and/or an enclosed gimmick
- **Interest:** Developing the **Interest** of the reader, making the reader to read on
- **Desire:** Develop the reader's **Desire** (I want this product or service and I want it now!).
- **Action:** Translate the desire into **Action**. Provide a means for the reader to buy your product/service in the easiest and most convenient way possible. The more difficult you make it and the more effort it takes, the fewer people will move into the action stage. Make it easy to respond. Ask for a response. Consider the carrier again. Which one enables the best response? Does it fit with your image?

The last 10% of the success is achieved by the creative package, which is the design of the letter and envelope, the enclosure of gimmicks, etc.

If at all possible, follow up the direct mail-shot to get feedback and to increase the response rate. The more follow-up you do, the more you will learn – it is an opportunity to open a dialogue with your customers. Ask for feedback and most people will give it to you. Combine direct mail with your ongoing market research.

But remember that your response will be lower than the number of mailing items that you send out. Depending on the lists you use, it could be as low as 1%! So check your lists carefully before mailing – and mail more than you need.

And make sure that what you mail is as professional as possible – in keeping with the image you want to project of your business (see **Exercise 5.19**). Use a professional designer, if necessary.

EXERCISE 5.36: DIRECT MAIL

What does it cost to post a letter?   € _____

What does stationery cost? (two sheets of paper/one envelope)   € _____

What does it cost to have letters inserted into envelopes and mailed?

€ _____ per 1,000

How much does it cost to rent a mailing list?   € _____ per 1,000 names

What is the cost per 1,000 names of a mailing?   € _____

What is the cost of designing your mailing item?   € _____

Identify five mailing lists, in addition to your own network, that you could rent for direct mail:

List	Number of names	Total Cost € per 1,000 names	Source

Now you have the information you need to determine your direct mail budget. Look back at **Exercise 5.33** to determine the balance of spending between the different promotion objectives – indeed to decide whether direct mail is an appropriate promotion tool for your customers/target groups. Then decide which lists to use and record their cost in **Exercise 5.37**.

EXERCISE 5.37: DIRECT MAIL BUDGET

Summarise your planned direct mail spend:

Objective	List	Number of names	Total cost per 1,000 names	Budget	Timing Months 1 - 12
Total					

The total of this exercise will feed forward into Exercise 5.47, your Promotion Summary.

The Internet

Earlier (in the section on *Preliminary market research* in **Chapter 3**), you saw how valuable the Internet is as an information source. However, depending on the nature of your business, it can be equally valuable as a marketing method or selling tool. For relatively little cost, your business can have its own home page or web-site on the Internet. A local Internet service provider will happily give you a quotation.

Why should your business have a web-site?

A web-site offers a window onto a world-wide networked market-place, making it easy for you to reach customers whom you would probably never have considered targeting.

For example, software companies can provide updates and new releases of software for downloading from their web-sites, reaching customers at the other side of the world. Newspapers and magazines have discovered a treasure trove in their back issues, which they can sell on-line to people looking for specific information.

Sales is one reason for establishing a web-site – and probably the best, since it most clearly recovers your investment – but there are others:

- A web-site can act as an on-line brochure, attracting potential customers to contact you about doing business
- It can also establish your credibility in a certain field, if your site is full of authoritative information on a specific topic
- Last (though not a good reason for incurring the expense, if that is all it is) is that it can act as a symbol of "corporate up-to-dateness".

E-commerce is the term that is used to describe selling on the Internet (in fact, it goes beyond mere selling to the way you organise your business – but that's another discussion).

Your approach to e-commerce should be similar to the way you approached marketing. You must:

- Analyse your customers (to decide whether you need a web-site?)
- Research your competitors (are they using e-commerce and, if so, why and how?)
- Decide what you want to achieve with the web-site (sales, awareness, image or information).

Exercise 5.38: Internet/E-Commerce Research

Customers:
◊ Is your business suitable? – Are you providing goods or services that can be delivered easily world-wide (or, at least, remotely from your present location)? Or, if not, can you attract customers to come to you (hotel, tourist resort)?
◊ Are your customers (and potential customers) connected to the Internet? – Compare your customer demographics with the Internet's (primarily single males 18-35 well-educated, no dependants – ideal for many businesses, but not all)

Competitors:
◊ How many of your closest direct competitors have web-sites?
◊ Analyse each web-site on (score between 1 and 5): (If you don't know enough about the Internet to do this, get an expert to help you while you learn)

Score

Contents of the web-site
Quality of graphic and design
Brand and image projected
User effectiveness of the web-site
Navigation through the site
Listing on search engines
Regularity of updates
Interaction between web-site and users
Technology used

Allies:
◊ Who could be your allies on the Internet? (Non-competing sites? Sites owned by people within your network?)

Targets:
◊ What targets have you set for your web-site?
◊ How will you measure that they have been achieved?

The Internet: So big, so powerful and so pointless that for some people it is a complete substitute for life.
ANDREW BROWN

Setting up a web-site

There are two aspects to a web-site: Content and Appearance. Content **always** wins. People will browse an attractive-looking web-site once but, as soon as they discover that the information they want is not available, they will leave and probably will not return. However, if they find the information they want, they will come back for more, even if your site is a little hard to navigate.

But it's not an either/or situation. You can – you must – have great content **and** great appearance in your web-site.

Before you rush into setting up your own Web-site, stop and think. Ask yourself the questions in **Exercise 5.39**.

EXERCISE 5.39: SETTING UP A WEB-SITE

Are you clear about what you are trying to do? – A Web-site can be used for a number of purposes (often simultaneously). Which of the following do you want to achieve?
◊   Providing product support to existing customers
◊   Providing product information to potential customers
◊   Selling on-line
◊   Identifying prospects
◊   Receiving feedback from customers
◊   Advertising your business' existence, capability and excellence.
Have you decided what content you want on the web-site?
What image do you want to project?
Which search engines are you going to register with?
What are the key words you are going to use to enable Internet users to find you through these search engines?
Are you going to link with other web-sites?
Will you place advertisements on those other web-sites?
Where else will you advertise your web-site?
In what other ways will you promote your web-site?
How often will you update your web-site?
What follow-up is needed for queries from visitors to your web-site?
What statistical packages do you need to track the visitors to your web-site?
What information do you want from the statistical packages?
How much will it cost to set up and maintain your web-site?

Note that trends on the Internet include:

- Faster modems with greater possibilities for graphics and sound
- Full entertainment web-sites unaffordable by small companies
- Enforcement of electronic property laws, which means you must be careful about the copyright of any material you use on your Web-site
- Electronic commerce and on-line shopping, which opens great opportunities but also poses risks of fraud, etc.

Make sure you plan for these trends when setting up your web-site.

Now you have the information you need to determine your Internet budget. Look back at **Exercise 5.33** to determine the balance of spending between the different promotion objectives – indeed to decide whether the Internet is an appropriate promotion tool for your customers/target groups. Then record your Internet costs in **Exercise 5.40**.

EXERCISE 5.40: INTERNET BUDGET

Summarise your Internet promotion spend:

Objective	Activity	Budget	Timing Months 1 - 12
Set-up			
Maintenance			
Updating			
Other			
Total			

The total of this exercise will feed forward into Exercise 5.47, your Promotion Summary.

Personal selling

The aim of this chapter is to identify what sales you expect to make and how you expect to make them.

In most cases, in the early stages at least, you are going to be your own salesperson. Therefore, you must:

- Prepare your sales talk well
- Write down the buying motives of your customers and also the reasons why they do not buy
- Think of reasons to counter those objections.

For lot of people, selling still has a negative connotation – the image of the slick sales person pushing un-needed (and often un-wanted) products down someone's throat. Not any more! Modern-day selling is about partnership and communication. It is important to build a relationship with your customers. The customer has to trust and respect you.

Build a database with the names and addresses of your customers (keep them in a notebook, if you prefer). Memorise the names of your customers, remember what they bought the last time, or what they asked about last time. Get as much information as you can about your customers' hobbies, family situation, job, etc. Use that information when you next talk to them.

Of course, the key is to get appointments with potential customers. Nine out of 10 appointments result in a "No". But if you get "No" nine times, you are likely to get one "Yes". So you need to get 10 appointments, as often as you can. Therefore self-motivation is critical. Selling – day in, day out, year in, year out – is the most underestimated element in business.

Note that marketing studies have identified four types of people involved in a purchase decision, in addition to the end-user of the product. The types are:

- **Recommenders:** People whose opinion is valued
- **Influencers:** People whose use of the product may be critical
- **Supporters:** Advocates of the product
- **Deciders:** The people you MUST reach, who make the buying decision.

> The average salesperson spends less than 25% of their time face-to-face with their clients. Personally, I spend 90%. That's the only way to make money in sales.
> EDNA LARSEN

It is important that you know who occupies which role when you are selling to a business or organisation. For example, a software company selling a special-purpose package to accountants in businesses found it necessary not only to sell to the accountants (the end-user) but also to the accountants' bosses (the deciders). They understood the decision-making process and acted accordingly. They quickly became market-leader in their niche.

The checklists in **Figure 5F** and **5G** may be helpful to you in developing your personal selling techniques.

FIGURE 5F: QUESTIONS TO ASK YOURSELF *BEFORE* YOU START SELLING

Do you know enough about the product?	☐ Yes ☐ No
What is the product core?	
What is the product surround?	
Are you talking to the right person?	☐ Yes ☐ No

Who are:
◊ The recommenders?
◊ The influencers?
◊ The supporters?
◊ The deciders?

Do you know what the customer wants?	☐ Yes ☐ No
Does what he wants fit with what he needs?	☐ Yes ☐ No
Why does the customer want it?	
Have you had any previous experience with the customer?	☐ Yes ☐ No
Has the customer had experience with your competition?	☐ Yes ☐ No

Who is the end user of your product?
How will your product be used?
How will the customer's life be better or easier after he/she uses your product?

FIGURE 5G: SELLING TECHNIQUES   E

Are you prepared?	☐ Yes ☐ No
Do you know your customers' needs?	☐ Yes ☐ No
Do you listen?	☐ Yes ☐ No
Are you clear in your language (no jargon!)?	☐ Yes ☐ No
Do you talk about benefits instead of the product's features?	☐ Yes ☐ No
Do you have answers to your customers' objections?	☐ Yes ☐ No
Do you know when to close the sale? And how?	☐ Yes ☐ No
Are you persistent?	☐ Yes ☐ No

Now you are ready to determine your promotional spend on personal selling. It probably won't be much, since the main cost will be time – paid for by salaries, which will be covered in **Chapter 7, People** (make sure you include these salaries at that point). Look back at **Exercise 5.3** where you identified your customers to determine the balance of spending between the different promotion objectives – indeed to decide whether personal selling is an appropriate promotion tool for your customers/target groups. Then record your personal selling costs (excluding salaries and sales commissions) in **Exercise 5.41**.

> *Salesman: A man who knows nothing of what he is selling save that he is charging a great deal too much for it.*
> OSCAR WILDE

> *The art of selling is not to prove to Mr Prospect that he is wrong, but to help him reach a decision which he, Mr Prospect, knows is right.*
> JOHN A McMILLAN

Exercise 5.41: Personal Selling Budget

Summarise your personal selling spend:

Objective	Activity	Budget	Timing Months 1 - 12
Total			

The total of this exercise will feed forward into Exercise 5.47, your Promotion Summary.

Public relations (PR)

Public relations embraces all the activities you undertake to get positive attention for your business among the public in general. Good PR creates a positive image for your business and helps to ensure that people recognise and remember your business, especially over the long term.

Good PR is also useful for your contacts with your suppliers. If you need a quick delivery, a special order or a credit, PR will help make sure that your supplier will go out of their way to help you. The same applies for your neighbours, local authority, etc. Good PR will also lead to free publicity for your business.

But public relations is not just about getting your business in the papers. Public relations is exactly what it says: Building a relationship with the public.

Let's define "public". From the perspective of where your business is located, it includes:

- Neighbours
- The neighbourhood
- The local community.

Within the business, it includes:

- Staff
- Suppliers.

In a wider context, public includes:

- Colleagues
- Unions
- Government (local, regional, national)
- Politicians
- Consumer groups
- Financial institutions
- Trade organisations.

Public relations builds and maintains a good reputation. If your business is well-regarded by the groups you want to influence, your marketing mix will be strengthened and it will be easier to get things done (planning permission, recruiting staff, word-of-mouth sales, etc.)

It goes back to your mission statement and what social profile you want to project. You have to decide which groups you want to maintain a positive relationship with and how you plan to do this. Keep it practical and within your means (both money and time).

Local newspapers are always looking for news. If you have good news about your business, make sure you let them know. Build a profile for yourself and your business through your local paper. And while the relationship you build will not protect you totally when bad news has to be reported, it means the reporter knows and trusts you already and may go out of their way to check facts with you before going to print.

Use **Exercise 5.42** to help you develop your public relations activity.

EXERCISE 5.42: PUBLIC RELATIONS

E

Which groups are important for your company?

◊ Neighbours   ☐ Yes ☐ No
◊ Local banks   ☐ Yes ☐ No
◊ Local politicians   ☐ Yes ☐ No
◊ Local authority   ☐ Yes ☐ No
◊ Local press   ☐ Yes ☐ No
◊ Trade organisations   ☐ Yes ☐ No
◊ Unions   ☐ Yes ☐ No
◊ State agencies   ☐ Yes ☐ No

How good are your public relations now?

◊ Neighbours   ☐ Good ☐ Fair ☐ Poor
◊ Local banks   ☐ Good ☐ Fair ☐ Poor
◊ Local politicians   ☐ Good ☐ Fair ☐ Poor
◊ Local authority   ☐ Good ☐ Fair ☐ Poor
◊ Local press   ☐ Good ☐ Fair ☐ Poor
◊ Trade organisations   ☐ Good ☐ Fair ☐ Poor
◊ Unions   ☐ Good ☐ Fair ☐ Poor
◊ State agencies   ☐ Good ☐ Fair ☐ Poor

Will your value, vision and mission statements appeal to these groups?

◊ Neighbours   ☐ Yes ☐ No
◊ Local banks   ☐ Yes ☐ No
◊ Local politicians   ☐ Yes ☐ No
◊ Local authority   ☐ Yes ☐ No
◊ Local press   ☐ Yes ☐ No
◊ Trade organisations   ☐ Yes ☐ No
◊ Unions   ☐ Yes ☐ No
◊ State agencies   ☐ Yes ☐ No

Why?

How will you reach these groups?

◊ Sponsorship?   ☐ Yes ☐ No
◊ Press releases?   ☐ Yes ☐ No
◊ Visits/Open Days?   ☐ Yes ☐ No
◊ Information/newsletter?   ☐ Yes ☐ No
◊ Profile in local newspapers?   ☐ Yes ☐ No
◊ Donate your services?   ☐ Yes ☐ No

Now you are ready to determine your promotional spend on public relations. You may be able to do a large part of the work yourself (include the time spent on PR in your own or one of your staff's workload and include when considering salaries in **Chapter 7, People**) or you may prefer to use a professional PR consultancy. Look back at **Exercise 5.33** to determine the balance of spending between the different promotion objectives – indeed to decide whether public relations is an appropriate promotion tool for your customers/target groups. Then record your public relations costs (excluding salaries) in **Exercise 5.43**.

EXERCISE 5.43: PUBLIC RELATIONS BUDGET

Summarise your public relations spend:

Objective	Activity	Budget	Timing Months 1 - 12
Total			

The total of this exercise will feed forward into Exercise 5.47, your Promotion Summary.

Trade shows and exhibitions

Another useful promotion activity is attendance at trade shows and exhibitions. A targeted exhibition attracts thousands of potential customers, most of whom want information about the products/services on display. They are potential customers.

The steps involved are:

- **Plan your budget:** Remember trade shows are part of your overall marketing budget
- **Select your shows:** Pick those that will attract your core customers/target groups
- **Book space:** Book the best you can, but look for bargains in spots that other exhibitors neglect
- **Set objectives:** These must be measurable and measured – otherwise how will you know whether the show was worthwhile?
- **Start planning your stand several months in advance:** Don't leave it until the last minute
- **Invite customers (existing and potential) to visit you at the show:** Send them complimentary admission tickets
- **Brief the staff who will be attending:** Make sure they all know why your business is exhibiting, what you are exhibiting, what you expect from them
- **Manage your stand during the exhibition:** Make sure that the stand is manned at all times, that your have adequate supplies of the appropriate materials and that your staff have a system for logging customer enquiries, with full contact details for immediate follow-up after the exhibition
- **Afterwards, follow-up:** Send out all the materials you promised, contact everyone you met – but do it immediately, not four to six weeks later like most exhibitors.

Use **Exercise 5.44** to help you decide on how best to use trade shows and exhibitions.

Exercise 5.44: Trade Shows and Exhibitions

Identify five trade shows that are relevant to your business:

Show	Dates	Target audience	Expected attendance	Cost of basic stand

What products/services have you to display at the show?
Can you provide working models (if appropriate) or give demonstrations?
Can you provide samples?
Have you suitable display material?
What other costs will there be, in addition to the cost of the basic stand?
Have you the resources (staff, time, money) to attend?
What will be the benefits of attending the show?

Now you are ready to determine your promotional spend on trade shows and exhibitions. Look back at **Exercise 5.33** to determine the balance of spending between the different promotion objectives – indeed to decide whether trade shows are an appropriate promotion tool for your customers/target groups. Then record your trade show costs in **Exercise 5.45**.

EXERCISE 5.45: TRADE SHOWS AND EXHIBITIONS BUDGET

Summarise your trade shows and exhibitions spend:

Objective	Trade show/ exhibition	Budget	Timing Months 1 - 12
Total			

The total of this exercise will feed forward into Exercise 5.47, your Promotion Summary.

Other promotion

Don't forget the basics – a clear letterhead, readable business cards and an attractive brochure. Record your costs for these in **Exercise 5.46**.

Exercise 5.46: Promotion Basics Budget

Summarise your spend on promotion basics:

Objective	Item	Budget	Timing Months 1 - 12
	Letterheads		
	Business cards		
	Brochure		
Total			

The total of this exercise will feed forward into Exercise 5.47, your Promotion Summary.

Promotional budget

Now that you have considered the main types of promotional activity, it is time to plan your promotional budget, which will be included in your financial projections.

For each relevant product or service you plan to sell, complete **Exercise 5.47**, based on the information in **Exercises 5.35, 5.37, 5.40, 5.41, 5.43, 5.45, and 5.46**.

Don't be too concerned that a significant part of your promotion budget is allocated to awareness-creating, image-creating or information-giving. These are essential parts of the promotional cycle and you need to spend on these aspects. But don't overspend. The aim of promotion is to make sales – and you can't do that if you don't keep some of your budget for sales-generating activity.

Exercise 5.47 will link in with **Exercise 5.49** later.

EXERCISE 5.47: PROMOTION — SUMMARY

Repeat this exercise for each relevant category of product/service that you plan to sell.

Activity	Months 1 to 12	Costs			
		Sales-generating	Awareness-creating	Image-creating	Information-giving
Advertising (Ex. 5.35)					
Direct mail (Ex. 5.37)					
Internet (Ex. 5.40)					
Personal selling (Ex. 5.41)					
Public relations (Ex. 5.43)					
Trade shows and exhibitions (Ex. 5.45)					
Letterheads, business cards, brochures (Ex. 5.46)					
Total					

Summarise in text form your promotion plan:

DEVELOPING A MARKETING PLAN

Developing a marketing plan consists of pulling together all the information you have collected and decisions that you have made in the course of your work on this chapter – in particular, the specific combination of the 4Ps of the marketing mix that you plan to use.

You will be expected to include a paragraph or two about your marketing plan in your business plan. Use **Exercise 5.48** to record a first draft.

EXERCISE 5.48: MARKETING STRATEGY

My marketing strategy can be summarised as:
◊ Direction
◊ Targets
◊ Image
◊ Marketing mix
◊ Spend

Ensure that your marketing mix is fully integrated with the image you have defined (**Exercise 5.20**) and that it supports the position you want to take on your market or markets (**Exercise 5.13**).

SALES FORECAST

Effective sales forecasting is a critical activity that determines the level of business activity for the year and may involve:

- Organising all relevant information from company records
- Assessing the product range to identify "winners" and "losers"
- Attempting to identify opportunities for market and product development
- Defining the outcomes from the above in terms of a forecast of sales of each product or category
- Supporting the forecast with evidence of how the sales will be achieved.

The work you have done to date in developing a marketing plan will now be of great assistance to you in determining your sales forecast.

Evidence – a core element of the **TENBizPlan** approach – to support the sales forecast should be compiled, ideally in the form of orders or enquiries. Since yours is a new business, much of the evidence may be in the form of market studies and letters of comfort from target customers.

Because of the crucial importance of the sales forecast, every effort must be made to ensure that it is realistic. Try to keep a balance between being overly optimistic (which means you will probably not achieve your forecast sales) and being unduly pessimistic (which means no one will support you since your business appears to have no prospects of survival). Base your sales forecast firmly on the market research that you have done in this chapter.

Also look for a balance between thorough planning accuracy and the sheer complexity of dealing with very large product ranges. Instead of listing every single product line that your business offers, consider grouping similar products. So perhaps "Bags" could be a product line, rather than each individual type of bag being a separate product line in its own right. Obviously, the ideal is to include all products individually, since this gives the most accurate forecasts. However, a sensible balance may have to be struck between the precision of the projections and the amount of work involved both in creating them and in subsequent monitoring.

If you group product/services, you will have to use average selling and purchase prices in your forecasts. A simple way to do this is to set the selling price at €1, and relate the purchase price to this. For example, for a group of products with a margin of 40%, your selling price is €1 and your purchase is €0.60. Your sales forecast then reflects sales values, not unit volume.

If you sell the same product at different prices to different participants in the channel(s) of distribution (for example, at full price in your own shop and at a discount to other retailers), treat them as two separate products with different prices or aggregate the sales and use a weighted average price.

Your sales forecast is informed by your market research as this will indicate which target groups you will aim for, what price they are likely to pay, when and where they can buy your product/service, etc.

Your sales forecast is also determined by your marketing mix – in particular, by your promotional activity. However good your product, sales do not just happen – they must be generated by activity.

In **Exercise 5.49**, you will estimate your sales in volume and money terms for the first year of your business. You may need to use several worksheets to provide space for all your products, or perhaps you can group your products/services.

To complete **Exercise 5.49**, first write in your estimate of unit sales for each product/service or group of products/services for each month in the first year. Total these downwards (to give total sales per product for the year) and across (for total sales of all products per month).

When you have done this, multiply total unit sales for each product/product group by its price (**Exercise 5.31**) to get the total sales value for the year.

Then list the VAT rate applicable for each product/service group.

Then go back to **Exercise 5.47** and transfer your promotion budget into the right-hand columns of **Exercise 5.49**. You will now be able to relate the sales-generating element of your promotion budget to the sales expected to be achieved. (As a result, you may want to revise either your promotion budget, the split in your promotion budget between sales-generating and other aims, or your sales forecast – you can now do so with the relationship between promotional activity and resulting sales clearly in view.)

In each case, remember that your sales depend largely on the "sales-generating" element of your promotional activity. When you come to revise your sales forecast, or your promotional budget, later in your planning, remember this interdependence and take account of it in your revisions.

Last, estimate the number of customers you expect – either on a product-by-product basis or on a total basis. Calculate the average sale in value and units per customer. This will give you useful information – and a reality check (Do you really expect every customer to pay €200 or that you will have 200,000 customers? – check again!).

Forward orders

It is important that you take a realistic approach to your sales forecast, since it is on this that the rest of your business plan will depend.

Forward orders – orders placed by customers for delivery when your business is up and running – can be a very useful way of backing up your sales forecast, since they show that:

- There is a genuine demand for the product/service you are offering
- You can sell
- Your sales forecast has a tangible base.

Letters of comfort, where a customer indicates his intention to buy from you without giving a specific order, are the next best thing at this stage.

Now go out and get those orders and letters!

EXERCISE 5.49: SALES FORECASTS   **E N**

	Products/product groups				Promotion budget (from Exercise 5.47)		
	A	**B**	**C**	**Total**	**Sales**	**Other**	**Total**
Unit sales							
Jan							
Feb							
Mar							
Apr							
May							
Jun							
Jul							
Aug							
Sep							
Oct							
Nov							
Dec							
Total							

	Products/product groups				Promotion budget (from Exercise 5.47)		
	A	**B**	**C**	**Total**	**Sales**	**Other**	**Total**
Price (Ex. 5.31)							
Total sales value							
VAT rate (Ex. 4.3)							
Number of customers							
Average sale per customer – value							
Average sale per customer – units							

These sales forecasts will form part of your input into the financial projections.

Now check what evidence you have to support these estimates. Does the evidence truly support them – or could you improve on it? When you are satisfied, file your evidence with your working papers.

THE TENBIZPLAN APPROACH TO BUSINESS PLANNING

Text

In this chapter, you have created draft text for input into your business plan document in relation to:

Project Overview

- Mission statement – **Exercise 5.16**
- Industry Trends – **Exercise 5.10**
- Targets – **Exercise 5.14**

Marketing

- Summary of Marketing Plan – **Exercise 5.48**
- Customers – **Exercise 5.6**
- Competition – **Exercise 5.9**
- Products/Services – **Exercise 5.24**
- Place – **Exercise 5.30**
- Price – **Exercise 5.31**
- Promotion – **Exercise 5.47**
- Sales forecasts – **Exercise 5.49**.

Evidence

File copies of all of the exercises that you have completed in **Chapter 4**, for ease of reference later. They will be a crucial part of your evidence supporting your business plan.

In this chapter, you will also have identified other information that will be good evidence for your business plan – for example, information regarding, your competitors' pricing, or promotion activities available to you or letters of comfort from potential customers. File these safely as part of your working papers also.

Numbers

The numbers created for input into your financial projections as part of the process of business planning in this chapter are:

- Sales forecast – **Exercise 5.49**
- Promotion budget – **Exercise 5.47**
- Credit terms agreed with customers – **Exercise 5.32**.

Key Question

The key question for this chapter is:

> **What sales do I expect and how will I generate them?**

To answer the question, you will need to consider:

- Your business' mission statement and marketing direction
- Your customers and competitors
- The four Ps: Product, Place, Price and Promotion
- Your marketing plan
- Your sales forecast.

PROCESS &

RESOURCES

The key question for this chapter is:

How, and with what resources, will I meet my planned sales?

This chapter deals with how you propose to produce and deliver your products/services. It seeks to define your business process and the facilities, space and people (the resources) you will need to get your products/services to your customers in the quantities predicted by **Chapter 5, Marketing & Sales**. Whether your business involves the provision of a simple service, or requires a complex manufacturing operation, you need to think through the process step-by-step.

Process is deliberately placed AFTER marketing in the **TENBizPlan** approach because, too often, in people's minds, production comes before marketing – to the detriment of the business. Too many entrepreneurs, because they know that they can make something, believe that customers will want to buy it. But that's not how the real world works. Marketing comes first, identifying what customers want – then Process supplies whatever it is that meets that need.

Each company's process is specific to itself, even if it shares common elements with other companies in similar businesses. This guide cannot, therefore, address specific situations in detail but help you to think through your business process by:

- Defining the main stages in your business process.
- Calculating the staff, space and equipment needed to set up and sustain the process
- Identifying the indirect costs (overheads) required to support and administer business activities – these are the mundane, sometimes forgotten activities that allow all the other parts of the business to function smoothly.

This chapter identifies the staff resources required to support your process. However, because of the importance of staffing to your business, People is covered separately in **Chapter 7, People**. However, you will include People under the heading "Process & Resources" in your business plan document.

Output from this chapter

In your business plan, you will need to be able to explain (perhaps only in outline, if it's very technical or complicated) the process and facilities that you use to deliver your product or service. That's what the text output of this chapter is: A clear explanation that will appear as the **"Process & Resources"** section in your business plan.

In addition, as always, you must be aware of the links between this and the other elements of business planning:

- **Personal assessment (Chapter 2)**: What do you want to do? What do you want to achieve?
- **Idea assessment (Chapter 3)**: This chapter focused more on the development of your business idea than on the process and resources required to achieve it. As you work through **Chapter 6**, you may want to return to **Chapter 3** to re-examine your product development.
- **Marketing & Sales (Chapter 5)**: The fact that a level of demand exists which would allow you to sell millions of units does not mean that you will be able to put in place the process and resources needed to service such high numbers. When you have worked through your process and identified sensible levels of capacity and timetables of when you will reach those levels, you need to go back to **Chapter 5** to reconcile these two pivotal areas. You also build here on the findings of your market research

- **People (Chapter 7)**: How your process is organised will determine (at least in part) how many staff you will require and how they should be organised.

As always, each chapter of the guide – each stage of the business planning process – informs and creates the need for revision in others.

WHAT IS A BUSINESS PROCESS?

Once a business has identified its customers and designed products or services to meet their needs, it must then establish a process to provide the products/services to customers as a matter of routine business practice.

Each organisation has its own specific process but there are core activities, some or all of which every business will require. These are:

- Buy
- Make
- Sell
- Manage.

FIGURE 6A: THE PRIMARY ACTIVITIES OF A TYPICAL BUSINESS

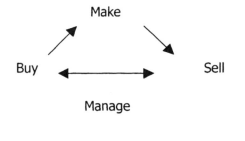

The relative importance of buying and making varies between businesses.

Businesses that sell physical products must buy in items and add value to them. They do this through processes that range from simply holding items until the customer wants them, up to complex manufacturing processes that mix and transform many raw materials into a product ready for delivery to the customer.

Smaller businesses that sell services without a physical product, or where the physical aspect is insignificant, may not need a specialist purchasing function. Although such businesses will almost certainly have to procure services such as telephone and electricity, as well as goods such as stationery and promotional materials, neither purchasing nor inventory control are as significant as for physical businesses.

However, all independent businesses must:

- **Sell:** Without sales, there is no business

- **Manage:** From implementing a strategy, to day-to-day running of the business, through to maintaining records for legal and management information purposes.

In developing your business plan, you must think through your process and the core activities that are relevant to your situation. You will also need to identify the resources and people needed to establish and maintain those functions.

Your own process

In the remainder of this chapter, we will consider each of the core activities, highlighting the important issues you will need to plan for and providing exercises to capture the information required for your business plan.

But first, pause for a moment and consider your own process, as you currently understand it.

Think about your product or service. What are the stages in its movement through the business, from the stage when a potential customer phones for a price to the delivery of the product or service? What activities are involved?

Use **Exercise 6.1** to help document an initial description of your process.

> A McDonald's outlet is a machine that produces, with the help of unskilled machine attendants, a highly polished product. Through painstaking attention to total design and facilities planning, everything is built integrally into the technology of the system. The only choice open to an attendant is to operate it exactly as the designers intended.
>
> GEORGE COHON, President, McDonald's Canada

EXERCISE 6.1: DEVELOPING YOUR OWN PROCESS

Close your eyes. Imagine that you have transported yourself six weeks, or six months, ahead in time to a date when your new business is fully operational. Everything is working perfectly (thanks to good planning!).

Ask yourself these questions:

◊ What do you see? Size, layout of premises? Furniture, phone systems, etc? People?
◊ How do things get done? Is it busy or quiet? Does it appear organised?
◊ Who does what?
◊ How are customers' orders fulfilled?
◊ How are products made? From what? With what?
◊ What machinery is used?
◊ Where is inventory stored?
◊ What items are used to make the products?
◊ How are your products delivered to customers?
◊ How are your services delivered?
◊ What equipment do you need for your services?

When you have completed **Exercise 6.1**, refine it by working through the relevant sections of the following systematic approach to defining your process.

Buying

Once the product/service you plan to sell has been defined, whether through idea assessment or R&D, and confirmed as suitable through market research, the next question is "How to supply it?".

For many businesses, buying-in is the answer. In other cases, the business will manufacture the product itself, but will need to buy-in parts or raw materials.

You also need to buy supplies to keep the office going and someone needs to have responsibility for acquiring equipment for your business now and in the future.

Outsourcing

Outsourcing is a technique whereby parts of the business are handled by specialists outside the business. Common examples of outsourcing include:

- Sub-contractors for specific tasks
- Consultants for professional advice
- Freelancers to help with peak workloads.

But a more modern view of outsourcing is based on cost-effectiveness. Many activities make up a business' process from product conception to final delivery to customer. In only a few of these can the business expect to enjoy a competitive advantage over other similar businesses. For example, you may be a brilliant designer, but are all your administration systems world-class too? So, increasingly, businesses are identifying parts of their business process that can be outsourced to specialists – the accounting function, debt collection, product design, etc. Many of these functions, though not all, are administrative in nature – some businesses even contract out their marketing. The advantages lie in a saving on resources that would otherwise be committed to non-core activities (although it's difficult to argue that marketing is a non-core activity!). As you work through your business process, consider where outsourcing could benefit your business.

Another reason for considering outsourcing is scale. Perhaps your business plans to manufacture and sell a new form of car tyre. Your skills lie in selling and you already have a well-established network of potential sales outlets within the motor industry. Your preliminary market research, and further research in this chapter, identifies a minimum investment of €10 million for the factory and equipment needed to make your new tyre – well beyond your capacity to finance. By outsourcing the manufacture under licence to a manufacturer with spare capacity, you might be able to reduce your investment significantly, and free your time to concentrate on what you do best – selling.

The buying process

In most cases, the buying process consists of purchasing and inventory management. Effective purchasing requires:

- Negotiating skills
- Knowledge of the industry in terms of sources of supply
- Ability to specify and verify quality standards

Inventory management requires:

- A detailed assessment of the reliability of sources of supply in terms of quality, order quantities, delivery lead times
- Design of your stores area to provide easy access and physical verification of inventory levels
- A rational approach to classifying stocks.

Purchasing

In all cases, the aim of the purchasing function is to buy:

- The right items
- At the right price
- At the right time.

The starting point therefore is the right items, which involves specifying exactly what you want. Depending on the product involved, the level of specification may be critical or it may not. There is a balance to be maintained here between:

- On the one hand, specifying an item so exactly that it becomes a special order for most suppliers and thus incurs unnecessary costs for you
- On the other hand, making do with items that are not quite right and that damage the overall perception of your product in customers' minds for the sake of small amounts of money.

This balance is informed by your values, your attitude to quality, the image you want to project for your business and other factors (including your customers' requirements). The purchasing function is often driven by the materials planning function within Operations (see later in this chapter).

In purchasing large value items, it may be helpful to enter into a formal contract with your supplier – first having carefully negotiated all the terms of the contract. For smaller items, particularly generic items that can be bought almost anywhere, this is not necessary.

There are efficiencies to be gained by centralising your purchases with a single supplier. These efficiencies are sometimes offset by your vulnerability to that supplier. Good purchasing practice suggests that, where possible, you should always have more than one supplier for critical or important items.

How products, supplies and equipment are bought has an enormous impact on your organisation. Imagine:

- Buying a new computer that is incompatible with your existing computers
- Critical parts arriving too late to fulfil a customer order

- Running out of letterheads or business cards
- New furniture looking old and battered when delivered
- Machines being out-of-date and unserviceable only months after buying
- Machines breaking down due to missing parts.

Purchasing is a key part of your business process that must be planned, if it is to be effective. Use **Exercise 6.2** to help you define your purchasing function.

Exercise 6.2: Purchasing Function

Answer these questions:

◊ What are the main materials, products and services will you need to buy to support the day-to-day operation of your business?
◊ Who will supply these items?
◊ Can you classify them into low-cost quick-delivery and high-cost long-lead-time items?
◊ How are you going to ensure the right timing and quantity of your purchases?
◊ What will they cost?
◊ Do you have evidence to support these prices?
◊ What are the critical factors with regard to your planned suppliers? (Price, service, delivery times, quality, availability of stock)
◊ Have you considered alternative suppliers (regional, national and international – use the Internet to find them!)
◊ What resources will your purchasing function require?

Resource	Detail	Costs	
		Once-off invest-ment	**Ongoing cost**
Space			
Equipment			
Staff			
Other			
Total			

These costs will feed through into Exercise 6.22: Capital Expenditure; Exercise 6.23: Product/Service Costs; and Exercise 6.24: Overheads.

Inventory management

Now think about the physical on-the-ground impact of your purchasing. You have made arrangements to have items (whether products or parts of products) delivered. What will happen when they arrive? Use **Exercise 6.3** to help you decide how to organise your inventory management function.

EXERCISE 6.3: INVENTORY MANAGEMENT

Answer these questions:
◊ Where and how will you store inventory?
◊ What special conditions will your inventory require?
◊ How often and how will deliveries inwards arrive?
◊ How often and how will deliveries be made to customers?
◊ How will you check to make sure that the right items, and the right quantities of them, are delivered and put into inventory?
◊ How will you check to make sure that the right items, and the right quantities of them, are taken out of inventory for manufacture or delivery to customers?
◊ How often will you restock the shop area (if you have one)?
◊ Will your layout allow for the shop to be restocked while customers are in the store?
◊ If you run low on a particular item, due to poor ordering/supplies or unexpectedly high sales, how will this impact the display of items for sale in the shop area?
◊ How will you co-ordinate inventory control with purchasing and sales?
◊ What resources will your inventory control function require?

Resource	Detail	Costs	
		Once-off invest-ment	**Ongoing cost**
Space			
Equipment			
Staff			
Other			
Total			

These costs will feed through into Exercise 6.22: Capital Expenditure; Exercise 6.23: Product/Service Costs; and Exercise 6.24: Overheads.

Credit terms

An important aspect of negotiations with suppliers is credit terms. Their importance lies in their impact on cashflow. If you have to pay your supplier 30 days after purchase, this is not as good for cashflow as being allowed to wait 60 days but better than having to pay on the day of purchase. Record the credit terms you have agreed in **Exercise 6.4**.

EXERCISE 6.4: CREDIT TERMS

Will your suppliers offer you credit?   ☐ Yes ☐ No

If "Yes", on what basis?

If "No", why not? Is this standard in your industry?

Summarise the impact of your credit terms in the table:

What percentage of your purchases do you estimate you will pay:	%
Within 0 to 30 days?	
Within 31 to 60 days?	
Within 61 to 90 days?	
Within 91 to 120 days?	
In more than 120 days?	

In summary, you need to establish that you:

- Can buy the raw materials or goods for resale at the prices and in the quantities projected in your forecast

- Have thought through your sources and are not vulnerable to disruptions from suppliers

- Have clear policies for inventory and that your plan assumptions show a reasonable balance between the need to meet sales and the costs and funding requirements of carrying inventory

- Know the resources you will need to establish and maintain an effective purchasing function.

MAKING

Production is the part of your business process that provides products and/or services to your customer. It may be as simple as inventory-holding and bulk-breaking (selling in smaller quantities than were bought) or as complex as a multi-stage manufacturing operation. Or it may be delivery of a service such as a training programme or consulting services.

In manufacturing businesses, it can be a highly detailed and complex process of forecasting requirements, scheduling work through the production process and balancing capacities to ensure delivery targets are met. Many service businesses also require meticulous planning and organising to ensure that projects are completed to meet clients' deadlines. Retail/distribution-type businesses have to design their operations carefully in terms of layout, stacking/retrieving customer service and checkout/despatch.

The production process

Effective production is the core of your business and requires the knowledge and skills to:

- Define and set up a logical and cost-effective sequence of activities to ensure that products and services are available to meet sales
- Schedule the resources needed to meet the sales demand at the times they arise, dealing with peaks and valleys to achieve a balance between the risk of losing sales and carrying unproductive staff and/or inventory
- Maintain quality standards.

Use **Exercise 6.5** to describe your production process.

> Engineering is the ability to do for one dollar what any damn fool
> can do for five dollars.
> ARTHUR MELLEN WELLINGTON

EXERCISE 6.5: PRODUCTION PROCESS

Break the production process down into its operations – for example, in manufacturing it might be:

◊   Cut to size
◊   Machine to shape
◊   Assembly
◊   Store
◊   Despatch.

In a service business, it might be:

◊   Carry out an assessment of client needs
◊   Draw up an offer to the client specifying the terms and scope of the service
◊   Provide the service on dates agreed.

Identify the stages within your production process.

What resources will your production process require?

Resource	Detail	Costs	
		Once-off invest-ment	**Ongoing cost**
Space			
Equipment			
Staff			
Other			
Total			

These costs will feed through into Exercise 6.22: Capital Expenditure; Exercise 6.23: Product/Service Costs; and Exercise 6.24: Overheads.

You need to go over this process several times, looking for flaws and ambiguities. Ask yourself:

- Where is it not clear?
- Where could it go wrong?
- Where could it be made simpler?
- What happens if ...?

Materials/services planning

Materials planning consists of identifying the parts that make up the product that will be manufactured. Where the product is a stock item (that is, it is made regularly to a pre-agreed specification), materials planning is a less onerous responsibility than where products must be customised to clients' specifications.

Although materials planning is typically associated with manufacturing operations, the same principles of confirming that all is ready apply for services.

Use **Exercise 6.6** to help with your materials/services planning.

EXERCISE 6.6: MATERIALS/SERVICES PLANNING

For each product, identify:
◊ Parts required
◊ Materials required
◊ Other details

For each service, identify:
◊ Nature of service
◊ Duration
◊ Equipment needed
◊ Whether performed at customer's location or in-house.

Identify:
◊ Critical equipment/machines.

What resources will your materials/services planning function require?

Resource	Detail	Costs	
		Once-off invest-ment	Ongoing cost
Space			
Equipment			
Staff			
Other			
Total			

These costs will feed through into Exercise 6.22: Capital Expenditure; Exercise 6.23: Product/Service Costs; and Exercise 6.24: Overheads.

Production planning/Scheduling

If you are to meet customers' needs, your production process must make sure that the required products or services are delivered on time. This leads to the need for a system of production planning, which balances demand for products against available resources.

For product-based businesses, this can be part of an integrated production management system, using the latest computer technology, or it may be no more complex than a wall-chart.

For services-based businesses, the critical resource is usually staff time and so scheduling is the service equivalent of production planning.

Develop targets for your production process – for example:

- How quickly do you want to be able to respond to orders?

- What percentage of defective products is acceptable?

- How much stock is acceptable?

- What are the production targets for specific machines?

- What are the production targets for specific staff?

If you have targets, you need feedback on how well (or indeed, whether) you are achieving them. What information do you want back from the process? How will you arrange for this?

Use **Exercise 6.7** to help you decide on your production planning/scheduling.

EXERCISE 6.7: PRODUCTION PLANNING/SCHEDULING

Answer these questions:
◊ Will you use formal production planning techniques?
◊ If not, can you quantify staff time and machine time directly to your different products/services?
◊ Have you clearly defined the tasks and responsibilities of the production function?
◊ Is your production seasonal?
◊ What targets will you set for your production process?
◊ How will you measure achievement of these targets?

What resources will your production planning/scheduling function require?

Resource	Detail	Costs	
		Once-off invest-ment	Ongoing cost
Space			
Equipment			
Staff			
Other			
Total			

These costs will feed through into Exercise 6.22: Capital Expenditure; Exercise 6.23: Product/Service Costs; and Exercise 6.24: Overheads.

Distribution/logistics

Logistics is about getting your product and services into your business, through your business' process and out to your customers. As a function, it is becoming increasingly critical for the efficiency and cost-effectiveness of many businesses. Information technology, e-commerce, automation, and just-in-time systems all rely heavily on items arriving, leaving and being in the right place on time.

As soon as items – product parts, supplies, equipment, etc. – arrive, you must have a system in place to ensure that they go to the right place in your business at the right time. Next, you need to get the product or service to the customer. How critical is delivery in the sales promise? Do clients need (or want) quick delivery? Can the products be damaged easily? How are they packaged? All these questions need to be answered.

Good logistics can save you a lot of money. Use **Exercise 6.8** to help you here. Link this exercise back to **Exercise 6.3** on inventory management.

EXERCISE 6.8: LOGISTICS/DISTRIBUTION

List every movement of your parts, materials, supplies and equipment:
Are the places that items are moved from and to close beside each other?
If not, why not?
Could they be moved? At what cost? With what benefit?
Do the items to be moved require special equipment (because they are heavy, hazardous, fragile, etc)?
How much time is spent on movements of items?
How many people are involved in movements of items?
How much is that in money terms?
Can movements of items be eliminated, reduced, simplified, or made more efficient?
List the stages in the movement of the products or services to the customer.
Where is intervention from your business needed?
What stages are critical?
Look at your distribution chain again. Can it be done differently?
How?
At what cost?
With what benefit?

What resources will your logistics/distribution function require?

Resource	Detail	Costs	
		Once-off invest-ment	Ongoing cost
Space			
Equipment			
Staff			
Other			
Total			

These costs will feed through into Exercise 6.22: Capital Expenditure; Exercise 6.23: Product/Service Costs; and Exercise 6.24: Overheads.

Before you finalise your production process, you must ensure that it answers the Key Question of this chapter: Meeting planned sales. Your process must deliver enough products/services to meet your planned sales – or it's not good enough and must be re-designed.

Use **Exercise 6.9** to check your production capacity.

Exercise 6.9: Capacity Check on Production

To be sure that your production facility can meet the demands of sales, complete this exercise for each activity.

If the hours short are significant, you must develop coping strategies:

◊ Use over-capacity (if there is any) in earlier months that you can use to build up stocks

◊ Re-design the products/services so that they require less time in the bottleneck activities

◊ Raise the capacity by improving methods or increasing resources

◊ Reduce your sales forecast.

Months	Hours available	Hours required	Hours short	Coping strategy
Jan				
Feb				
Mar				
Apr				
May				
Jun				
Jul				
Aug				
Sep				
Oct				
Nov				
Dec				

Irrespective of the level of complication in your production process, you need to be able to demonstrate that you have:

• Thought through your business process and can describe it concisely (by words and flow chart)

• Identified any capacity limits that might constrain your ability to deliver the sales you forecast and have clear plans to deal with them

- Calculated and specified the resources you need to establish and maintain an effective production function.

Technological development

As your business grows, it is likely that technology will play a larger role in its success. It is important that you are aware of new developments in technology generally and of specific developments that might impact your business (positively or negatively). In particular, whatever your business, take time to study the trends in e-commerce, which is creating both opportunities and threats for businesses everywhere. Using technology to your own benefit will become a success factor and will cross-over into all functions in your business.

Technological development involves:

- Product development
- Innovation
- Intellectual property
- Development of the production process
- Quality.

Product development

Although research and development (R&D) is very often seen as applying only to science and technology-based businesses, it is in fact applicable to **all** businesses, regardless of industry, market or size.

The exercises in **Chapters 3** and **5** that progressively refined your initial idea definition into a product or service with a place in the market is a key element in R&D. Your on-going market research, as you monitor developments in the marketplace that might affect demand for your product/service, is also part of R&D. And, for many businesses, this is all that R&D need involve. These businesses – and perhaps yours too – do not need laboratories, testing grounds or other specialised facilities. Their research is more market-based. This is the approach that this guide will take to R&D. If your needs involve science or technology-based R&D, you should take specialist advice locally.

Complete **Exercise 6.10** to identify the extent of your R&D.

EXERCISE 6.10: RESEARCH & DEVELOPMENT

Is your product/service science or technology-based?   ☐ Yes ☐ No
Do you have specialist technical skills in this area?   ☐ Yes ☐ No
If"Yes", outline your qualifications:

If "No", outline how you propose to acquire the necessary technical skills:

If your product/service is not science or technology-based, how have you arrived at your current design/definition? (See **Chapters 3** and **5**)

How do you propose to keep your product/service up-to-date?

What resources will your R&D function require?

Resource	Detail	Costs	
		Once-off invest-ment	Ongoing cost
Space			
Equipment			
Staff			
Other			
Total			

Increasingly, R&D looks beyond the mere development of the product and considers what happens at the end of the product's life. Is it thrown away? Or can parts be recycled and used again? Is there a system in place for this? How your business will deal with this stage will depend very much on your personal and business value statement. Use **Exercise 6.11** to consider the implications of the end of product life for your product/service.

> Technological progress is like an axe in the hands of a psychopath.
> ALBERT EINSTEIN

EXERCISE 6.11: END OF PRODUCT LIFE ACTION

How long will your product last in normal use?
What parts of it can be recycled?
Could the product be redesigned so that more of it could
be recycled?   ☐ Yes ☐ No
If "Yes", what parts and at what cost?
Have you a recycling process in place for your product when
it comes to end of its life?   ☐ Yes ☐ No
If "Yes", how will it operate?
How will you communicate this process to your customers?

Innovation

Innovation is one of the key success factors in any modern business. The importance of innovation in the future is going to be even more significant due to constant change in technology, globalisation and the increased availability of information from the Internet, TV, computer, telephone and fax. To keep up with increasing competition, it is essential to be aware of those changes and constantly adjust the business to take account of new developments.

Within innovation, there are three main directions:

- **Adjustment:** These are small changes that do not alter the function of the product or service
- **Modification:** Maintaining the technology used but changing the function (from clock to watch)
- **Renovation:** Same function, different technology (from vinyl records to compact disc).

You must decide which of these directions (or what combination) is right for your business.

Innovation does not have to be a "giant leap forward". It can be a small step or, better still, a series of small steps (the "continuous improvement" that is so much a part of Quality Management Systems).

Always be on the look-out for ways to improve your product or service:

- Watch people using your product for a while
- Swap jobs: Let technicians do the selling and let the sales team manage production
- Arrange service contracts with your customers to get constant feedback
- Let clients set the quality criteria.

You will always face resistance when you try to innovate. Don't let it get you down. Without innovation, your business will stagnate and die.

Organising innovation

Innovation does not happen; it must be planned for, organised and managed, through:

- Constant feedback and direct contact with customers (client panel)
- Monthly review of information
- Regular brainstorm sessions with a group of people from different backgrounds
- A budget for innovation
- Appointing someone or making time yourself to search for new ideas (3M allows R&D workers to spend 15% of their time on their own ideas and initiatives and has a rule that 30% of turnover must come from products developed in the last five years)
- Creating an "idea box" (like a suggestions box) with cash prizes if ideas are used by the business
- Creating project teams (made up of both technicians and sales people) to work with clients on particular ideas and giving the team the power and authority to implement changes
- Creating a positive atmosphere in your business towards change.

To manage innovation and harness it to its true role in product development, it is important to create a constant flow of information through the business. To do this, you need to set up an information system. This will bring together feedback from within your own business (for example, comments from your staff, clients and suppliers – all of which links with quality management) and combines it with outside sources such as competitors, newspapers, trade magazines, etc.

To prevent any restriction of vision, the information sources should be widespread and some should be unrelated to business – to help you keep an open mind.

Answering the following questions will help you to develop your information system:

Internal

- How are you going to organise a system of feedback from your staff, clients and suppliers?
- What information/comments should you be looking for?

External

- What information sources are you going to access to keep informed?

Innovation should be part of your strategic plan (call it your "innovation plan" to get the message across), as well as being part of on-going product development.

Intellectual property

Intellectual property is a catch-all term used to cover a number of separate rights relating to the protection and exploitation of ideas. It is an important area to understand in the context of R&D.

The value of intellectual property rights lies in the fact that they allow the owner of the rights the freedom to exploit the ideas to which the rights attach and protection from others who may want to do the same. Thus, if your business discovers a new way of making something, invents a new product or even simply publishes a book, the law provides a means protecting your right to exploit the value of these, while preventing others from doing so without your permission. This makes intellectual property rights very valuable.

Business' interest in intellectual property lies in two areas:

- Protection of its own rights
- Use of other people's rights, through technology transfer, licensing, etc.

First, let's look at the different types of intellectual property.

Patents

A patent is an exclusive right given by the State and enforceable in the Courts. It gives the "patentee" a monopoly to make, use and sell the invention for a fixed period of time and the right to stop others manufacturing, using or selling the patented invention during that period unless they have obtained the patent owner's authorisation to do so. In return for this monopoly, the patentee pays fees to cover the costs of processing the patent application and granting the patent. Annual renewal fees are also paid in order to keep the patent in force.

The European Convention (EPC) came into force in 1977 and established the European Patent Office (EPO). A European patent application can be filed either with the Patents Office in any one of the EU member states or directly with the Hague Branch of the EPO. The applicant can choose to designate any of the 18 contracting states.

When granted, a European patent has the effect of a national patent in each of the countries designated. Therefore, an applicant may find it considerably cheaper to lodge a single patent application to the EPO, designating a number of contracting states, as opposed to lodging individual patent applications with each of the countries.

The Patent Co-operation Treaty (PCT) came into effect in 1978. Its main aim is to streamline patent application filing and novelty search procedures for applicants wishing to obtain patent protection in a wide number of countries around the world.

The PCT provides a system whereby a single international application in one of the contracting states allows for the designation of up to 80 other countries in which one wishes to have patent protection. The applicant designates those in which a patent is desired and eventually the relevant national authority may grant a patent.

Trade marks
Once a business has a product to sell, it needs something that distinguishes its goods and services from those of competitors. A trade mark is a sign that is capable of being represented graphically (in words or pictures written down) and which is capable of distinguishing the goods or services of one business from those of other businesses. It may consist of words (including personal names), designs, letters, numerals, or the shape of the goods or of their packaging. An applicant for a trade mark is required to pay fees to register it and renewal fees to keep it in force.

Industrial designs
A design is a new idea or a conception of the external "shape, configuration, pattern or ornament" intended to be assumed by any article. Designs may be registered in respect of such diverse items as toys, lamps, articles of furniture, containers, clothes, fabrics and wallpaper. A design applied to an article should not be confused with what may be a patentable invention, or a "device" trademark (a trademark containing or consisting of a picture or drawing).

Copyright

Copyright is the creator's (or legal owner's) rights in creative works like paintings, writings, photographs, drawings, sound recordings, films and television broadcasts.

The author of a work is the first owner of copyright in the work, except in the case of a work made under a contract of service in the course of employment, or of photographs or portraits made under contract for some other person.

It is advisable for an author to sign, date and witness his/her work as proof of ownership and to display the international copyright symbol © prominently on his/her work.

EXERCISE 6.12: INTELLECTUAL PROPERTY

Do patents apply to your business?   ☐ Yes ☐ No
How is patenting law organised in your country?
How much does it cost to get a patent (in your own country
and in other countries that might be important to your business)?   € _____
Do trade marks apply to your business?   ☐ Yes ☐ No
How is trade mark law organised in your country?
How much does it cost to get a trade mark (in your own country
and in other countries that might be important to your business)?   € _____
Do industrial designs apply to your business?   ☐ Yes ☐ No
How is industrial designs law organised in your country?
How much does it cost to get a patent (in your own country
and in other countries that might be important to your business)?   € _____
Does copyright apply to your business?   ☐ Yes ☐ No
How is copyright law organised in your country?
How much does it cost to get a copyright (in your own country
and in other countries that might be important to your business)?   € _____

Technology transfer

Technology transfer is an "umbrella" term for a range of methods by which third parties can avail of ideas protected under intellectual property law.

In your research (it may even have been what started you thinking of starting your own business), you may have identified a product/service, or process, that you believed had potential in your market. However, on further research, you discover that the idea is protected. Can you go any further?

Yes. You can approach the owners of the intellectual property rights that you are interested in and discuss the possibility of licensing those rights from them, or coming to some other arrangement.

Usually, technology transfer is specific to a market (you would license the rights for Europe, or for your own country only) and a period (perhaps five years). The owners would share their protected information with you, enabling you to replicate their product/service, in return for a fee or royalty, usually calculated on the income you generate from the rights.

Technology transfer is a complex area and you are recommended to take specialist advice.

EXERCISE 6.13: TECHNOLOGY TRANSFER   E

Which areas of your business might benefit from technology transfer?

Have you identified a source of appropriate technology?   ☐ Yes ☐ No

If "Yes", have you approached the source?   ☐ Yes ☐ No

If "Yes", with what result?

If "No", when/how do you propose to do so?

What benefit will the technology transfer provide you?

What is this worth to you?   € _____

What is the asking price for this technology?   € _____

Development of the production process

As in other areas of your business, it is not enough to design your production process once and then forget about it. Technological development is too fast-moving to allow this approach. Use **Exercise 6.14** to help you determine how you should keep your production process up-to-date. In the same way as you analysed your idea in **Chapter 3**, you should now put your production process under the microscope. Record your answers to the questions below in your working papers file.

EXERCISE 6.14: DEVELOPMENT OF THE PRODUCTION PROCESS

How many times a year will you review your process?
On what type of information will that review be based?
Where will that information come from?
How will customers be able to influence production to get customised products?
Have you considered maintenance of machines, etc?
Has your process been tested?
How would you lay out your production floor in an ideal situation?

Quality

Quality is in – big time! Quality has always been important as a means of differentiating products and delivering higher value-added but there is no escaping the current management focus on quality as a means of achieving higher profits through customer satisfaction.

Quality is an attitude of mind that results in everyone in a business working together towards:

- Eliminating (or minimising) errors and faults
- Meeting deadlines
- Mapping out clear lines of responsibility
- Continuous improvement.

Think about what quality means to you. What does it mean for your customer? What does it mean for your product/service?

Quality systems and certification

Quality systems help ensure that quality is delivered every time. Quality certification provides independent assurance that the quality systems meet approved standards.

The key international quality standards are:

- **ISO 9000/2000:** The Quality Standard (revised in 2000), the most successful international standard ever produced and currently in use in over 70 countries world-wide
- **ISO 14000:** The Environmental Standard.

ISO 9000 is a strategic management tool, facilitating effective control over design, manufacturing and service delivery processes. Applying an ISO 9000 system for Quality Management within an organisation can result in significant benefits including:

- **Management effectiveness:** Through structured, organised and defined authorities, responsibilities and reporting structures
- **Operating efficiency:** Through clearly documented practices and procedures
- **Cost reduction:** Through the identification and elimination of potential system deficiencies and product failures
- **Increased marketability:** Through the identification of a registered company with a quality philosophy and international standard
- **Customer satisfaction:** Through the receipt of enhanced service or product quality levels.

As ISO 9000 is a harmonised European and international standard, certification to the standard opens up international markets to companies where previously technical trade barriers may have been a major impediment.

The standard (in fact, there are four standards: ISO 9000, 9001, 9002 and 9003) requires an organisation to implement a documented quality management system addressing all organisational activities from the definition of its quality policy and objectives to the detailing of the various methodologies and controls applicable to its service delivery or product manufacturing processes.

This takes the form of a Quality Manual, supported by procedures manuals, work instructions, etc, defining:

- **What** must be done
- **Who** is to do it
- **When** it is to be done
- **How** it is to be done.

The business's Quality Manual is assessed to ensure that it adequately and completely conforms to the requirements of the relevant standard. The assessment is conducted on the applicant's premises by an experienced team of assessors. On approval, the business is awarded "Registered Firm" status and can use the mark on advertising material, letterheads and for other promotional purposes. Once registered, on-going inspections ensure that quality standards are maintained.

ISO 14000 is a standard for the management of the environment and a business' relationship with it. It is applicable mainly to larger process and chemical industries.

Because of the importance of quality, you should include a reference to it in your business plan. Think through your attitudes to quality and how you intend to implement it in your process. Then complete a draft of your business plan input in **Exercise 6.15**.

EXERCISE 6.15: QUALITY

Write a draft of the paragraph in your business plan on "Quality assurance systems" – how you intend to ensure that your business only produces quality products/services:

> *Quality is no longer a competitive advantage.*
> *It is a minimum entry requirement in any market.*
> *BRIAN TRACY*

Environmental concerns

As explained in the section on *Developing a marketing direction* in **Chapter 5,** customers increasingly expect companies to be concerned about the impact on the environment, both socially and physically, of their products and services. At the same time, regulations on environmental issues are becoming stricter.

Businesses can react in three ways:

- **Do nothing:** Wait to be pushed into complying with emerging regulations
- **Act now:** Identify potential environmental hazards and take steps to eliminate them. Use this as a "competitive edge"
- **Anticipate:** Identify new businesses that will be created by these trends and get in first.

Areas to consider include:

- Materials used, both in manufacture and packaging (toxic, recyclable, replaceable)
- Machines used
- Smell
- Noise
- Risks (health, fire, etc.)
- Waste.

In the meantime, control over the impact of your activities on the environment is an important part of the management of your business. There are, of course, legal requirements in this area but, more than that, good environmental management can lead to cost savings, enhanced customer relations and a positive product image.

If you are interested in exporting your product, you will find that compliance with an environmental management standard is invaluable, especially when dealing with other European businesses.

Health and safety

Health and safety in the workplace has become a major issue in industry in recent years, driven largely by EU and national regulations and by an increasing awareness of employers' social responsibilities.

Put simply, in general, an employer is responsible in so far as is reasonably practicable for the safety, health and welfare of his/her employees.

Employees also have a duty to ensure their own health and safety as well as that of other staff and others in the workplace.

 Check what regulations apply to your business with a lawyer experienced in health and safety matters or a professional consultant.

SELLING

Most of this essential business process function is covered in **Chapter 5, Marketing & Sales**. The generic sales skills are communications, influencing and negotiation. Specific product knowledge will be needed and other skills, such as formal presentation skills, copy and letter writing skills, may be needed if mailings and group demonstrations are planned. Your sales function has to have someone who "knows the business" – someone who knows the best trade fairs, the right time to get orders, the people who matter and how to get access to them. If you are not that person, you must recruit someone with the right experience. Because there are so many different aspects to marketing, sales and after-sales service, we will only consider order processing in this section, as a model for other aspects.

Order processing

It's all very well getting orders, but you don't make money until you supply them. So you need a process that takes orders and converts them into satisfied customers. Typically, an order process consists of the following stages:

- **Order receipt:** You receive the order – How? By telephone, fax, post, e-mail, face-to-face in your shop or at the customer's premises?
- **Order verification:** You check that you understand the order and can supply the product/service
- **Credit check (if appropriate):** You decide whether to allow the customer to buy on credit and, if so, what terms to give. This is your credit policy, which you have decided as part of your marketing mix (**Chapter 5**)
- **Input to production plan/inventory control:** You must make arrangements to make the product, supply it from inventory, or schedule a service, depending on your business
- **Billing:** You must bill your customer, if you extend credit to him
- **Cash receipt:** You must get paid and bank the cash
- **Query resolution:** You must resolve any queries your customer has with his order.

Use **Exercise 6.16** to help you develop your own order process.

EXERCISE 6.16: ORDER PROCESSING AND OTHER SELLING FUNCTIONS

Which of the following stages are needed in your order process?
◊ Order receipt
◊ Order verification
◊ Credit check (if appropriate)
◊ Input to production plan/inventory control
◊ Billing
◊ Cash receipt
◊ Query resolution.

What other stages are needed in your order process and why?
How will you organise each stage?
What resources will your order processing function require?

		Costs	
Resource	**Detail**	**Once-off invest-ment**	**Ongoing costs**
Space			
Equipment			
Staff			
Other			
Total			

These costs will feed through into Exercise 6.22: Capital Expenditure; Exercise 6.23: Product/Service Costs; and Exercise 6.24: Overheads.

What resources will other aspects of your selling process require?

Resource	Detail	Costs	
		Once-off invest-ment	Ongoing costs
Space			
Equipment			
Staff			
Other			
Total			

These costs will feed through into Exercise 6.22: Capital Expenditure; Exercise 6.23: Product/Service Costs; and Exercise 6.24: Overheads.

After you have considered the process(es) needed for other aspects of Selling, your business plan must show that you have:

- Provided for the resources needed to establish and maintain a sales function capable of delivering the sales forecasted each month
- Made realistic provision for sales and sales-related costs in your projections.

Managing

Management requires the discipline to improve business strategies by monitoring and reacting to the threats and opportunities created by internal and external events. It requires a formal process and the ability to listen to and work with external advisers and or, non-executive directors.

Information systems

Keeping informed on what is happening outside your business is difficult and you can be snowed under with too much information very quickly. But the outside world is where you sell your products/services and it is where the opportunities lie, particularly in a world that is becoming more and more competitive.

The obvious sources of information on the outside world are the ones that you used earlier in your market research. Analyse which sources you should use on a regular basis in **Exercise 6.17**.

EXERCISE 6.17: SOURCES OF INFORMATION

Which trade magazines will you subscribe to?

How will you keep informed of international developments?

What are the addresses of useful web sites?

What are the trade organisations that you should join?

Who are the people in your network (**Exercise 2.6**) who can keep you aware of developments?

How will you store the information you research? Think about filing structure and information technology.

How will staff use the system and when?

How will you want information presented for use?

What resources will your sources of information require?

		Costs	
Resource	**Detail**	**Once-off invest-ment**	**Ongoing costs**
Space			
Equipment			
Staff			
Other			
Total			

These costs will feed through into Exercise 6.22: Capital Expenditure; Exercise 6.23: Product/Service Costs; and Exercise 6.24: Overheads.

Become an expert in prioritising. Some information is "nice to know", other information can make or break your business – you have to learn how to see the difference and gather only the important bits.

Exercise 6.18: Information for Your Business

What type of information do you need across the following functions:

	Importance	Frequency	Source	Who is responsible?
Buying				
Internal				
Inventory levels				
Re-order levels				
Delivery speed				
Response time				
Logistical costs per unit				
Vendor rating				
External				
Feedback from suppliers				
Making				
Internal				
Productivity				
Material usage				
Use of equipment				
Wastage				
Use of capacity				
Quality control problems				
% Defaults				
Selling				
Internal				
Number of customers				
Number of repeat orders				
Sales expense in % of sales				
Journey planning				
Order size				

	Importance	Frequency	Source	Who is responsible?
Sales funnel				
Call volume				
Price per lead				
Price per converted lead				
Sales per distributor				
Average call time per customer				
% success rate				
Discounts given				
Response time				
New contacts				
External				
Competition				
Market				
Economy				
Society				
Feedback from customers				
Stake holders				
Colleagues				
R&D				
Internal				
Number of improvements				
Number of new ideas				
Customer feedback				
Supplier feedback				
External				
Technological developments				
New product introductions				
Customer feedback				
Staff feedback				
Supplier feedback				

Some more tips include:

- **Intuition:** Do not under-estimate the power of intuition. Allow intuition to guide you and note ideas as they occur. Try to find out why
- **Enquiries:** Enquiries are a great way to look for opportunities. Make sure you are made aware of them
- **Idea bank:** Write down all the ideas that you, your staff, suppliers and customers generate and review them on a regular basis. You might miss a great opportunity if you don't
- **Learning:** Most businesses are now knowledge-based, so you need to find a way to collect the learning. Set up regular sessions to identify what has been learned and how that learning could improve your organisation. Consider how training (yourself and your staff) could add to that learning.

Administration

Administration is an area that is easily forgotten in the excitement of sales and production. However, it is a critical business function and your business plan must show that you have thought through the back-up support your core business activities need – for example:

- Records and clerical functions
- Accounts and wages systems
- Control systems to manage core activities such as purchases and sales
- Reception and telephone facilities.

You must also show that you have made realistic provision for administration costs in your projections.

In established businesses, administration is usually spread across departments with specialist purchases, sales and production administrators. There will usually be a dedicated accounts and wages department and reception will be a full-time operation.

In a start-up business, all the clerical and administrative tasks are usually centralised and often carried out by one person or by the owner or the owner's partner working in the evenings to "catch up".

Purchases administration

The aim of controlling purchases is to make sure that you pay only for sound goods that you have received in response to valid orders placed by you or your duly authorised staff.

There are four aspects to effective control over the purchasing function:

- Clearly specify who is authorised to order goods and the value limits to which they can order
- Use effective documentary evidence such as purchase order forms and goods inwards advice notes
- Maintain checks on incoming goods for quality and match them to the suppliers' delivery notes and your purchase order
- Pay suppliers' invoices only when they can be matched to your control documentation (your order and goods inward advice note).

Good documentation also helps in expediting overdue deliveries and reducing waste caused by over ordering.

Sales administration

The aim of controlling sales is to make sure that you achieve the levels of sales planned and that you get paid for all goods or services you provide.

Break the sales generation activities shown in **Chapter 5** into weekly and daily targets and monitor them relentlessly. If you don't, you simply will not meet your sales forecasts.

Establish a system of documentation appropriate to the nature and scale of your business. Use enquiry, sales orders and goods outward advice documents to verify delivers and support sales invoices.

Cash control

Very simply, to manage cash you need to know:

- How much you have
- How much is due in
- How much is due out.

Money is just something to make book-keeping convenient.
HL HUNT

Your bank balance will tell you how much money you have – except that the information is out-of-date by the time you receive it. Manage your cash by putting in place a manual or computer-based system.

- For example, buy a ledger book with five columns. This is your "bank balance book". Keep a separate ledger, or section in the same ledger, for each bank account that your business operates. Use the columns in the bank balance book to record every transaction that goes through your bank account, as it happens, with the following information:
- **Date:** When the transaction happened
- **Type:** Whether it was a cheque or a lodgement or a direct debit (more later)
- **Money in:** Lodgements and other credits – just write in the amount, no more details
- **Money out:** Cheques and other withdrawals, again just the amount will do
- **Balance:** Keep a running balance all the time.

Don't wait until the end of the month to write up the cheques you send out or to note down lodgements you make to your bank account. Do it immediately you write a cheque or make a lodgement.

Arrange your direct debits and standing orders so that they all fall on the same day of the month and you can include them once a month in your bank balance book.

Equally necessary is that you know how much money is due to your business, who owes it and whether it has been paid. If you do not plan to use a computerised system, use a "still to be received" file – a manilla folder. Into this file, place a copy of every invoice issued by your business. As payment for each invoice is received, tear up the copy in your file and throw it away. What remains in the folder represents your business' accounts receivables.

You can record your notes of debt-chasing on the copy invoices and can see instantly from the thickness of the folder how good (or how bad) your collections process is.

The first step in settling accounts payables is to know how much is due and when. That helps you plan your finances and make sure you have enough money when you need it.

Create a "still to be paid" file by buying another manilla folder. Into this, place copies of every invoice you receive for credit purchases. When you pay the invoice, remove it from the folder. This way, the size of the folder tells you instantly how much you owe.

Instead of tearing up the copy invoice when you pay it, staple it to your cheque instead and send it to your creditor, so they can tell what invoices you are paying.

EXERCISE 6.19: ADMINISTRATION

Identify the main administration areas within your business.
Document (in words and/or flowchart) the process you intend to use for each.
What resources will your administration processes require?

Resource	Detail	Costs	
		Once-off invest-ment	Ongoing costs
Space			
Equipment			
Staff			
Other			
Total			

These costs will feed through into Exercise 6.22: Capital Expenditure; Exercise 6.23: Product/Service Costs; and Exercise 6.24: Overheads.

INFRASTRUCTURE

Infrastructure consists of all those things that you take for granted but which are essential to the smooth running of your business.

Premises

Chapter 5 explained how important place is as part of the marketing mix (4 Ps). In the property business, they say that only three things matter in choosing a property: Location, location, location. For certain kinds of business – shops, hotels, restaurants – location can make or break the business. But in all cases, the right working environment is important.

Essentially, you have two choices:

- Work from home
- Set up an office/shop/workshop somewhere else.

Working from home

Working from home is the simplest, and often the cheapest, alternative. It suits certain kinds of business and does not suit others. Consultants and other people whose main contact with their customers is in the customers' own premises can work from home easily – but your neighbours might not appreciate a factory being built in your garden! So this option is best suited to service businesses.

If you work from home, you need to set aside a clearly-defined "workspace". In this area – and in this area only – you work. When you leave it, you are "at home". If you do not do this, you will never get a break from your business.

Make your workspace a "Do not disturb" zone. If you are to do your work properly, you must be able to put aside the distractions of home life (telephone calls, children, visitors, chores).

Next, you need to check with your local authority about planning permission for your workspace. Then consider insurance.

Think about combining working from home with serviced offices, where you will have a professional telephone answering/message-taking service, a "business" address and access to meeting rooms for times when your customers want to come and talk to you.

Working elsewhere

This is a more expensive option – not only in rent or mortgage, but also in travel time and convenience. But for most businesses, it is a necessary step.

If you are looking for offices, consider somewhere that offers secretarial support (for example, telephone answering, message taking, fax, photocopying, reception, etc.) – it will save you hiring a secretary until the volume of work justifies it. And you save on buying equipment.

For workshops and factories, you need to check lay out, logistics, transport, weight of machinery, health & safety regulations, environmental issues, availability of three-phase electricity, etc. This is critical to make sure that:

- You do not end up in an unsuitable premises
- You do not pay for space that you cannot use
- You do not pay for costly refitting.

Go back through the exercises you have completed earlier in this chapter, where you identified the resources you require for each part of your process. Extract the Space requirements (make sure you eliminate any overlap) and use them to help you design your premises layout in **Exercise 6.20**.

EXERCISE 6.20: PREMISES LAY OUT

How much space do you need in total? _____ m²
How is this divided between the different parts of your process:
◊ Buying – Purchasing, Inventory control, etc?
◊ Making – Production, Production planning, Logistics/distribution, etc?
◊ Selling – Order processing, etc?
◊ Managing – Administration?
Draw your ideal space, based on the natural flow within your process.
Revise this until you have considered all the options. Summarise them as two options:
◊ **The ideal:** The exact layout of premises that you want, with everything exactly where you want it
◊ **The acceptable minimum:** The basics, below which you will not be able to function in a business-like manner.

Only when you have done this exercise, should you start to look for accommodation. Otherwise, it's too tempting to plump for the first apparently suitable space you are offered, without thinking through all the consequences.

Although drawing an ideal space based on your process seems best suited to retail and manufacturing businesses, where layout can add or take significantly from a business, it also helps in an office environment to promote efficiency.

Retail location

Picking the right location for a shop or restaurant needs lots of market research. Major retail and food chains are known to spend months monitoring pedestrian traffic outside a possible location before coming to a decision.

For any apparently suitable premises, be prepared to spend several days checking:

- Traffic flow (both vehicles and pedestrians)
- Types of customers in the area
- Their spending patterns in other premises close by
- The timing of any rushes
- What other traders in the area think about the location
- What development (if any) is proposed for the area that might have an effect (positive or negative) on your plans.

Check insurance premiums, compliance with food hygiene and health and safety regulations, planning permission, etc.

Buy or rent?

This depends on how much money you have. But consider your motives also: are you acquiring a property for your business or investing in the property business. It's very easy to get involved – and get your business' cashflow involved – in improving a property you have bought, instead of getting on with making your business a success.

And whatever you do, don't fall into the trap of taking a very much larger space than you need because you have been assured by the real estate agent that "there will be no problem letting it". If you want to be a property landlord, start a property business. By all means take enough for sensible expansion, but don't let trying to cover the cost of excess space distract you from your real business.

Leases for rented properties should be checked very carefully. They may not always include all the terms the letting agent told you about – and, by the same token, will probably include some clauses not mentioned at all. Have the lease checked by a lawyer.

And, whether leasing or buying, don't be rushed to sign anything until you have completed your business planning, made sure of your financing and know what you are signing. Use **Exercise 6.21** to help you make sure that you have thought of everything.

EXERCISE 6.21: PREMISES

E

How important is location for your business?	Very ☐
	Reasonably ☐
	Not at all ☐
Do you intend to buy or rent your premises?	☐ Buy ☐ Rent

What is your budget for premises?

Once-off capital costs:

◊   Purchase   € _____

◊   Renovations   € _____

◊   Fixtures & Fittings   € _____

On-going revenue expenditure:

◊   Rent (annual)   € _____

◊   Services   € _____

How much space do you need?   _____ m²

Will your customers visit your premises?   ☐ Yes ☐ No

◊   Do those visitors need to be impressed?   ☐ Yes ☐ No

◊   Is parking an issue?   ☐ Yes ☐ No

◊   Will you need space for deliveries?   ☐ Yes ☐ No

Could your work be done from home?   ☐ Yes ☐ No

◊   Have you a suitable space?   ☐ Yes ☐ No

◊   Have you planning permission?   ☐ Yes ☐ No

If renting, are you and your solicitor happy with the lease:

◊   Period of the lease?   ☐ Yes ☐ No

◊   Rent (+ other charges)?   ☐ Yes ☐ No

◊   Your responsibilities?   ☐ Yes ☐ No

◊   The landlord's responsibilities?   ☐ Yes ☐ No

◊   Terms for renewal/termination?   ☐ Yes ☐ No

Other issues

Wherever you locate, you need to consider a wide range of other issues, including: Lighting, heating, alarms, signs, locks, insurance, toilets, interior decor, fittings, telephone (including ISDN lines, if you want high-speed Internet access), storage and parking.

> In retailing, the first consideration in the design of a shop should be ease of shopping for the customer. Being able to find what you want is the key thing, and only after that do aesthetics come into it.
> SIR SIMON HORNBY, chairman, WH Smith

CAPITAL EXPENDITURE

Expenditure in business is classified as capital or revenue.

Capital expenditure – items expected to be used over a number of years – are called fixed assets (examples include vehicles, computers and office furniture). Their cost is charged against profit over the years of their useful life – as "depreciation" – rather than in full in the year in which they were bought. The aim is to show a fair picture of the costs incurred in earning the company's turnover for each year. So a machine bought for €50,000, which is expected to last for 10 years, will be depreciated at 10% and shown in the profit and loss account (or income statement) as an expense of €5,000 each year.

Revenue items are those that will be used in the next twelve months – for example, stock for resale and stationery -- and are fully charged as a cost in the year in which they are bought.

There are no monetary guidelines to help you distinguish between capital and revenue items. However, most businesses use common-sense and treat low value items as revenue, even if they have a long life – for example, there's little point depreciating a €5 stapler or €12 kettle over 10 years. Often an arbitrary amount of €100 (or €500 or €1,000, depending on the size of your business) is appropriate – anything above the limit is capital, anything below is revenue.

Go back through the exercises earlier in this chapter where you identified the resources required to support your process. Identify the fixed asset items – usually in the "Once-off investment" column – and list them in **Exercise 6.22** under the appropriate categories. Make sure you eliminate any overlap between functions – for example, both the purchasing and order-taking functions will require a telephone but, if one person will do both jobs, only one telephone is needed.

As you identify the fixed assets you require, you may realise that you have some already. For example, if you intend to set up as a computer consultant, it is likely that you already have a PC and printer, etc. In the section on *Owner's Equity* in **Chapter 8**, we will explain how to handle this. For now, simply indicate in **Exercise 6.22** that you have this item already and that there's no need to allow for the cost of buying it.

It is a good idea to back up any costs that you plan to include in your financial projections for the purchase of fixed assets with appropriate evidence – suppliers' quotations or estimates, price lists, advertisements, etc. File this evidence in your working papers.

EXERCISE 6.22: FIXED ASSETS TO SUPPORT YOUR PROCESS

Fixed assets	How many?	Cost €	Have already? Yes/No	Need to buy? Yes/No	Deprec-iation rate %	Month of acquis-ition
Premises						
Equipment						
Transport						
Furniture						
Information technology						
Other						
TOTAL						

EXPENSES

Expenses consist of:

- Product costs
- Overheads.

Product costs

How do you know what your product will cost to make or your service cost to provide?

The bad news is that this can often be a very difficult area. In the past, accountants have had to struggle with measuring direct costs such as materials, arguing over how much labour cost should be allocated to a product and then trying to apportion overhead expenses to get the total cost

The good news is that the only costing concept that you need to understand is the difference between costs that will not change in response to increases and decreases in volume ("fixed" costs) and those that will ("variable" costs).

So-called "Fixed Costs" such as salaries and rent don't automatically change as volume increases though they obviously will have to sooner or later if the business expands to the stage where larger premises and more staff are needed. Their response to increases in volume follows a stepped pattern – for example:

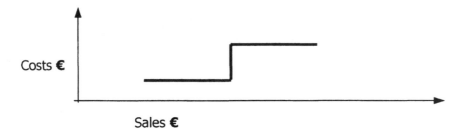

Variable Costs such as materials and sales commissions will rise in direct proportion to sales – for example:

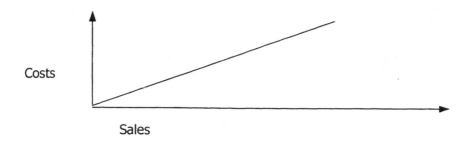

By thinking through your costs to identify fixed and variable costs, you will develop a highly realistic financial model. This will give you very accurate feedback later when you explore options that involve changes to sales.

Complete **Exercise 6.23** – look back at the exercises you completed earlier in this chapter, especially **Exercises 6.2** and **6.5** – and file your evidence of why these costs are reasonable in your working papers.

Complete **Exercise 6.23** for each product/service defined in your sales forecast and modify the number of rows to suit your own situation. Direct costs are costs such as materials and labour that can be directly measured and allocated to the product. Measurement of direct costs can be a vexed area, so keep this as simple and clear as possible:

- Show only materials that are clearly part of the product
- Do not include any overheads (they will be included in **Exercise 6.25**)
- Only include labour costs that are paid on a sub-contract or piece work basis – the cost of employees paid on an hourly or other time-based rate is covered in **Chapter 7**.

Exercise 6.23: Product/Service Costs

(repeat exercise for each product/service you intend to sell)

Direct Cost Description	Product A €	Product B €	Product C €	Product D €
Total				

Notes:

◊ Only a Total cost is required for retail/distribution businesses, as they will have only one direct cost – the purchase price.

◊ Service businesses with no direct costs have no cost of sales element, since all their costs are included in overheads.

How many months' inventory do you intend to hold at a time?	**Months**
What minimum order value have you (or your suppliers) set?	€
Do you intend to buy at the start to stock your business? If so, what is the value of this inventory? In what month will this purchase be made?	€

Spare no expense to make everything as economical as possible.
SAMUEL GOLDWYN

Overheads

Each part of the business will have its own day-to-day running costs – overhead expenses such as staff salaries, costs of telephone calls, stationery etc. In small businesses, these overheads are usually taken in aggregate for the business rather than being allocated across departments.

Exercise 6.24 will record the overhead costs for your business. Typical overhead categories are shown – add new categories or amend those offered to meet your specific situation. Use the Miscellaneous category for small items that do not fit elsewhere.

Staff salaries will be dealt with in **Chapter 7, People**.

If the overhead varies with Sales (for example, delivery costs), enter the planned percentage in column 3. Identify which expenses have their cost spread evenly throughout the year and which must be allocated month-by-month.

Go back over earlier exercises to identify overheads – these will appear in the "Ongoing costs" column – and include them in the appropriate category in **Exercise 6.24**.

You will then need to identify other overheads, not captured thus far. Make sure that you don't include expenses such as promotion that have already been dealt with elsewhere. Also make sure that you eliminate overlap and double-counting.

EXERCISE 6.24: OVERHEAD EXPENSES

Overhead	Annual cost €	Percentage of Sales (%) (if a variable cost)	VAT Rate (%) (If applicable)	Even spread/ allocate?
Audit & Accountancy Fees				
Books, Magazines & Information				
Computer supplies				
Delivery costs				
Insurance (Exercise 4.6)				
Legal Expenses				
Light, Heat & Power				
Motor & Travel Expenses				
Postage & Telephone				
Printing & Stationery				
Rent & Rates				
Repairs & Renewals				
Training				
Miscellaneous				
Total				

THE TENBizPlan APPROACH TO BUSINESS PLANNING

Text

In this chapter, you have created draft text for input into your business plan document in relation to:

Process & Resources

- Process – **Exercise 6.5**
- Quality – **Exercise 6.15**.

Evidence

File copies of all of the exercises that you have completed in **Chapter 6**, for ease of reference later. They will be a crucial part of your evidence supporting your business plan.

In this chapter, you will also have identified other information that will be good evidence for your business plan – for example, information regarding, your technology transfer, costs of fixed assets and overheads, etc. File these safely as part of your working papers also.

Numbers

The numbers created for input into your financial projections as part of the process of business planning in this chapter are:

- Product costs for each product/service (or group of products/services) – **Exercise 6.23**
- Overheads – **Exercise 6.24**
- Fixed assets – **Exercise 6.22**
- Credit terms agreed with suppliers – **Exercise 6.4**.

Key Question

The key question for this chapter is:

> **How, and with what resources, will I meet my planned sales?**

To answer the question, you will need to consider:

- Your production process – Buying, making and selling
- Your infrastructure – Premises, administration, etc
- Your product/service costs, your capital expenditure on fixed assets and your overheads.

7

PEOPLE

The key question for this chapter is:

Can I describe the people I will need & how I will organise them?

At an early stage, you need to begin to estimate how many staff you may need and how this number will grow – and where you will recruit staff. There's not much point planning to develop a buisness if you can't get the people to do the work.

Where marketing is the key driver of your business, determining its direction, people are its engine, determining whether the business reaches its objectives. How many times do you hear business-owners saying "I could do so much, if only I had the right staff"? How often do you see people in positions for which they are clearly unsuited – and doing a bad job, for the customer and for the business that employs them. Unless you plan for your staff, before you ever need to recruit them, you may end up like these other business-owners, unable to reach your objectives.

People is part of the core planning stage. You have done your personal and idea assessments, considered your marketing and process; it's time now to consider the other elements. People is one of these.

In your business plan, you need to consider People under a number of headings:

- Management
- Overall employment numbers
- Organisation.

Those reading your business plan will expect you to have clear explanations of these points – in particular, management.

Output from this chapter

Earlier, in **Chapter 2**, *Self-Assessment,* you wrote a first draft of a paragraph on "Management" to be placed within the "**Project Overview**" section of your business plan. That draft focused on yourself as a manager, without any exposure to the concepts and techniques of management, or any consideration for the skills and abilities of other staff who may be working within the business.

By the end of this chapter, you will have rewritten that paragraph, on a much more informed basis. You will know what staff you will require, and when, and to do what; you will know how they will be organised; and you will have given some thought to their cost. All of these are key inputs from this chapter into your business plan.

And let's not forget that People cannot be seen in isolation. There are links to most of the other parts of the business too:

- **Personal Assessment (Chapter 2):** Your own view of your skills and experience is the starting point for recruitment of additional staff. You need to balance your weaknesses or lack of knowledge or experience with suitable staff

- **Idea Assessment (Chapter 3):** In deciding on your idea, you assumed that you would be able to find staff with the right skills and experience to help you grow your business. If that's not the case, how does this affect your idea; or, being positive, suppose you find someone with very special skills, could they take your business into areas that you might not have considered?

- **Marketing & Sales (Chapter 5):** Particularly in the area of customer service, the quality of the staff you recruit is critical. But your staff are critical to the implementation of all areas of your marketing strategy

- **Process & Resources (Chapter 6):** Again, in planning the process by which you deliver your product or service, you must assume the availability of suitable staff. But, here in People, you have an opportunity to check the validity of that assumption and to revisit Process, if necessary

- **Finance & Funding:** You need to pay your staff and you must plan for the cost. If you can't afford all the staff you would like, can you manage with the staff you can afford? Which staff positions are "essential" and which just "nice to have"?

The links, as you can see, all inform and revise one another. As you work through this guide, you will become better informed about all the different aspects of your new business and be able to fit them together.

> In a hierarchy, every employee tends to rise to his level of incompetence ...
> in time, every post tends to be occupied by an employee who is incompetent to
> carry out its duties ... Work is accomplished by those employees
> who have not yet reached their level of incompetence.
> LAURENCE J PETER, The Peter Principle

Planning for Staff

In **Chapter 6, Process & Resources**, we looked at the main functions in a business, and the operations and tasks they entail. Our next step is to consider the people needed to carry out the functions and how to recruit, train and organise them into an effective team.

Start-up businesses are characterised by a few people carrying out tasks over a diverse skills area. As the business grows and more people are recruited, there is a higher degree of specialisation and the business develops a more formal structure.

You must anticipate this and adopt a planned and systematic approach to recruiting, training and managing staff from the start. This section will provide you with the basic skills and knowledge to do this.

Staff is a key success factor for any business. If you not have the people who can do the work – and do it right – you do not have a business. Staffing is likely to be one of the biggest cost factors in your business, particularly in a service environment.

Organisational structure

People work best when they are part of an effective organisation structure. The following techniques will help you establish an effective structure for your company.

- **Clear lines of management:** Avoid confusion and conflict by making sure that each member of staff knows where they fit in and who they report to
- **Unity of objective:** From the very beginning, use your vision and mission statements to make sure that everyone understands the ultimate goals of the business and their roles in achieving them. As your business grows, it is easy for people to put their own interests and/or the interests of their own department before what is best for the business overall
- **Delegation:** The further down the organisation's hierarchy that a job is done, the lower the cost of that task. This means that you should train and motivate staff to take on more responsible tasks and then trust them to do the tasks effectively
- **Span of control:** As your business expands, make sure that the numbers of people that any one person must supervise does not become too great for them to manage

- **Job descriptions:** Support the organisation structure with up-to-date job descriptions (see **Figure 7A**). They are an invaluable way of allocating work fairly and effectively and avoiding confusion.

Even if you are currently the only person involved in the business, drawing up an organisation structure to show the main business functions will get you off on the right foot. You can fill in more names to the boxes as you take on staff.

FIGURE 7A: ORGANISATION STRUCTURE

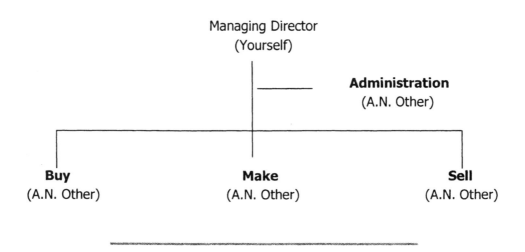

Other specialist functions may be important to your business – information technology, accounting, etc – and can be added to the structure above or included within the key functions. Make sure that you include responsibility for taxation and other regulatory matters within one of the positions (seethe section on *Taxation* in **Chapter 4**).

You need to decide which functions are necessary for your business. This doesn't mean that you have to staff them with specialists now – it just means that there is a job to be done and someone will have to do it, perhaps along with several other jobs as well. It is not uncommon for a single person within a start-up businesses to have several very different job-roles. It's one of the exciting things about working for a start-up (use this in your recruitment approach) – the opportunity to develop skills in a way that a larger, more structured business would never permit.

EXERCISE 7.1: AN ORGANISATIONAL STRUCTURE FOR YOUR BUSINESS

Draw the organisational structure that you would like to see for your business.

Look at the chart and the function boxes and think about who will fill these positions initially.

◊ You alone, while holding another wage-earning position   ☐
◊ You alone, full-time   ☐
◊ You and your partner: Full-time   ☐
◊ You and your partner: Part-time   ☐
◊ You and your business partner(s)   ☐
◊ You and your business partner(s) with employees at a wage   ☐
◊ How many employees full-time?   _____
◊ How many employees part-time?   _____

Fill in names against each function.

Then consider the situation in 12 months' and 3 years' time and repeat the exercise.

Having identified the functions required and allocated the existing staff to them, the next step is to check the general workload. Are some people going to be too busy? Are more people required for some functions? Complete **Exercise 7.2** to find out.

Exercise 7.2: Calculating the Workload

Write the names that you have filled in against functions in your organisation structure in the first column of the table below and estimate the number of hours estimated needed to perform each function.

Where the "Total Hours" column exceeds a reasonable level (say 35 to 40 hours per week), you should:
◊ Check that the original estimated hours are reasonable
◊ Reallocate the extra hours across qualified existing staff, training as required
◊ Recruit new staff and amend your table to reflect this.

Go through this process as many times as it takes to get it right. Note the training and recruitment implications and file them with this exercise in your working papers.

Staff Name	Hours per week					Total Hours
	Buy	Make	Sell	Manage	Other functions	

In working through the time required by each function, you will need to define and describe the work that has to be done by the holder of each function on your organisation chart. Record this in a Job Description, similar to **Figure 7B**.

> *A compact organisation lets all of us spend time managing the business rather than managing each other.*
> WARREN BUFFETT

FIGURE 7B: JOB DESCRIPTION

Job Title:
Reporting To:
Primary Objective
Key Tasks:
General Responsibilities:

Start the task of writing job descriptions with your own job because, until you have defined your own job, it will be virtually impossible to allocate jobs to other staff. But remember, because it's your business, any jobs that cannot be done by other staff – whether through lack of time or ability – will fall back to you. Don't take on too much for yourself initially – especially try to avoid taking on jobs that other staff can do (remember to delegate!).

In the section on *Self-assessment* in **Chapter 2**, you identified your drive, personality and experience and skills. Now you consider very carefully, in the light of the deeper insight that you now have into your new business, what is your own range of skills and how do they benefit the business?

Consider your:

- Technical skills
- Personal qualities
- Business skills.

In assessing yourself, be honest. Ask yourself these questions:

- Would you give yourself the job of general manager of your new business?
- Are your keyboard and literary skills really up to sending out customer letters and writing marketing blurbs? Perhaps you excel in production and technical innovation instead?
- Are there key areas of the management of your business that you have left out of the job description above?
- If there are, does this mean that you need to expand your management team?

- Maybe you need to acquire other skills? If so, can you get by with a little training for yourself or should you buy in these skills on a freelance basis as and when required?

Go back now to **Chapter 2, Personal Assessment** and complete **Exercise 2.5** again, this time focusing on the needs of your own new business, as identified by your research to date. Use the answers to direct the next exercise.

Would a partner or key manager supply some of the skills you are missing? Use **Exercise 7.3** to identify critical areas in your business and those where a partner or key manager could make a difference.

EXERCISE 7.3: CRITICAL BUSINESS AREAS

Which of these areas are most critical to the development of your business? Where would a partner or key manager make the most difference? Rank them 1, 2, 3, etc.

	Critical	**Difference**
Marketing	_____	_____
Sales	_____	_____
Financial control	_____	_____
Production	_____	_____
Management	_____	_____

Then consider:

- Could your business bear the financial impact of another salary? One that would make a critical difference to the speed at which your business develops?

- Could you reduce your own salary for a while to compensate (a real test of commitment!)?

How much will my staff cost?

Summarise your staff costs in **Exercise 7.4**.

Remember that salary is not the only cost in employing someone. Social insurance usually must be paid on their earnings and they may be entitled to bonuses, commissions, overtime payments, etc.; they will need training – and there will be other costs you have not thought of.

You need to know:

- The average salaries for the functions you are considering
- The average conditions
- The average reward "package".

Recruitment agencies in most countries publish this information – often free of charge. Other good sources are trade associations and employer representative bodies.

You then need to decide whether you are going to pay just average – or a little more, or a lot more, to get the people you want. Or, are there special circumstances that mean people will work for you for less than for other employers – for below average salaries – perhaps because you are prepared to offer them stock options or other incentives?

Wages: What you get paid for doing what you are told, as opposed to salaries which are what you get paid for doing things without being told.
HERBERT V PROCHNOW & HERBERT V PROCHNOW Jr.

EXERCISE 7.4: STAFF COSTS

Staff by function	Salary €	Social Insurance, Bonus, etc €	Total annual cost €	Start date	Effective first year cost €
Manage					
Your own salary (Exercise 2.9)					
Buy					
Make					
Sell					
Other functions					
Other					
TOTAL					

These figures will help you in developing your financial projections and in making applications for employment subsidies, if you are eligible.

Can you afford all these people? Which people are essential and which "nice to have"? Deciding this will help you to explore the financial consequences of staff recruitment.

Further, although it won't show in salary costs, every extra person you employ will add other costs:

- Fixed assets, such as furniture, machinery, computers
- Overheads, such as telephone and postage costs, canteen costs, etc.

You need to take these into account as well and refer back to **Exercises 6.22** and **6.24** if necessary.

Next, you need to consider issues such balance in:

- Gender
- Age profile
- Ethnicity
- Disabilities.

Does your mix of staff reflect your customers? Does it reflect the real needs of your business? Is there local legislation that imposes requirements on you in relation to any of these issues?

Next we will consider where you will recruit staff, since there's not much point planning expansion if you can't get the people to do the work.

RECRUITING STAFF

Recruiting staff is a major stumbling block for many small businesses. It takes time and effort. But the results can have an enormous impact on your bottom line. Hire the right people, and you will have a strong staff who will move your company forward. But the wrong person will pull down morale, waste your time, and cost you more than just an extra salary.

The key steps are:

- Knowing what you're looking for
- Finding applicants
- Interviewing.

Knowing what you're looking for

Before you begin looking for someone to fill a vacancy, you need to know what you're looking for. The work you have already done on your organisational structure will now prove immensely helpful. You should:

- **Create a detailed job description:** Write down the specific tasks that you expect this employee to perform. Think about every detail. Then summarise and put the tasks in order of priority. Use **Figure 7B**

- **Develop a list of skills required:** What skills are essential? What skills are merely desirable?

- **Decide whether there are other things you want?:** Specific educational background? Experience in a particular industry? What else is necessary for the person to develop in your company?

- **Think about personality:** You need people who share your vision and your standards.

- **Take a reality check:** Look at what you have written down. Which areas are priorities? Where are you willing to compromise? Will you get the person you want for the salary you are offering?

Use **Exercise 7.5** to help you to create a candidate profile. Each time you plan to recruit, complete this exercise.

EXERCISE 7.5: CANDIDATE PROFILE

Is a job description available for this position?	☐ Yes ☐ No	
What skills are required?	**Essential**	**Desirable**
◊	☐	☐
◊	☐	☐
What else do I require in a candidate?	**Essential**	**Desirable**
◊	☐	☐
◊	☐	☐
What personality do I want in a candidate?		
◊		
◊		
Am I being reasonable?	☐ Yes ☐ No	
Where can I compromise?		
Where must I **not** compromise?		

Finding applicants

Requirements defined, you now need to find people to meet them. Here are some suggestions:

- **Look in your files:** Starting out, you should draw on your network of personal contacts (see **Exercise 2.6**). As your company develops and becomes visible and successful, you will have people writing in looking for jobs, even though no vacancies are being advertised. If any of these people look promising, make time to meet and find out more about them. Then, when you need a particular mix of skills, you may find the perfect candidate in your files already

- **Ask your staff:** Your own staff may know someone with the right skills whom they would be happy to recommend (for a bonus, perhaps). And they will come with a built-in guarantee, since they won't want to let down the staff-member who sponsored them

- **Ask around:** Ask everyone you know (including customers and suppliers) whether they know anyone they would recommend. Have some background information available on the job ready to give out

- **Advertising:** Make it clear what you are looking for and write the ad to attract candidates. But make sure you have the time to handle a deluge of responses

- **Use a recruitment agency:** A sensible route if you do not have the time or ability to screen applicants, but it can be expensive. Through their contacts, agencies can often find people whom you would otherwise not reach with an advertisement

- **Look on-line:** The World Wide Web has opened up a new set of places to post your job vacancy. These are best used for high-tech vacancies

- **Use your own web-site to attract candidates:** List current vacancies and use a "We're always looking for good people" message to attract candidates even when you don't have any vacancies

- **Contact University/college/school career offices:** They are always looking for jobs for their graduates and will usually circulate your listing free

- **Job fairs:** An opportunity to give your company some visibility and talk to a variety of candidates in an unpressured environment

- **Non-traditional workers:** Don't overlook older or part-time workers or those with disabilities – they can be very capable and committed

- **Use interns or people looking for work experience:** Very often students or people returning to work after an absence look for work experience to help them identify the career path they should follow. If their skills appear to fit, give them a short trial – perhaps a week or two – with a view to employing them formally at the end of the trial if they suit. Usually, interns are more interested in experience than pay, though they do require more managing because of their lack of experience.

Whatever route you choose, it is a good idea to insist that every candidate completes a standard application form (see **Figure 7C**). Keep the form simple but make sure that you get all the information you need to decide whether a candidate has the skills you require for the specific position – and make sure it complies with local employment legislation in the information it asks for. Use the candidate's CV as a back-up.

FIGURE 7C: JOB APPLICATION FORM

POSITION _____

NAME (Mr/Mrs/Miss/Ms) _____
ADDRESS _____
_____

TELEPHONE (Home/Work) _____
DATE OF BIRTH _____
STATUS   [] Single   [] Married   [] Divorced   [] Separated
CHILDREN (Number/Ages) _____
HEALTH (Illnesses/Disabilities) _____
_____

EDUCATION
           Year(s)   *School/course*   *Degree/certificate*
From _____ to _____   _____   ☐ Yes ☐ No
From _____ to _____   _____   ☐ Yes ☐ No

WORK EXPERIENCE
           Year(s)   *Organisation*   *Position*
From _____ to _____   _____   _____
From _____ to _____   _____   _____

OTHER EXPERIENCE
Describe other significant experience that could be useful in this position
_____
_____

HOBBIES/INTERESTS
_____
_____

OTHER INFORMATION
_____
_____

I wish to apply for the position of _____ .
I declare the information above to be correct to the best of my knowledge and belief.

Signed _____   Date _____

Make a shortlist

Before you start looking at candidates' CVs or application forms, write out again a summary of the main points you are looking for in a candidate. Screen quickly looking for these – and only these.

Put all applications that do not meet these criteria into a separate bundle. If you want, review them later to see whether they include any candidates you might want to keep for your files for other positions that might come up later. Otherwise, remove them from consideration immediately. Write to them to say that you will not be calling them to interview – from the candidate's point of view, it's better to get bad news than not to hear at all.

Concentrate on the candidates that meet your criteria. Read their application forms again more carefully. Look for little things: gaps in employment, jobs that don't quite fit a career path, hobbies that don't sit well with the personality type you are looking for, inconsistencies and even, if the job involves written communication, misspellings and poor grammar.

Make a shortlist. Decide which candidates you want to interview and contact them to arrange dates and times. Although interview candidates should do their own research on your business before coming for interview, it is helpful to include some background information on your business with the letter confirming the interview.

Interviewing

When interviewing, you only have a short time to find out all you need to make an informed decision about investing in someone who should become an asset to your business. Therefore:

- **Use an interview checklist:** Develop a list of points that you want to cover during the interview (see **Figure 7D**)

- **Ask open-ended questions:** Avoid questions that can be answered "Yes" or "No"; use questions like "Why did you like working in sales?", "What are your strengths and weaknesses?" or "Why are you leaving your current job?"

- **Ask unconventional questions:** See how candidates think (and how fast) by asking them questions they may not have prepared for. For example, "Why shouldn't all staff be paid the same?", "If you didn't have to work, what would you do with your time?". But avoid straying into areas often protected by law – like candidates' personal lives, etc

- **Find out what's important to the candidate:** What is he/she looking for: growth opportunities, regular hours, training, new responsibilities? Will he/she finish the job or just clock-watch?

- **Listen:** Spend 20% of the time talking and 80% listening. The purpose of the interview is to help you learn about the candidates, not to talk about yourself

- **Interview more than once:** Use the first interview to find the top two or three candidates; use the second to make sure you choose the best

- **Involve other staff:** If you are particularly pleased with a candidate, let them meet some of your existing staff with whom they will be working. Get these staff-members' opinion

- **Check references:** Ask what the relationship between candidate and referee is. Confirm previous positions, responsibilities and achievements. Ask about working habits, ability to get along with others, problems, etc.

Be open with candidates. Tell them that you are interviewing others. Give them a date by which they can expect to hear from you – one way or the other. Keep to it.

> When you hire people who are smarter than you are,
> you prove that you are smarter than they are.
> RICHARD GRANT

> Start with good people,
> lay out the rules, communicate with your employees, motivate them and reward
> them. If you do all these things effectively, you can't miss.
> LEE IACOCCA

Figure 7D: Interview Checklist

Candidate name _____

Meets educational criteria?	☐ Yes ☐ No
Meets experience criteria?	☐ Yes ☐ No
Passed competence test?	☐ Yes ☐ No
Has essential skills?	☐ Yes ☐ No
Has desirable skills?	☐ Yes ☐ No
Has additional skills?	☐ Yes ☐ No
Has good oral communication skills?	☐ Yes ☐ No
Has good written communication skills?	☐ Yes ☐ No
Has foreign language skills?	☐ Yes ☐ No
Has good personality?	☐ Yes ☐ No
Would fit in well with other staff?	☐ Yes ☐ No
Is currently employed?	☐ Yes ☐ No
Notice period needed?	_____
Has clean driving license?	☐ Yes ☐ No
Is a smoker?	☐ Yes ☐ No
Has a good health record?	☐ Yes ☐ No
Permission to contact referees?	☐ Yes ☐ No

Check with your local professional adviser, a business lawyer, or a local business support/advisory body about the employment legislation applicable to your business and take appropriate steps to ensure compliance with this in interviewing and recruiting staff.

The job offer

You should have already discussed the job offer with your ideal candidate at interview, before writing to offer the job – in some cases, you may make the offer at the interview and shake hands on a deal. Either way, you should write to the selected candidate and set out clearly:

- The job title and description
- The salary: how it is to be paid and any overtime, bonuses, etc
- The normal hours of work
- Holidays
- Period of notice required on resignation or dismissal
- Grievance procedures
- Any other "house" rules.

Send two copies of this letter, both signed by you, and ask for one back, signed by the new appointee to signify their acceptance of the position on the terms offered.

In some cases, before you offer a job, you may want to ask the candidate to undergo a medical examination. This is usually done for management positions or positions where good health is important. Where appropriate, make it clear at the interview that this further hurdle exists.

Managing Staff

Businesses go through different stages of development and the management style appropriate to one stage may not be right for another. For example, a person who runs a one-person business does not need to worry about delegating – but when he/she has a dozen employees delegating becomes more important than doing.

You should be thinking about managing long before you have anyone to manage. The starting point is your own strengths and weaknesses as an entrepreneur. Go back to **Chapter 2, Self-assessment**. Refresh your memory on your own skills.

If you are to build a strong business team, you need to become a good manager yourself. There are lots of books and courses available to help you here. You need to build skills in delegation, time management, coaching, appraisal and communications to name but a few.

But one of the most important points to make is that successful managers show, in lots of little but important ways, that they care for their staff, that they trust them and that they are willing to allow them to use their initiative (and to make mistakes!).

Good managers listen, they are interested in people in and outside work, they share information and knowledge, they are open to new ideas, they are enthusiastic and have a sense of humour.

Delegating

Delegating is difficult for entrepreneurs. Their whole business, their way of life, is built on their own vision. What should be done, when and how are all determined by the entrepreneur. And now parts of the business, even decisions, are to be handed over to someone else.

This is very often the way that entrepreneurs see delegating – in a negative light, as giving up control. But that's not delegating – that's giving up control!

You should ask yourself why you want to put in the long hours, work very hard and want to deal with all the stress. The reason why is likely to be the freedom to make your own decisions, make your own mistakes and achieve results. Surely you should apply the same motivating factors to your staff.

Delegating is a specific sequence of techniques that empowers one person (the person to whom work is delegated) while freeing up the time of another (the person delegating).

Delegation consists of the following steps:

- **Communicate your mission statement:** This need only be done once, when the person joins the organisation, to put their work into context
- **Communicate the targets:** What do you want to achieve?
- **Define the task:** Do this in terms of resources available and outcome required, not in terms of method: What specifically is to be done?
- **Transfer a clear understanding to the person who is to do the work:** Check that they understand; ask them to explain the task to you
- **Stand back and let them do the work:** Be available to help – but only when asked
- **Careful, shared evaluation of the outcome:** Focus on outcome, not methods.

The important points in delegation are the task definition and the evaluation. You must sit down with the person after the task is complete and talk through what they achieved. Because you have more experience, you may know faster, better, cheaper ways of doing the task – but you should let the person identify these on their own. If you tell them, they will never learn. Worse still, they will give up, saying to themselves "I did the job. Got the right result. But all the boss was concerned about was doing it his way".

The other difficulty that entrepreneurs have with delegation is a lack of recognition that their own drive differs from that of their employees. You will quite happily stay at work late into the night, work through weekends and public holidays, but you cannot expect that your staff will always want to do the same. Good staff will be prepared to work extra hours to get the job done – but not just for the sake of doing. You need to learn to motivate (not just with extra money for working late) – and be reasonable in your demands. To help yourself decide where you should be delegating, complete **Exercise 7.6**.

> *Managers are the basic and scarcest resource of any business enterprise.*
> PETER F DRUCKER

EXERCISE 7.6: DELEGATION

How much does your time cost?   € _____
(The standard formula is three times salary, divided by 200 days,
divided again by 8 hours in a day = € per hour)
Do you really want to take work home in the evenings and at weekends?

☐ Yes ☐ No

What areas do think you **must** deal with yourself?
What areas are most critical to the business?
What areas are you comfortable delegating to another person?
Delegate to whom? Develop a profile of the right person for each task you want to delegate and match staff to tasks.

Person	**Profile**	**Tasks**

Employment legislation

Employment law differs from country to country but, in general, full-time employees are entitled to:

- A written contract of employment
- Equal pay for equal work
- Protection against discrimination
- Holidays
- Maternity leave (and paternity leave in some countries)
- Trade union membership
- Minimum notice on termination of employment
- Protection against unfair dismissal
- Protection against redundancy, and minimum payments if it should occur.

 You must check the legal requirements that apply to your business with a lawyer who is familiar with local employment legislation.

Training

Whatever the skills of your staff when you recruit them, there is little doubt but that you will have to invest in training them at some point – whether because you want them to learn new skills, because of changes in technology or processes, or because you are sufficiently enlightened to realise that a well-trained person is an asset.

At the very least, you must have an effective induction programme to ensure that new recruits:

- Are aware of the business' commitment to training and their own personal development
- Become competent members of staff as early as possible.

Training requires a Training Needs Analysis. This simply means that you list your present skills, compare them against the skills you believe that you need and plan to do something about the difference. Answer the questions in **Exercise 7.7** to prepare a Training Needs Analysis for each member of staff

You should complete the Training Needs Analysis yourself too, as should your business partners

Remember also that you cannot know everything. Whatever your own background, you will have to buy in some expertise – from accountants, solicitors, computer experts or consultants. But to give yourself a general understanding of a range of topics, even if the detailed work is done by someone else, attend courses outside your own immediate area of interest.

EXERCISE 7.7: TRAINING NEEDS ANALYSIS

What skills do you think you need to start your business?
What skills do you think you need to run your business, once it has been started?
What skills are you missing?
What existing skills would you like to improve?
What training do you need?

Staff retention

It may seem strange to consider retaining staff before you have even recruited your first member of staff but, as in many things, forward planning pays off.

Staff are a key success factor in any business. Managing staff has implications in every part of the business as very often your staff will be responsible for implementing all the bright ideas and strategies you come up with. They can make or break your ideas. And, properly encouraged, they can have bright ideas of their own. Therefore a lot of time and thought should be given not only to considering whom you want to recruit, but also to how to keep your staff happy and productive.

To see why this is important, consider the costs of staff turnover:

- **Loss of capacity:** There's no one there to do the work
- **Loss of knowledge:** All the person has learnt, before joining and while with your business, is gone
- **Loss of experience:** All the experience that the person had is gone
- **Loss of network:** All the contacts the person had is gone – as well as the new contacts the person built up while working with your business. Some other employer has these now – are they a competitor of yours?
- **Loss of training:** All the training you gave the person is gone
- **Cost of recruitment:** You have to spend time and money recruiting a replacement and may have to pay the new person more than the person who left
- **Cost of induction:** The new person will take a little while to settle in, during which time they are producing below expected output and are a drain on other people's time
- **Cost of new training:** You may have to provide the new person with specialised training.

Add all these up and very quickly you will decide that you don't want to have staff turnover any higher than is absolutely necessary.

But a warning! If you have a staff member who is under-performing or not working as part of the team, and will not accept the need to change their ways, get rid of them fast – subject only to local employment legislation. Poor staff eventually drag all the other good staff down to their level.

Reward systems

To keep your staff happy and productive, you need to develop a reward system which appeals both to you (that is, it is cost-effective) and to your staff (that is, it is motivating). Usually reward systems consist of a mix of money, working conditions, benefits, time off, personal development opportunities, personal freedom and respect.

What balance of these will you offer? Will it be the same for all staff, or will seniority or ability provide better rewards?

You should look outside your business at other businesses' rewards systems. In most countries, recruitment consultants publish surveys of salary and benefits packages across industries. Although these are averages, they may give you a starting point for your own system.

If you plan to introduce a motivational reward system, you need to have in place some measurement or appraisal system that is clearly fair to staff. It must fit with your mission statement, your marketing, your business culture and your process. It must be easy to calculate and visibly fair.

As well as the obvious productivity or output targets, consider measuring and rewarding on targets such as:

- Absenteeism
- Quality of work
- Client complaints (or the absence thereof).

PROFESSIONAL ADVISERS

Of necessity, an entrepreneur must be a master of all trades. But, as your business expands, you may need to hire a professional adviser to help you in areas such as computers, accounting, taxation and law (depending on your own skills).

Reasons for hiring an outside consultant include:

- To save time
- You need information, knowledge and expertise in a specific area
- You want an independent view
- You want a second opinion.

Choosing an adviser

Choose carefully – a good adviser can add immeasurably to your business, while a bad one could cost you a lot of money with nothing to show for it. Ignore qualifications – they are necessary but not the basis for choosing an adviser. Look instead for experience. A good adviser will refer you to his/her previous clients. Ask other entrepreneurs whose opinions you value for recommendations.

Consider:

- The adviser's knowledge of your business area and your specific project/problem: You don't want to have to teach the adviser about the problem
- His/her experience as an adviser to other entrepreneurs: Unless the adviser understands the constraints within which start-up entrepreneurs operate, they will not be able to give you the best advice
- His/her way of working: Will they be dedicated to you until the project is done, or available as necessary?
- Ethics/confidentiality: Can you trust him/her?
- Costs: How and when will you be billed?
- Time-frame: Can the work be done when you want?.

Develop a clear briefing of what you expect from the adviser and ask for several quotes before you decide who you are going to deal with.

Most advisers will not charge you for a first meeting. Use this to help you decide whether you want to engage them or look further.

Mentors

Loneliness and a sense of isolation are the two most common complaints among entrepreneurs (after the difficulty in getting anyone to finance their business!). That's why it is so important to have the support of your family when you run your own business. But sometimes you need more than support – you need someone who has been there, done that, someone who has experienced what you are going through. This is where a mentor can be helpful.

A mentor is an experienced businessperson who makes available their experience and expertise to small businesses, usually for very modest reward. Most mentors are "putting something back into the system". Your bank or local enterprise support agency may be able to suggest a suitable mentor.

When selecting a mentor, act as if you were interviewing for a vacancy with your business (you are – for a trusted adviser to yourself). Aim to meet about three potential mentors and prepare carefully (re-read "Recruiting Staff" again). Go through the skills/experience match carefully. You may not be able to judge how good the mentor is at his/her specialist area but you can judge the chemistry between the two of you. This will be important, especially if you are looking for a confidante rather than an expert to solve a problem. Above all, do not let an agency "assign" a mentor to you.

Your mentor must keep totally confidential everything you say to him/her. By the same token, you must be totally honest with your mentor. You are wasting your time (and theirs) if you are not telling them the full picture – and you may get wrong advice as a result.

Structure the mentor/business relationship:

- Express your expectations from the mentoring process. (Write them down)

- Allow the mentor to express their expectations. (If you have selected carefully, there will be no surprises)

- Agree on what the mentor will do and what they will not do. Confirm confidentiality

- Decide on what information the mentor needs to be able to help you properly

- Decide on the frequency and venue of meetings. Don't be too ambitious. Keep it practical.

THE TENBizPlan APPROACH TO BUSINESS PLANNING

Text

In this chapter, you have created draft text for input into your business plan document in relation to:

Promoter(s)

- Update the draft text on Management, based on your re-assessment of yourself in this chapter

Project Overview

- Employment – **Exercise 7.1**

Process & Resources

- People: Indicate the key responsibilities within your process, who holds/will hold them and why each person is suitable – **Exercise 7.2** and **Figure 7B (Job Description).**

Evidence

File copies of all of the exercises that you have completed in **Chapter 7**, for ease of reference later. They will be a crucial part of your evidence supporting your business plan.

In this chapter, you will also have identified other information that will be good evidence for your business plan – for example, salary surveys, etc. File these safely as part of your working papers also.

Numbers

The numbers created for input into your financial projections as part of the process of business planning in this chapter are:

- Your own salary and staff salaries — **Exercise 7.4.**

> All commercial operations can, in the final analysis, be summed up in three words: Personnel, products, profit. Personnel comes first.
> Without a good team, it is impossible to expect anything from the other two.
> LEE IACOCCA

Key Question

The following Key Question was posed at the start of the chapter to focus your thoughts as you read through it.

Can I describe the people I will need & how I will organise them?

In answering the question, you should consider:

- The organisational structure best suited to your business
- Your staffing plan
- Your own position
- Relevant employment legislation.

FINANCE & FUNDING

The key question for this chapter is:

How will I fund my business?

Most start-ups, at this stage in their planning, will show a funding gap – the maximum negative point of the cash balance in their cashflow projections. It occurs because, although most of the planning process has been completed, the business is only now reaching the stage where it can identify its real cash need and, therefore, is still unable to obtain specific commitments of external funding.

In fact, the figures shown by the financial projections at this stage may not even be what the business needs by way of funding. These are merely a first rough draft of the projections that will appear in the business plan. There's still a lot of work to be done.

In the next chapter, you will be provided with the techniques and knowledge to quantify the right amount, and type, of funding for your business. This will allow you to seek funding, based on a sound understanding of your true needs.

For now, let's learn about the different types and sources of funds that may be available to you.

Output from this chapter

The aim of this chapter is to define the types and sources of funding available to you.

Later, as you identify the "funding gap" in your business – the difference between the funding you need and the funding you already have in place – you will see how you can use this knowledge to source the appropriate funding to ensure the right capital structure for your business.

Links to other stages in the business planning process include:

- **Formalities (Chapter 4):** The legal status you have chosen for your business may influence the types and sources of finance appropriate to your business and vice versa

- **Marketing & Sales (Chapter 5):** The type and source of finance that you raise for your business may be influenced by the image you wish to communicate – for example, venture capital for a high-tech start-up

- **Process & Resources (Chapter 6):** The purpose(s) for which you are raising finance – to fund the purchase of property, to buy fixed assets or to provide working capital – will help decide the type and source of finance appropriate to your business.

It takes more than money to make a business a success.
MARY KAY ASH

TYPES OF FINANCE

At start-up, your need for finance is at its greatest and yet, perversely, this is the time when it is most difficult to raise funding.

There are basically only two types of finance:

- **Equity:** Capital invested in the business, usually not repayable until the business closes down finally
- **Debt:** Capital lent to the business, usually repayable at a specified date.

There are also only two sources:

- Your own money
- Someone else's money.

Combining these gives the following matrix:

		SOURCE	
		Owner's	**External**
	Equity	Share capital	Share capital
TYPE	**Debt**	Directors' loans	Overdraft
			Bank loan
			Leasing, etc

This chapter will consider each type of finance and point you towards sources.

> *Finance:*
> *What you have when you don't have as much as if you had nothing.*
> *T GRANDON GILL*

EQUITY

Owner(s)' equity

If you are putting equity into the business (and you MUST – if you won't, who else will!), you should recognise that this investment will be at risk.

It is important that you raise as much as you can from your own resources, since most financiers work on a "matching funds" basis – that is, they will invest no more than you are investing.

This may mean that you should formally include as part of your investment some items that would have been available to the business on an informal basis anyway. For example, if you plan to start a software business, you probably have your own PC and peripherals and probably intended using these in the business until it could afford to buy newer (and faster) machines. Put a value on them and include them as part of your investment, which might now be made up of €3,000 cash and €10,000 equipment – which looks better than just €3,000 cash!

Return to **Exercise 2.10** and review your capital available for investment.

Then use **Exercise 8.1** to identify your personal assets and how you will handle them in the context of your business start-up. For each asset, you have four choices:

- Keep the asset as a personal possession, separate from your business
- Mortgage it, if it is suitable, to raise funds to invest in the business
- Sell it, to raise funds to invest in the business
- Invest it directly into the business.

If you decide to invest certain of your assets in the business, you should:

- Check that they are necessary – see the fixed asset requirements you identified in **Exercise 6.23**
- Obtain an independent valuation if they are significant
- Formally transfer them – write a note acknowledging the transfer and keep copies in both your personal and business records.

EXERCISE 8.1: PERSONAL ASSETS

Personal assets (See Exercise 2.10)	Action: ◊ Keep ◊ Mortgage ◊ Sell ◊ Invest	Mortgage value €	Sale value €	Value to business €

Before you mortgage your family home as security for your business funding, you should take professional advice from your lawyer. You need to consider:

- Ownership of the property
- The impact of relevant legislation
- What would happen to the family home and your family should the business fail
- The approach that the banks and the courts take in such circumstances.

External equity

Before you raise external equity, you need to be prepared to allow other people to own part of your business. This sounds logical, but many entrepreneurs forget and react badly when their investors begin to want some involvement in the business in return for their investment.

If you are looking for external equity, there are three types to consider:

- **Seed capital:** Less than €100k, for start-ups
- **Venture capital:** Between €100k and €500k, for businesses at an early stage of development
- **Development capital:** €500k+, for companies ready to expand.

Seed capital is the one you probably want. Unfortunately, it is also the hardest to get.

Sources of external equity

The first sources you should try are:

- **Family and friends:** Depending on your personal circumstances, this can be a fruitful source. But make sure they understand the risks involved and can afford to lose their investment. And put any agreement in writing, with professional advice

- **Business contacts:** It's worth checking to see whether someone you know in business will help you get started with a small investment. Use your network (**Exercise 2.6**).

Summarise the equity investment that you expect in your business in **Exercise 8.2**. Only include amounts that have been committed which, at this stage, since you do not have a business plan, are likely to include only your own personal investment and those of people close to you.

EXERCISE 8.2: EQUITY – SUMMARY

	Cash €	Assets €	Total €	Date cash/ assets due
Owner(s)				
External				
TOTAL				

DEBT

Owner(s)' debt

This is not a major source of finance for start-ups, since other investors prefer to see the owners' investment in the form of equity (more permanent than loans). However, it may be appropriate to put some part of your investment in the business as a loan (and thus repayable). Take your accountant's advice here.

External debt

Debt comes in a variety of forms, from a simple loan from a friend with few conditions attached, through overdrafts, term loans, long-term loans, mortgages, etc.

Debt finance available to start-ups includes:

- **Overdraft:** The simplest form of bank finance. Basically, this is no more than permission to have a negative balance on your bank account. However, overdrafts must be cleared (and stay cleared for at least 30 days during the year, though not necessarily consecutive days) on an annual basis and the overdraft is repayable on demand
- **Term loan:** A loan for a fixed period, usually at a variable rate. Repayments include both interest and capital
- **Long-term loans:** Often subsidised by government or EU schemes, these aim to provide businesses with capital for 7 to 10 years
- **Mortgages:** Loans to buy business property, secured on the property itself, with fixed or variable rate options
- **Leasing:** A way of acquiring the use of fixed assets (for example, plant and machinery, cars, office equipment) with the minimum up-front cost. Instead, you pay a regular monthly or quarterly payment, which is usually allowable for tax purposes. At the end of the lease, depending on the terms, you may have the option to continue using the asset for a small continuing payment or to buy it outright from the lessor
- **Invoice discounting:** A facility linked directly to sales, which maximises the cash value of current assets. The bank will pay you, say, 80% of the face value of an invoice when it is issued. The balance, less charges, will be paid to you when the invoice is paid. Useful for the company that is

expanding and in danger of being choked for lack of cash, though not usually available to start-ups.

When considering financing your business with debt, you must consider:

- Fixed or floating
- Long-term or short-term.

Fixed debt is a loan that is secured on a specific asset – for example, on premises. Floating debt is secured on assets that change regularly – for example, debtors.

"Secured" means that, in the event that the loan is not repaid, the lender can appoint a "receiver" to sell the asset on which the loan is secured in order to recover the amount due. Thus, giving security for a loan is not something to be done lightly.

Because you have to pay interest on debt, you should try to manage with as little as possible. However, few businesses get off the ground without putting some form of debt on the balance sheet.

The issues are usually:

- What is the cheapest form of debt available?
- What is the correct balance between debt and equity?
- Are there methods of reducing the amount of borrowing required?
- To what extent will personal assets back borrowing?

It is a good idea to try to match the term of the loan to the type of asset that you are acquiring:

- To avoid constant renewing or restructuring problems
- To ensure that each loan is covered by the break-up value of the assets in case of disaster.

The Lord forbid that I should be out of debt, as if, indeed, I could not be trusted.
FRANÇOIS RABELAIS

For example, a loan to buy premises should be a long-term loan, unless you can see clearly that you will have enough money within a short space of time to repay it. Taking out a short-term loan or overdraft to buy premises is a recipe for disaster. You will have to renegotiate it time and again – and, if your business runs into temporary difficulties, you run the risk of losing everything if the bank calls in the loan.

Short-term loans, or even overdrafts, are more suited to funding inventory or receivables because you should be able to repay the loan once you have sold the goods or got the money in. Short-term loans should always be repaid within the year – even if at the end of the period you still need to borrow more to fund future cashflow. If you have to borrow the same sum of money against the same asset for longer than a year at a time, you should be considering longer-term finance.

If disaster strikes and you have to repay the loan, it will be much easier to do so if the value of the assets it was used to fund is roughly equivalent to the value of the loan. Thus, for instance, you would hope to sell your premises for at least as much as you borrowed to buy them. Machinery may be more difficult, as the resale price is rarely comparable with the purchase price. For this reason, where possible, consider buying good second-hand machinery for your start-up.

If you can, you should arrange your loans so that unrealisable (or slow to realise) assets are purchased out of your own equity, using borrowing only for realisable assets. If an asset is easily realisable, the bank is much more likely to accept it as security.

Sources of debt

Sources of debt you should try first include:

- **Family and friends:** Depending on your own circumstances, this can be a fruitful source. But make sure they understand the risks involved and can afford to lose their investment. Put any deal in writing, with professional advice on both sides

- **Business contacts:** It's worth looking to see whether someone you know in business will help you get started with a small investment. Use your network (**Exercise 2.6**)

- **Banks:** The main source of debt for start-ups

- **Credit cards:** If you have a credit card with a high credit limit (and a low balance!), this may provide a source of funding (though more expensive than most). Bear in mind that if you do not clear the credit card balance at the end of each month, you will pay very high interest rates. However, once your business is up and running, a company credit card not only provides an additional credit line but can cut purchasing costs and simplify administration

- **Credit unions:** Increasingly willing to help members start businesses
- **Finance companies:** Sometimes more willing to lend than a bank, as long as they can secure the loan with assets or personal guarantees. Finance companies are rarely cheaper than banks, but may sometimes be prepared to lend when banks refuse.

When looking for finance, beware of "specialists" who claim that they can find you money at favourable rates of interest if only you pay an up-front fee. Don't pay **anything** until you have the money.

Often, if you only need a small amount of money, the best way to raise it is to approach a bank with which you have already built up some relationship, whether on a personal basis or in a business capacity. The larger borrower may feel it worthwhile to seek professional help to put together a more sophisticated fund-raising package. Your accountant is the best person to give you advice in this area and may have contacts that will ease your path.

Summarise the debt investment that you expect in your business in **Exercise 8.3**. Only include amounts that have been committed which, at this stage, since you do not have a business plan, are likely to include only your own personal loans and those of people close to you.

Exercise 8.3: Debt — Summary

Type	Amount committed €	Date cash due	Interest rate %	Number of repay-ments	Source
Owner(s) loans					
Overdraft					
Term loan					
Long-term loans					
Mortgage on property					
Leases					
TOTAL					

Subsidies

Most countries recognise the contribution that the entrepreneur makes to the economy, and provide a range of State bodies to assist entrepreneurs and potential entrepreneurs to develop their businesses. The assistance they provide is often in the form of cash subsidies or grants but may also include advice, workspace, etc.

It is important that you know just what assistance is available to you as you start your business. It may be vital in providing the final piece of the jigsaw to get your business up and running, or it may provide just the push you need to get going. Sometimes, it may even be just the fact that someone else has confidence in you that gives you the push to move forward.

Subsidies, or other assistance, are good. They can help your business to grow. Just going through the application process, whether or not you are successful, will focus your planning. But don't let the need to meet subsidy-givers' criteria push your business where you don't want to go.

Too often, entrepreneurs start by asking "Where will I get a subsidy?". Subsidies are not the aim of the business – your work on this programme so far should tell you that. They are an extra, which may help you do something that you couldn't otherwise have afforded. They come at the end of the funding process – not at the start of the planning process! However, if there are subsidies available, you would be foolish not to take advantage.

You should now identify subsidies and other aid available to entrepreneurs locally that may be relevant to your business.

When you find a scheme that may be of assistance to you, complete **Exercise 8.4**. Repeat the exercise for each scheme.

Exercise 8.4: Assessing Subsidy Schemes

How is the subsidy scheme organised?
What are the conditions of eligibility?
Can you meet the conditions?   ☐ Yes ☐ No
Do the conditions help or hinder your business?   ☐ Yes ☐ No

Consider whether subsidies are available and useful to your business in areas such as:

- **Financial management:** To help you establish an accounting system, with regular management reporting
- **People:** To subsidise salaries for key staff
- **Training:** To subsidise the cost of specialised training for key staff, or management training for yourself
- **Research and development:** To assist with new product development
- **Feasibility:** To test the feasibility of a new product or service in the marketplace
- **Marketing support:** To help spread your marketing budget or to assist you with your market research
- **Income support:** To provide supplementary income to you in the early stages of starting your business, when your business cannot afford to pay you a salary (mostly provided as an encouragement where an entrepreneur leaves the Unemployment Register to start a business)
- **Export support:** To assist in the cost of exporting, always expensive for a small business.

Use **Exercise 8.5** below to record the value of any subsidies you are likely to receive. Add them to your sources of external funding.

EXERCISE 8.5: SUBSIDIES

	Subsidies			
	1	**2**	**3**	**4**
Source				
Subsidy type				
Subsidy value				
Conditions				
Timing of receipt				

> I am convinced that the more money a new business needs to begin with,
> the less chance it has of success.
> MARK McCORMACK

YOUR FUNDING

In the previous pages, you have identified the extent of the funding that is now committed to your new business, in terms of:

- Equity – **Exercise 8.2**
- Debt (Loans and leases) – **Exercise 8.3**
- Subsidies – **Exercise 8.5**.

Figure 8A shows the application of the financiers' rule: "long to long, short to short". This means that only long-term funds should be used to finance long-term investments (for example, fixed assets), while short-term funds (overdrafts, etc) should be used only for short-term assets (receivables, inventory, etc).

When you come to input your funding into your financial projections, you will see immediately whether you have sufficient funding to start your business and keep it going.

If you have a negative cash balance at any point during the year or at the end of the year, you have a funding gap that must be bridged. We will fill the funding gap in the next chapter, when we have completed a rigorous analysis of your financial projections.

> *People don't realise that if you have an idea, you only have one-third of what you need. You also need the money to turn your idea into a product, and the money to get the business off the ground.*
> MARCUS BROOK, Entrepreneur

FIGURE 8A: TYPES OF FUNDING

Funding type	Advantages	Disadvantages	Comment
External Equity	◊ Long-term ◊ Suitable for funding property and equipment purchases ◊ No profit impact ◊ No repayment	◊ Some loss of control ◊ Will require significant growth in business to justify investment (not suited to "lifestyle" businesses ◊ Sometimes difficult to raise in small amounts	◊ Ideal if you can get it ◊ Make this your first choice, if you can live with loss of control and value safety over risk
External Loans	◊ Can be split between long-term and short-term or overdraft to suit need	◊ Interest will impact profit ◊ Must be repaid	◊ Check Interest cover ratio ◊ Reschedule repayments to suit business' cashflow
Leases	◊ Suitable for equipment purchases ◊ Offers an additional line of credit ◊ May give tax advantages (check locally)	◊ Interest will impact profit ◊ May be more expensive than bank borrowings ◊ Fixed repayments may not suit business' cashflow	◊ Use for equipment where bank borrowings are not available
Subsidies	◊ Often non-repayable	◊ May have conditions attached	◊ Worth looking out for, if available

When your business is up and running, you will have access to the following additional sources of funding:

- Profits from operations
- Credit extended to you by your suppliers.

If you're short, take a loan.
Never ask for a small amount.
Ask for what you need, and always pay it back, the sooner the better.
ARISTOTLE ONASSIS

THE TENBIZPLAN APPROACH TO BUSINESS PLANNING

Text

In this chapter, you have created no draft text for input into your business plan document.

Evidence

File copies of all of the exercises that you have completed in **Chapter 8**, for ease of reference later. They will be a crucial part of your evidence supporting your business plan.

In this chapter, you will also have identified other information that will be good evidence for your business plan – for example, details of banking facilities, sources of subsidies, etc. File these safely as part of your working papers also.

Numbers

The numbers created for input into your financial projections as part of the process of business planning in this chapter are:

- Equity (your own and external equity) – **Exercise 8.2**
- Debt (your own and external loans and leases) – **Exercise 8.3**
- Subsidies – **Exercise 8.5**.

Key Question

The following Key Question was posed at the start of the chapter to focus your thoughts as you read through it.

How will I fund my business?

In answering, you should consider:

- Your own equity
- External equity
- Your own loans
- External loans and leases
- Subsidies
- Your funding requirement.

9

FINALISING THE
PROJECTIONS

The key question for this chapter is:

 **Have I the best plan possible?**

Over the last eight chapters, you have entered information about your own new business into your draft business plan. In your financial projections, you have built a financial model of your business. However, those projections are no more than a first draft, a "first look" in financial form at your thinking on your new business. Now you need to refine those projections in order to produce a solid business plan, one that you have tested in every way possible.

Planning is the process through which entrepreneurs shape the future of their business. Planning develops tentative initial forecasts into clear plans of action to achieve specified goals. It is not about hit-and-miss attempts to predict the future but is a pragmatic management activity to control it. Planning involves quantifying ultimate and intermediate goals in terms of profit and cashflow and thoroughly exploring the actions that might influence them.

In this chapter, you will learn how you can assess and refine your financial projections, subjecting them to analysis similar to that used by bankers and financiers. Ratio analysis on the financial statements, sensitivity analysis to changes in key variables, What If scenarios – all these techniques will be explained and explored.

This is the core of the planning process – a dynamic and directed appraisal of all aspects of your plan, to ensure that your financial projections are soundly based, stand up to rigorous review and truly represent "the best plan possible".

Output from this chapter

The purpose of this chapter is to lead you through techniques for reviewing your financial projections and making them more robust. When you finish, you will have fully thought through the plan for your business.

In this chapter you will:

- Develop a clear understanding of the linkages between business activities and financial statements so that you can identify the areas that will help improve your plan

- Learn the systematic **TENBizPlan** approach to exploring financial projections

- Work through the financial ratios using the **TENBizPlan** Performance Analysis Sheet

- Quantify the break-even point and sensitivities of your business

- Round off your exploration by carrying out What If analysis and looking at ways to reduce the risks your business will face.

Again, as in other chapters, your work in this chapter will lead you back and forth across the guide, improving, refining and re-evaluating earlier research.

YOUR FINANCIAL PROJECTIONS

To date, you have created the following input into your financial projections from the previous eight chapters of this book:

- Tax rates – **Exercise 4.3**
- Bank interest rates – **Exercise 4.4**
- Sales forecast – **Exercise 5.49**
- Promotion budget – **Exercise 5.47**
- Credit terms agreed with customers – **Exercise 5.32**
- Product costs for each product/service (or group of products/services) – **Exercise 6.23**
- Overheads – **Exercise 6.24**
- Fixed assets – **Exercise 6.22**
- Credit terms agreed with suppliers – **Exercise 6.4**
- Your own salary and staff salaries -- **Exercise 7.4**
- Equity (your own and external equity) – **Exercise 8.2**
- Debt (your own and external loans and leases) – **Exercise 8.3**
- Subsidies – **Exercise 8.5**.

Whether you use dedicated financial projection software, spreadsheets that you develop yourself, or paper-based models to develop your financial projections is immaterial.

The important point is that you are now happy that you have captured within your financial projections all the information necessary to reflect your research and thinking throughout the process of business planning.

Check back to make sure that your projections are complete.

Then review them to see whether they fit with your expectations. The question now is: "Is this the best plan possible?".

Unless you are very lucky, the answer must be: "Probably not".

Even on a brief review of your forecast financial projections, you will probably have spotted things you don't like. Perhaps your projections show:

- Too little profit – so little that no one will back you
- Too much profit – so much that no one will believe you

Which of these reflects your plan?

- Great profits but awful cashflow – you will run out of money just when you need it most (this is the most likely situation and reflects the funding gap carried over from the previous chapter).

In traditional business planning, that would be the end of the road – or very nearly. A critical lack of understanding of the connections between business activities and the financial statements (or financial projections) usually means that entrepreneurs:

- Accept poor plans and make the best of them
- Fudge their plan to achieve an apparently acceptable result, fooling others and, sadly, sometimes fooling themselves too.

TENBizPlan's dynamic approach

But there is another way. **TENBizPlan** provides a dynamic approach to business planning, which will be demonstrated in this chapter.

Let's accept as a starting point that you have not yet got the best plan possible, but that this is your target. Then let's try to improve it using a dynamic approach that combines some simple financial techniques, and the knowledge you have developed to date.

We will assess, rework and reassess the projections until we are satisfied that they represent the best plan possible. We will explore, explore and explore until we understand fully the connections between actions and results in business terms and we have a plan to which we can commit ourselves and discuss in confidence with any third parties such as bankers or investors. The difference between our present forecast and what we will have at the end of this chapter is the extensive exploration of options and sensitivities that goes into defining a genuine plan of action.

The process we will follow is shown in **Figure 9A**.

FIGURE 9A: FROM A FORECAST TO A PLAN

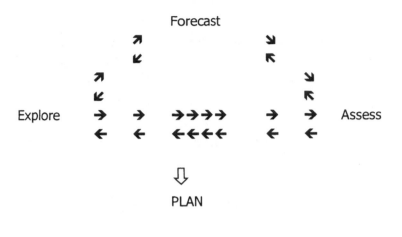

In the rest of this chapter, we will use your financial projections in the same way that airlines use flight simulators – to make sure that we eliminate as many errors as possible before we take off and face the real situation.

The benefit of this approach is that you can see the consequences of proposed actions **as you plan them** – just as you would in a flight simulator. You can have "second thoughts" and make changes **before** rather than after the event when the damage is done, or the opportunity lost. Take the opportunity to use this process as a simulator – every time you think "I wonder what would happen if …", try it and see what happens. If you like the result, incorporate it into your plan – if not, change the input back to what it was before your idea.

Note, however, that this is not a single pass exercise – not an exercise that you run once and accept the results. To turn your forecast into a robust and solidly based plan requires considerable thought and effort. It may require re-thinking sections of your planning to date, conducting fresh market research on new or amended ideas, considering alternative approaches to the same target – whatever it takes, your plan is not finished until you have completed a thorough exploration of all the variables.

The **TENBizPlan** approach provides five tools to assess your forecast and help you turn it into a robust plan:

- **Key Results analysis:** To show how your plan measures up on the primary business objectives of profit and cashflow
- **Break-even analysis:** A technique that identifies the sales volume at which the business breaks-even (the point where sales equal costs and profit is zero) and how far the current forecast is above or below that level of sales
- **Ratio analysis:** A way of looking at the financial results of your planning that identifies the elements which determine financial performance and uses them to direct a process of improvement
- **Sensitivity analysis:** A technique used to highlight areas where changes would have the greatest impact on profit
- **What If analysis:** A technique used to explore what happens when changes are made in the assumptions underlying the plan.

You will use these tools to identify areas in your plan that need to be changed, either because the proposed assumptions/actions will not produce acceptable profits and cashflow or because the proposed assumptions/actions are over-optimistic.

As you grow familiar with these tools, you will learn to use them to assess and direct your planned business activities. These five analysis tools are your pre-start-up diagnostic check. You should not consider starting your business until you have worked through all of them and you believe that they indicate a good chance of success.

> The difference between a forecast and a plan is ...
> the planning.
> ANON

TOOL 1: KEY RESULTS ANALYSIS

Although the financial projections – the projected income statement, projected balance sheet and projected cashflow statement – are the scorecards by which we judge the future of a business, the level of detail in the projections sometimes can obscure the essential message.

So, in assessing your forecast, analyse two Key Results:

- Cashflow
- Profitability.

Improving cashflow

For most start-up businesses, cashflow is the major problem area. Most likely, you ended the last chapter with a funding gap, because you were unable to confirm external equity or loans, or other sources of funding such as subsidies, in the absence of a business plan.

Start by using **Exercise 9.1** to review your cash position.

EXERCISE 9.1: REVIEW OF CASH POSITION

Answer these questions:

◊   In which months do your projections show negative cash balances?
◊   What is the maximum negative cash balance?
◊   What can you do about it?

Although each situation is different, here are some ideas that may help you to correct an unacceptable or unsustainable cashflow.

Go back and look at **Chapter 5**:

- What credit terms (if any) did you assume that you would give your customers?

- What proportion of your sales will have these credit terms?
- Can you do anything to reduce the proportion of credit sales – or to reduce the credit terms you offer these customers? (But, be careful, don't damage your business by imposing credit terms that are unacceptably out-of-line with industry norms.)

Look at **Chapter 6**:

- What credit terms did you agree with your suppliers?
- Again, can you improve on these without damaging relationships with suppliers?

Look at **Chapter 7**:

- When did you assume that individual members of staff would start work?
- Could some of them be delayed by a week? A month? Two months?
- Would this help your cashflow in any significant way without damaging your business?
- Could you postpone paying yourself a salary for a month or two?

It's not unreasonable to postpone paying yourself a salary for a month or two but don't be tempted to improve your projections by omitting your salary altogether. You calculated your minimum salary in **Exercise 2.9**. Unless your circumstances have changed (in which case you should update the exercise), anything less than this minimum salary will put you under financial pressure personally.

Some advice:

- Don't fool yourself by omitting your salary from your projections
- Discuss any proposed downward change in, or temporary non-payment of , your salary with your spouse/partner and family before you include it in your projections
- Be aware that banks and other financiers are not fooled by plans that show low, or no, salaries to promoters and that they regard such tactics as an early warning signal of impending financial difficulties.

Go back to **Chapter 8**, and re-examine your sources of funding:

- Have you exhausted all the sources of funds that you can confirm at this time?
- Can you now make certain of additional funds?

As you identify potential for change, you can go back to your projections and update the cash balances and any other figures affected.

Improving profitability

Next, turn your attention to the projected profitability, using **Exercise 9.2** to review the profit position.

EXERCISE 9.2: REVIEW OF PROFIT POSITION

Answer these questions:
◊ Are the profit figures in your projections acceptable?
◊ Can you explain why some months are better than others?
◊ What can you do about the poorer months?

Repeat the chapter-by-chapter review of your original input to your projections in order to determine whether and where changes could be made that will improve profit, just as you did earlier for cashflow.

Think about your business and try to identify other changes that might be beneficial. In a later section, *Connecting Business to the Financial Statements*, we show business activities are reflected in the financial statements and the links that connect them. This will be a useful tool in improving profitability.

As a result of this work, your Key Results should show a more acceptable picture than it did when you started the chapter. This is Stage 1; Stage 2 is break-even analysis.

TOOL 2: BREAK-EVEN ANALYSIS

One of the key issues for a start-up business is to establish the level of sales needed to reach the point where it begins to make profits. This is called the "break-even point" and is the level of sales at which turnover exactly matches the costs of the business.

Break-even analysis indicates the ease or difficulty with which this milestone can be reached. Obviously, the more easily a company can reach (and sustain) its break-even point, the lower the risk to the promoters and investors.

Enter your original projections in **Exercise 9.3**. Even if you have reached break-even, complete **Exercise 9.3** before moving onto the next section of the assessment of your forecasts. The exercise will show you the margin of clearance above break-even, thus the sales volume you could drop before your business starts to lose money.

EXERCISE 9.3: SUMMARY OF BREAK-EVEN

Break-even achieved at	Original projections	Revised projections		
		1	2	3
Sales value				
Sales units				
% increase/ decrease to reach Break-even				

If you have not yet reached break-even, **Exercise 9.3** tells you how far you are away from break-even in the % Volume Increase box. Then you may revise your forecasts, until break-even is reached. For each new forecast, complete a column in **Exercise 9.3.** (Remember you must substantiate your revised forecasts, since it's too easy to change a forecast without taking account of the difficulty of achieving the same result in the real world.This is the "Evidence" element of the **TENBizPlan** approach, which we will see again in **Chapter 10**.)

What changes can you make to your financial projections to reach break-even? Intuitively, you can:

- Increase Sales price
- Increase Sales volume
- Reduce Cost of sales
- Reduce Overheads.

Look back at the earlier chapters of the guide to see where you can amend your original input into your financial projections to achieve one of these four objectives. Look also at the Performance Improvement model in **Figure 9G**.

A start-up business may not achieve break-even until its second or third year – but you should be clearly aware of your business' position relative to its break-even point in the first year.

CONNECTING BUSINESS TO THE FINANCIAL STATEMENTS

Although this section may appear at first to be a digression, it provides an introduction into the core of the **TENBizPlan** approach to dynamic business planning. It is important that you read and undertand it, since it forms the base for the next section on Financial Ratios. Specifically, as the financial statements are the scorecards of business, you need to understand:

- How they interact with the main activities of your business
- The techniques that allow us use the financial statements as part of a systematic approach to preparing sound business plans.

To illustrate how the statements reflect and interact with business activities, let's look at how we might approach an exercise to increase profit.

A simple income statement is shown in **Figure 9B**.

FIGURE 9B: INCOME STATEMENT

	€
Sales	500,000
Cost of sales	200,000
Gross profit	300,000
Overheads	200,000
Net profit	100,000

It is clear that the way to increase profit is to widen the difference between sales and costs – either by increasing sales or by reducing costs (Cost of sales and/or Overheads) – so these become the targets of our attention. Since each target is influenced by a number of factors – for example, Sales is determined by price, volume, etc – we must identify these factors and then identify the actions that will affect them. This process of exploding from the target to the many potential actions that might influence it is shown in **Figure 9C**.

Figure 9C: The Performance Improvement Model – I

Target	→	Influencing factors	→	Actions

For example, if we want to increase Sales income, we apply the process in **Figure 9D**, which shows the first step in the Performance Improvement model.

Figure 9D: The Performance Improvement Model – II

Target	→	Influencing factors	→	Actions
Increase Sales income		Price		
		Volume		
		Product mix		
		Seasonality		

The main drivers of Sales are, of course, price and volume – we can increase sales revenues by charging higher prices and/or by selling greater quantities.

We can also look to the mix of products to see whether we can sell more high-priced items at the expense of lower-priced ones and at the impact on profit of the peaks and valleys caused by seasonal sales trends.

This step of identifying the elements that drive our targets is mechanical and inflexible, since sales can only be affected by the four elements shown (there are no other elements). The next step offers a far greater range of possibilities.

Continuing our example, we might now decide that capacity constraints and customer requirements eliminate the volume and mix options. We can't make (or buy in) any more product units, so we can't increase volume. Instead, we decide to explore price increases as a means of boosting sales, and ultimately profits.

Some of the possible actions to increase prices include:

- Reduce discounting
- Improve quality
- Change packaging
- Re-design products
- Change distribution channels.

We have to assume that we cannot simply increase selling prices without damaging volume. So we have to find other ways of persuading customers to pay more. The full Performance Improvement Model for Sales is shown in **Figure 9E**.

FIGURE 9E: THE PERFORMANCE IMPROVEMENT MODEL — III

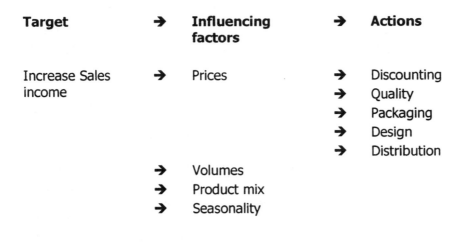

Target	→	Influencing factors	→	Actions
Increase Sales income	→	Prices	→	Discounting
			→	Quality
			→	Packaging
			→	Design
			→	Distribution
	→	Volumes		
	→	Product mix		
	→	Seasonality		

The process of exploring strategies or assessing decisions is usually more complex than the simple linear process described in this example, because an action may often produce not only the positive results desired but also some less desirable side-effects, as shown in **Figure 9F**.

Learn to make numbers talk!
They will speak to you about hard truths and also reveal the future.
JOHN D ROCKEFELLER

Figure 9F: Positive and Negative Effects of Actions within the Performance Improvement Model

Action	Positive effect	Potential negative side-effect
Reduce discounting	Increase in effective price	◊ Opportunity for competitors to offer discounts to gain business, leading to reduced volume
Improve quality	Customers see "better" product and are willing to pay more	◊ Cost of quality improvement ◊ Possible unwillingness of customers to buy "old" product, leading to inventory returned unsold
Change packaging	Customers see "better" product and are willing to pay more	◊ Cost of packaging change ◊ Possible unwillingness of customers to buy "old" product, leading to inventory returned unsold
Re-design products	Customers see "better" product and are willing to pay more	◊ Cost of re-design ◊ Possible unwillingness of customers to buy "old" product, leading to inventory returned unsold
Change distribution channels	Remove some channel costs, thereby increasing effective price	◊ Cost of change ◊ Confusion in market if customers' source changes, leading to reduced volume

This is where an effective modelling system delivers important benefits. Although it cannot identify negative side-effects for you, once they are identified it allows you take their impact into account in the financial projections quickly and easily.

We can use the Performance Improvement Model to analyse all the elements of sales and costs, as well as assets and liabilities. **Figure 9.G** sets out the "core" linkages between the financial statements and business activities in the Performance Improvement Model.

FIGURE 9.G: THE PERFORMANCE IMPROVEMENT MODEL

Target		Influencing factors		Action
Increase Sales income	→	Product mix	→	◊ Design & development
				◊ Rationalise product range
	→	Volume	→	◊ Develop new markets
				◊ Opportunities in current markets
	→	Price	→	◊ Competitors' responses
	→	Seasonality	→	◊ Price sensitivity
				◊ Sales & promotion tactics
				◊ Market information systems
				◊ Internal controls on sales
Reduce Materials costs	→	Price	→	◊ Product design
				◊ Materials specifications
				◊ Alternative suppliers
	→	Usage	→	◊ Negotiating price/discounts
				◊ Internal controls on purchases
Reduce Labour costs	→	Rate	→	◊ Wage negotiating
				◊ Planning to avoid idle time
				◊ Training
	→	Effectiveness	→	◊ Improved methods
				◊ Upgraded technology
Reduce Overheads costs (see note below)	→	Stable	→	◊ Alternative sources
				◊ Environment (insurances)
				◊ Work practices
	→	Dependant	→	◊ Driven elsewhere
				◊ Identify
	→	Volatile	→	◊ Formulate policies
				◊ Budgetary control
Control Credit	→	Debtors	→	◊ Cashflow planning
				◊ Credit assessment
				◊ Policy & management
	→	Creditors	→	◊ Internal communications
				◊ Negotiations/discounts

Target		Influencing factors		Action
Utilise Assets	➔	Fixed	➔	◊ Capital investment policy
				◊ Stock control
	➔	Current	➔	◊ Credit control
Manage Funding	➔	Structure	➔	◊ Profit performance
				◊ Gearing policies/funds
				◊ Sourcing skills
	➔	Interest rates	➔	◊ Credit control

When analysing overheads, it may be helpful to classify them as follows:

- **Stable Overheads:** These are predictable – for example, insurance, rent and rates, audit fees etc. Some options here involve "shopping around", negotiation and exploring the potential for changing environmental or work practices to reduce costs – for example, disposing of unused space, better records or preparation of records to reduce unnecessary audit and accounting fees, and improved safety practices to reduce insurance costs

- **Dependant Overheads:** These are overheads that arise from decisions made elsewhere – for example, depreciation, which results from decisions on investment, leasing charges and loan interest. These overheads cannot be considered in isolation from the factors that determine them

- **Volatile Overheads:** These are overheads requiring careful budgeting and control – for example, travel, motor expenses, maintenance costs, telephone and electricity, and promotion and advertising.

The Performance Improvement Model is a convenient framework within which to explore strategies to improve profits and cashflow. However, developing the model is not a static process – the actions shown in **Figure 9G** are given as examples only. Every business must develop its repertoire of actions by experience and exploration.

Now let's start to apply this knowledge to explore and improve our plan.

TOOL 3: RATIO ANALYSIS

One of the best ways to assess business performance is through ratio analysis. By relating key financial measures to one another, ratios highlight important cause-and-effect relationships within a business.

Ratios are widely used by third parties such as bankers who have access to comparative information for past periods of a business or for similar businesses in specific industries. Ratio analysis is also a useful tool for business managers when they have access to comparative data. Start-ups are at a disadvantage in not having data for previous years' trading but benchmark your business against data from other similar businesses as a substitute.

Ask your local business adviser, your accountant or a local economic data service for local norms (acceptable scores) for ratios that apply to your business.

The TENBizPlan approach to ratio analysis

There are two approaches to ratios:

- **Static:** Investors and bankers use them to form their own judgement of your business plan (and your subsequent performance against that plan) – therefore, you must be able to calculate the ratios that apply to your business and to discuss their implications

- **Dynamic:** Ratios provide a powerful tool to assess your forecast in a directed manner and, based on the conclusions drawn, to make changes that have a positive impact on profits and cashflow.

The first approach is typically used as an after-the-event check on financial projections. Ratios are taken as given, and decisions taken on the basis of conclusions drawn from the ratios. In most cases, no attempt is made to vary the financial projections, or the input on which they are based, in order to improve either the ratios or the underlying projections.

The **TENBizPlan** approach to business planning takes the second approach, using ratios as part of a dynamic assessment of forecast financial projections, with the aim of turning the forecast into a robust plan.

The ratios that you use depend on your perspective. For example, an investor will be interested in seeing what return he will get on his money and will construct ratios to provide that information. A banker, on the other hand, will be concerned about the ability of the business to pay its suppliers and lenders (its liquidity) and will construct ratios from that point of view. As a business manger, however, you must take a global perspective and will want ratios that answer all of the following questions:

- How profitable is my business?
- How easily will my business generate cash?
- What return does my business provide to investors?
- Does the capital structure (gearing) give me control over my business?

The power of ratios depends on the user's ability to discover the underlying causes that shape the ratios and to draw the appropriate conclusion as to corrective action. In the Performance Improvement Model (**Figure 9G**), you saw the connections between the financial statements and business activities and learned how these elements could help in analysing and improving financial projections.

These elements are:

- **Number** of products sold (sales volume)
- **Selling prices** of one or more products
- **Mix** of products that make up range
- **Trend** of sales and production
- Costs of **Materials** used
- **Labour** cost (in manufacturing businesses)
- **Overheads** cost
- Rate of **payment and collection** of payables and receivables
- **Capital tied up** in fixed assets and receivables
- **Sources of funding** to finance the business.

Changes to one or more of these elements will have an impact on the financial projections. If we understand the determinants of each ratio, we can use that knowledge to select the elements that will improve our plan.

The structure we will follow is:

- Compare your result for each ratio to an acceptable score based on norms for your industry (or a target that you set) and calculate the difference (**Exercise 9.4**)

- Where the differences are not acceptable, identify the elements that underlie the ratio and can be changed (Performance Analysis Sheet – **Figure 9H**)

- Define the actions that are required (Performance Analysis Sheet)

- Consider direct and indirect effects (Performance Analysis Sheet)

- Make the changes to the forecast

- Re-assess the situation (Review/Assess)

- Repeat process until you are satisfied that you have the best plan possible

- Explain why changes made are feasible (Performance Analysis Sheet).

The calculation of the main financial ratios is shown in the following sections of this chapter, together with suggestions as to how the ratio – and thus the underlying business activity – could be improved.

For each ratio that you consider unacceptable and in need of improvement, you should complete the Performance Analysis Sheet shown in **Figure 9H**.

EXERCISE 9.4: RATIO ANALYSIS

Record the ratios shown for your business and compare them to an acceptable local norm or a target that you have set for yourself. Identify the ratios that require improvement, using the Performance Analysis sheet (**Figure 9H**).

Ratio	Actual	Norm/ Target	Diff.	Accept Y/N?	Action Y/N?
Profit/(Loss) ratios					
Gross profit : Sales %					
Net Profit : Sales %					
Net Purchases : Sales %					
Overheads : Sales %					
Liquidity ratios					
Current ratio (times)					
Quick ratio (times)					
Stock Turnover (days)					
Debtor days					
Creditor days					
Investment ratios					
Net Profit: Total Assets %					
Net Profit : Capital Employed %					
Sales : Total Assets (times)					
Sales : Fixed Assets (times)					
Sales : Current Assets (times)					
Gearing					
Debt : Equity %					
Equity : Total Assets %					
Net Profit : Interest (times)					

FIGURE 9H: PERFORMANCE ANALYSIS SHEET

(Repeat for each ratio necessary)

Ratio _____

Your ratio		Acceptable ratio		Difference	

		Get more information in chapter									
Action checklist	**Tick**	**1**	**2**	**3**	**4**	**5**	**6**	**7**	**8**	**9**	**10**
Sales volume				X	X	X					
Selling prices				X	X	X					
Mix of products				X	X	X					
Sales trend				X	X	X					
Purchases						X					
Salaries						X					
Overheads			X			X	X	X	X	X	
Credit times								X			
Fixed assets				X		X					
Inventory				X		X					
Sources of funding										X	

What action should be taken to improve the ratio?

What impact will this action have on the ratio?

What impact will this action have on profits and cashflow?

What "side-effects" will this action have and how will you deal with them?

Original ratio		New ratio		Difference	

Why is the new ratio is realistic?

File the completed Performance Analysis Sheets in the **Chapter 9** section of your working papers.

Note that care must be taken in drawing conclusions from ratio analysis because:

- **Ratios involving balance sheet items are calculated at a specific date (the date of the balance sheet):** If the business has seasonal variations in the level of trading, the ratios may not be representative of other times in the year

- **Judgements on the results must be related to the business' circumstances:** For example, a business with high borrowings may appear unstable but the borrowings may be the result of rational management decisions when profits are high and the cost of borrowing relatively low

- **Local conditions:** Ratios may vary locally from international norms due to special circumstances – for example, especially high interest rates or difficulties in obtaining supplies (which may lead to greater than desirable inventory). You should look for local norms for the ratios used in – there is no point measuring your own business' ratios against ratios that are not relevant.

PROFITABILITY RATIOS

These ratios answer the question: "How profitable is my business?".
The two main ratios are:

* Gross profit: Sales

* Net profit: Sales.

There are also subsidiary ratios:

* Purchases: Sales

* Overheads: Sales.

Gross profit: Sales

Calculation

Gross profit / Sales X 100

This ratio is expressed as a percentage – for example, 47.5%.

Explanation

The Gross profit: Sales ratio shows management's ability to control the crucial factors of selling prices, cost of sales and, under certain conditions, sales volumes. The higher this ratio, the higher the gross profit, and the more money is available to cover overheads and to allow for profit.

Different industries have different gross profit structures. Some work on high gross profit margins, balanced by high overheads, while others have lower gross profit margins requiring them to run very tight control on their overheads.

Actions to improve this ratio

Gross profit = Sales – Cost of sales

Since Gross profit is the difference between Sales and Cost of sales, you can improve the Gross profit: Sales ratio by maximising that difference.
You can do this by:

* Increasing Sales income by increasing average selling prices

- Reducing Cost of Sales by negotiating a lower purchase price for your products/services
- Reducing Cost of Sales by reducing waste
- Increasing the difference by including more of the more profitable products/services in your sales in the sales mix
- Reducing any Direct Overheads included in Cost of sales ("above the line").

Observations

You might ask why increasing sales volume is not included as an action in the list above. The effect of sales volume on the Gross profit: Sales ratio depends on whether Cost of Sales contains any fixed cost – see the sewction on *Expenses* in **Chapter 6,** for an explanation of fixed and variable costs.

Where Cost of Sales is a variable cost, this ratio is independent of volume. For example, if you buy a book for €10 and sell it for €16, your Gross profit is €6 and as a percentage of sales is 37.5%. If you sell 100 books at the same price/cost parameters, your total Gross profit will increase to €600 but the ratio will stay the same – that is, 600/1600 = 37.5%. So, in this situation, increasing volume has no effect on this ratio.

However, where Cost of Sales is a fixed cost (or contains a fixed cost element), the volume of sales will have an effect on this ratio. For example, suppose you charter a 100-seater airplane for €10,000 for the day and sell tickets at €200 each. If you sell all the tickets, your Sales are €20,000 and your Cost of Sales is €10,000. Your Gross profit is €20,000 – €10,000 = €10,000 and the ratio is 10,000/20,000 = 50%. But if you sell only 100 tickets, your Sales are €10,000 but your Cost of Sales remains €10,000. Your gross profit is €10,000 -- €10,000 = 0 and the ratio is 0/10,000 = 0%. So, where Costs of sales is fixed, Sales volume has a significant impact on the Gross profit: Sales ratio.

None of this is to say that volume is not important to Gross profit. In absolute terms, obviously, the higher the volume the higher the gross profit. It is only the gross profit ratio that may not be affected.

The results of this example are summarised in **Figure 9I**.

FIGURE 9I: THE IMPACT OF VARIABLE AND FIXED COST OF SALES ON GROSS PROFIT

	Cost of sales variable		Cost of sales fixed	
Sales	16	160	10,000	20,000
Cost of sales	10	100	10,000	10,000
Gross profit	6	60	0	10,000
Gross profit: Sales ratio	37.5%	37.5%	0%	50%

Your own situation

Which tactics to improve Gross profit apply to your business? Can you:

- Increase Sales by increasing average selling prices?
- Reduce Cost of sales by negotiating a lower purchase price for your products/services?
- Reduce Cost of Sales by reducing waste?
- Increase the difference by including more of the more profitable products/services in your sales in the sales mix?
- Increase Sales by increasing Sales volume (only applies where all or part of Cost of sales is fixed)?

EXERCISE 9.5: EXPLORING THE GROSS PROFIT: SALES RATIO

Explore the effect of these tactics on your Gross profit: Sales ratio.

Use the Performance Analysis Sheet (**Figure 9H**) to record your actions.

Check your financial projections for the effects of your exploration on profits and cashflow.

Net profit: Sales

Calculation

$$\text{Net profit} / \text{Sales} \ X \ 100$$

This ratio is expressed as a percentage – for example, 10.5%.

Explanation

The Net profit: Sales ratio shows your overall performance in managing prices, costs of sales and all overheads to generate a return for the business. What constitutes good or bad results here depends on the type of business.

Actions to improve this ratio

$$\text{Net profit} = \text{Gross profit} - \text{Overheads}$$

Since Net profit is the difference between Gross profit and Overheads, the actions you can use to improve this ratio include those for the Gross profit ratio. In addition, you can:

- Reduce Overheads
- Increase Sales volume.

Observations

You might ask why increasing Sales volume has an effect on the Net profit: Sales ratio. Sales volume is important here because many Overheads in business are fixed.

Your own situation

The tactics you can use to improve Net profit include:

- Improve Gross profit
- Increase Sales by increasing Sales volume
- Reduce Overheads by reducing waste and controlling costs.

EXERCISE 9.6: EXPLORING THE NET PROFIT: SALES RATIO

Explore the effect of these tactics on your Net profit: Sales ratio.
Use the Performance Analysis Sheet (**Figure 9H**) to record your actions.
Use the Key Results Overview to see the effects of your exploration on profits and cashflow.

The subsidiary ratios look in more detail at the items that determine the gross and net profit.

Net purchases: Sales

Calculation

Net purchases / Sales x 100

This ratio is expressed as a percentage – for example, 22.7%.

Explanation

The Net purchases: Sales ratio indicates the economies achieved in buying and inventory management while controlling selling prices.

Your own situation

Because you may have already considered changes to Purchases as part of your actions to improve the Gross profit: Sales, it is probably unnecessary to complete a Performance Analysis Sheet for this ratio.

But, if Purchases is identified as a significant problem, the areas to look at include:

- Renegotiate better terms with suppliers
- Seek out alternative suppliers
- Identify cheaper replacement materials or products, whose quality will not damage sales
- Reconsider redesigning the product/service
- Re-examine inventory policy and stores to eliminate waste.

Overheads: Sales

Calculation

Overheads / Sales x 100

This ratio is expressed as a percentage – for example, 15.5%.

Explanation

The Overheads: Sales ratio indicates the level of performance in administering the business.

Your own situation

Because you may have already considered changes to Overheads as part of your actions to improve the Net profit: Sales, it is probably unnecessary to complete a Performance Analysis Sheet for this ratio.

But, if Overheads are identified as a significant issue, you should work through each individual overhead to identify areas where costs may be reduced. Use the classifications suggested in the Performance Improvement Model (**Figure 9G**) to help here.

LIQUIDITY RATIOS

These ratios answer the question: "How easily will my business generate cash?". They show the ability of the business to meet its day-to-day financial commitments by comparing the money it can expect to take in and pay out in the short term, based on the balance sheet position at the time the ratio is calculated.

The two main ratios are:

- Current ratio
- Quick ratio.

There are also subsidiary ratios:

- Debtor days – How long it takes your debtors to pay you
- Creditor days – how long you take to pay your suppliers
- Stock turnover days – how long it takes for your inventory to recycle.

Current ratio

Calculation

Current assets / Current liabilities

or

[Inventory + Debtors + Cash] / Current Liabilities

This ratio is expressed as a number -- for example, 1.4, representing the number of times that current assets cover current liabilities.

Explanation

Current assets are expected to convert into cash within the next 12 months at least and current liabilities are expected to be paid within the next 12 months. Therefore, a ratio of 1.4 says that, based on the business' current financial situation, for every €1.00 the business is currently committed to pay over the next 12 months, it expects to receive €1.40 and would therefore not anticipate problems in meeting its obligations.

Quick ratio

However, simply setting current assets and current liabilities against one another is often too blunt an instrument to provide a clear picture of liquidity.

The main items in Current assets – Cash, Debtors and Inventory – represent the main stages in the business cycle where items are bought and/or manufactured (inventory) before being sold to customers (debtors) who convert into cash when they settle their accounts. The further back in the business cycle, the higher the risk that the values recorded in the balance sheet may not be achieved – for example, inventory loses value through waste or obsolescence, and debtors may default. Obviously, a business whose current assets are comprised mainly of cash and debtors is better equipped to meet day-to-day payments than one whose current assets are made up predominantly of inventory. Inventory has a further limitation in that its value and the ease with which it can be converted into cash can be difficult to verify independently.

For these reasons, you should calculate an additional liquidity ratio -- the Quick ratio or Acid Test ratio, which eliminates inventory from the calculation.

Calculation
[Debtors + Cash] / Current Liabilities

Actions to improve the Liquidity ratios
There are two strands to improving liquidity:
- To improve overall liquidity, you must look to capital structure and to profits
- To improve the make-up of your liquidity, you must look to inventory control and credit control (see further ratios below).

Overall liquidity is determined in the first instance by the funding structure used in your business. Unless you have an effective capital structure in place – unless you have adequate Equity (Owners' or External) and Loans (Owners' or External) – you may find that your business is reliant on short-term measures such as bank overdrafts and extending the credit period taken from suppliers. This will lead to poor liquidity ratios and indicates that you may easily find your business pushed into disruptive activities solely aimed at shoring up cashflow without any consideration for profits and the long-term good of the business.

It is important, therefore, to get the right capital structure for your business. So far, all you have put into your financial projections (in **Chapter 9**) is the funding that you are sure of. Earlier in this chapter, you identified your funding gap – we will return to it as the final piece in the jigsaw before we finish the chapter.

Overall liquidity is also determined by your business' profit margin. A large profit margin on sales increases the value gap between debtors and creditors, thus improving the liquidity ratios. Although a large profit margin lessens the impact of a poor financial structure, it is no substitute for it.

Observations

Major differences between the two ratios – Current and Quick – could be a cause for concern and might indicate an undue reliance on Inventory. A reduction from 1.4. to, say, 1.1 might not create alarm but a drop to very low figures – for example, 0.6 for the Quick ratio – would be sure to raise questions.

Note that Current liabilities in both ratios include the short-term elements of loans – the principal that will be paid over the next 12 months – and this may make the liquidity ratios quite conservative.

Your own situation

Tactics to improve overall liquidity include:

*   **Introduce more long-term funds:** Use equity or long-term loans to reduce bank overdrafts and/or payables. Look at your business' Debt: Equity ratio (see below) to see whether your business can support further borrowings. Model the effect of different borrowing types and amounts

*   **Increase profitability:** Profit-increasing strategies will, indirectly, improve liquidity by increasing the value of amount receivable from debtors and/or reducing the value of amounts payable to creditors. In a start-up company, profit-increasing strategies are unlikely to be enough to correct a significant liquidity problem and so you will need to focus on sources of long-term funds, as the primary corrective action (this leads again to the funding gap, which will be covered later).

Exercise 9.7: Exploring Current and Quick Ratios

Explore the effect of these tactics on your Current and Quick ratios.
Use the Performance Analysis Sheet (**Figure 9H**) to record your actions.
Check your financial projections for the effects of your exploration on profits and cashflow.

To improve the make-up of your liquidity, look to subsidiary ratios on credit and inventory control.

The closer that Current assets are to cash, the more truly liquid the business. Your business should convert inventory and amounts receivable from debtors into cash as quickly possible, without impinging on customer service through stock-outs and over-aggressive credit control.

Important measures of a business' skill and commitment in managing liquidity are:

- The rate at which it settles amounts due to suppliers
- The rate at which it collects amounts receivable from debtors
- The levels of inventory it carries.

These are measured by the following subsidiary liquidity ratios:

- Debtors days
- Creditors days
- Stock turnover.

Debtors days

Calculation

Debtors / Credit sales x 360

This ratio is measured in days.

Explanation

This ratio is used to indicate the performance in collecting amount receivable from debtors. Note that if the debtors figure includes VAT (or other turnover taxes), the figure for credit sales should include VAT also, to ensure that like is compared with like. Ideally, this ratio should be minimised, insofar as is consistent with the business' marketing strategy.

Creditors days

Calculation

Creditors / Credit purchases x 360

This ratio is measured in days.

Explanation

This ratio is used to show the average credit period taken by the business from its suppliers. Ideally, this ratio should be maximised, although a ratio that is higher than the industry norm might be an early indication of cashflow difficulties.

Note also that if suppliers are prepared to offer extended credit, they must recoup the cost of the credit in some other way – through higher prices, slower service, etc. Make sure that you keep the right balance between pushing supplier credit to the limit and other factors that will impact on your business' success. Always bear in mind that your primary objective in business is to generate profit – don't sacrifice this by ruining your relationships with key suppliers.

Observations

Before you take action to improve your Debtor days and Creditors days ratios, you must remember that the credit timings that you entered into your financial projections (**Exercises 5.32 and 6.4**) represent your business' credit policy.

Bear in mind that the ratios you have just calculated may be distorted by trends, where your business has disproportionate sales or purchases in the period immediately before the balance sheet date. If half your customers pay within 30 days and the other half pay within 60 days, your true Debtors days ratio is 45 days -- irrespective of what the ratios say.

To test the truth of this, let's take a business where credit sales are €1,000 per month and half the customers pay within 30 days and the other half pay within 60 days. At the end of the year, the 30-day customers owe one month's sales (€500), while the 60-day customers owe two month's sales (€1,000). Amounts receivable from debtors at the year-end are thus €1,500. Annual sales are €12,000. The Debtors days ratio is calculated as:

Debtors / Credit sales x 360

1,500 / 12,000 x 360 = 45 days.

But, suppose the sales pattern changes and all the sales are made in the last two months (€6,000 in each month), with no sales earlier in the year. At the end of the year, the 30-day customers would again owe one month's sales (€3,000), while the 60-day customers would owe two month's sales (€6,000). The amount receivable at the year-end is now €9,000, while annual sales remain unchanged at €12,000. The ratio calculation is:

9,000 / 12,000 x 360 = 270 days.

The business' credit policy has not changed. All that has changed is the timing of the sales – it is this which distorts the ratio.

Changing the business' credit policy is a legitimate tactic in improving the Debtors days and Creditors days ratios.

EXERCISE 9.8: EXPLORING DEBTORS DAYS AND CREDITORS DAYS RATIOS

Explore the effect of these tactics on your Debtors days and Creditors days ratios.

Use the Performance Analysis Sheet (**Figure 9H**) to record your actions.

Check your financial projections for the effects of your exploration on profits and cashflow.

Make sure any significant differences between your ratios and your formal credit policy, caused by distortions in sales or purchases patterns, are explained in your working papers.

Stock turnover

Calculation

Inventory / Cost of sales x 360

This ratio is measured in days.

Explanation

This ratio is used to indicate the level of investment tied up in inventory. Ideally, this ratio should be minimised.

- **Minimum re-order value:** This is the value of the smallest quantity of the item that it is appropriate to order at a time from your supplier(s)
- **Opening stock:** The inventory at the start of the month (the previous month's closing inventory)
- **Used in Sales:** The quantity of items projected to be withdrawn from inventory during the month and sold – if this were valued, it would be equal to Cost of sales for that sales item
- **Purchases:** The quantity of this sales item bought during the month
- **Closing stock:** Inventory on hand at the end of the month (the next month's opening inventory).

By examining the closing stock figure for each sales item, you can identify those sales items that contribute most to the make-up of inventory. Focus your actions on these items.

Observation

Just like the Debtors days and Creditors days ratios, the Stock turnover ratio can be affected by seasonal patterns in trading.

For example, suppose a business makes half its year's sales in January, with the balance spread evenly during the rest of the year. Suppose also that deliveries from suppliers are erratic, so the business aims to have inventory to meet the coming month's sales in stock at the end of each month. Therefore, at the end of December, the business will aim to have sufficient inventory on hand to meet January's sales (half the year's turnover). Clearly the Stock Turnover ratio taken at the year-end will different from the ratio taken at some other time – even though the same inventory policy of holding inventory to meet the coming month's sales still applies.

Your own situation

The tactics available to you to improve your Stock Turnover ratio include:

- **Reducing the minimum re-order value:** This means that you will re-order more often but in smaller quantities. Your inventory at any given time will fall, but your purchasing costs may rise, since suppliers may charge you more since you are buying in smaller quantities, and delivery costs may rise since you have more deliveries

- **Buy more cheaply:** So far, we have considered only quantities held in inventory. But the inventory figure used in the ratio is made up of quantities held multiplied by the purchase prices of those quantities – reducing the purchase prices automatically reduces overall inventory.

Consider the issues here carefully before making any decisions, since it is easier to reduce inventory in than it may prove in practice. For example, the minimum re-order quantity may be set by your supplier and may not be negotiable.

Take a methodical approach to this important area. Explore the issues with your suppliers. Ask them for options. Check out the costs and benefits of each option before making any decisions.

EXERCISE 9.9: EXPLORING THE STOCK TURNOVER RATIO

Explore the effect of these tactics on your Stock Turnover ratio.

Use the Performance Analysis Sheet (**Figure 9H**) to record your actions.

Check your financial projections for the effects of your exploration on profits and cashflow.

Make sure any significant differences between your Stock Turnover ratio and your inventory policy, caused by distortions in trading patterns, are explained in your working papers.

RETURN ON INVESTMENT RATIOS

These ratios answer the question: "What return does my business provide to investors?". They measure the effectiveness of a business in using the assets it employs. Because assets require funding, any surplus assets tie up capital that could be invested elsewhere to earn additional income. Therefore, a business should aim to minimise the assets it owns.

The main return on investment ratios are:

- Net profit: Total assets (Return on Investment – ROI)
- Net profit: Capital employed (Return on Capital Employed – ROCE).

The subsidiary ratios are:

- Sales: Total assets
- Sales: Fixed assets
- Sales: Current assets.

Net profit/total assets

Calculation

Net profit / Total assets x 100

Explanation

This ratio is often known as the Return on Investment (ROI), sometimes also known as the "Primary" ratio. It shows the profit generated by all assets used in the business. Obviously, the lower the cost of the assets, the higher the ROI for the same level of profit.

Net profit/Capital employed

Calculation

Net profit / Capital employed

Explanation

This ratio measures the return on the long-term capital (owners' funds and loans) invested in the business and emphasises the goal of maximising return on investment. Again, note that the influences are profit and control of the assets that demand the capital employed.

Sales/Total assets

Calculation

Sales / Total assets

Explanation

The Sales: Total assets ratio shows the efficiency of management in generating sales from all the assets at their disposal. The determinants are effective use of productive assets such as machinery and tight control over inventory and receivables.

Sales / Fixed assets

Calculation

Sales / Fixed assets

This ratio is expressed as a number of times.

Explanation

The Sales: Fixed assets ratio is a subset of the Sales: Total assets ratio and indicates the performance in utilising the fixed assets to generate sales.

Sales/Current assets

Calculation

Sales / Current assets

This ratio is expressed as a number of times.

Explanation

The Sales: Current assets ratio is a subset of the Sales: Total assets ratio and indicates the ability of management to generate sales while controlling debtors and inventory.

Your own situation

Explore your own situation in **Exercise 9.10**.

These ratios are improved by actions that increase profit and that reduce unnecessary inventory and amounts receivable from debtors. You should also explore ways of reducing the levels of investment in fixed assets – for example, can you rent or lease rather than buy?

EXERCISE 9.10: EXPLORING THE RETURN ON INVESTMENT RATIOS

Explore the effect of these tactics (whichever you can use) on your Asset use ratios.
Use the Performance Analysis Sheet (**Figure 9H**) to record your actions.
Check your financial projections the effects of your exploration on profits and cashflow.

Gearing Ratios

These ratios answer the question: "Does the capital structure give me control of my business?". They look at the dependence of the business on outside funds and can give important indicators of loss of effective control by management to external providers of funding.

The main gearing ratios are:

- Debt: Equity ratio
- Equity: total assets.

A subsidiary ratio is the Interest cover ratio.

Debt: Equity

Calculation

$$\text{Debt} / \text{Equity} \times 100$$

or

$$\text{External loans} / \text{Owners' funds} \times 100$$

Explanation

This ratio is called the Debt: Equity ratio and examines the structure of the long term capital used in the business (the "gearing"). When this ratio reaches 100% or more, lenders have as much money invested in the business as the owners, and a business is considered to be "highly geared".

Observations

You should add the short-term element of loans (shown in Creditors on the balance sheet) to the long-term element (shown as long-term loans) to provide an accurate ratio.

It is impossible to give guidelines as to what constitutes the "right" gearing for a business. In times of low interest rates and high profit, it may suit businesses to be highly-geared but this strategy can be very risky if the business cannot pay down loans when the situation reverses and interest rates are high and profits low.

The key question is whether the current level of gearing is voluntary and determined by the business' strategy or has come about because the business is not making sufficient profits to pay loan instalments and suppliers on time. If a business is highly geared, it may be forced into a pattern of trading for cashflow and may need more drastic measures – such as a restructuring of ownership – to restore normal trading conditions.

A highly-geared company can expect more difficulty in raising further loans and its profitability may be vulnerable to an increase in interest rates. This susceptibility of a business to changes in interest rates is measured by the Interest Cover ratio.

It is unrealistic to expect banks to back a plan that is highly-geared from the start. If your projections show a high level of gearing, you will have to justify this in your plan.

Interest cover ratio

Calculation

Net profit / Interest

Explanation

The Interest Cover ratio is expressed as a number and shows the number of times the interest payable on loans is covered by profit. It allows a banker (and you) to assess the effect of an increase in interest rates on the business' profitability.

Observations

A low level of cover – say 1 to 5 – means that an increase in interest rates would significantly damage profitability. A high level of cover – say 10 or 20 – gives much greater comfort, even when interest rates are relatively stable.

The relationship between equity and dependence on external borrowing can be extended to include all external sources of funds by the Equity: Total assets ratio.

Equity: Total assets

Calculation

Equity / Total assets x 100

or

Owners' funds / Total assets x 100

Explanation

This ratio is the converse of the Debt: Equity ratio. It shows the true extent of the owners' ownership of the company's assets, since it identifies the percentage of the business' assets actually funded by the owners as opposed to all borrowing (including creditors).

Actions to improve the gearing ratios

The ultimate control over gearing in business is **profit**.

In most circumstances, a business that generates high profits will not need much in the way of borrowings. Where it does need to borrow, it will find it easy to do so.

In contrast, a business that struggles to generate adequate profits will always have cashflow difficulties, which it will attempt to alleviate by delaying payment to suppliers and, ultimately when suppliers' patience is exhausted, by seeking to raise more long-term capital to keep the business going. But, with its poor profit record, such a business will find it difficult to raise funds.

Since it may take two or three years before a start-up turns profitable, you may find it difficult to raise loans with no track record.

Get your capital structure right first time – see **Chapter 8.**

Your own situation

Explore your own situation in **Exercise 9.11**.

EXERCISE 9.11: EXPLORING THE GEARING RATIOS

Explore the effect of these tactics (whichever you can use) on your Gearing ratios.
Use the Performance Analysis Sheet (**Figure 9H**) to record your actions.
Check your financial projections for the effects of your exploration on profits and cashflow.

Summary

The key to understanding ratios is to watch for the ones that are relevant to you and your business – use **Exercise 9.3** to identify ratios that may be important to your business. You may not have any interest in the Interest cover ratio (you may have no borrowings, so it may not apply at all to your business) but you should fully understand your ratios and how they can be improved.

In general, the keys to effective financial performance are:

- Increase revenues from sales – preferably by raising effective prices
- Reduce cost of sales and overheads
- Minimise the investment in assets without compromising customer service
- Plan your capital structure and cash flows to avoid liquidity problems.

Like many worthwhile targets, these are often easier to say than to do.

Tool 4: Sensitivity Analysis

The purpose of sensitivity analysis is to highlight the areas in your business that will have the greatest impact on profit – where a lot can be achieved with very little effort.

On the positive side, it can identify where you can focus attention to get the best improvement in your business for the least effort. We want to use it in a more defensive way – to identify the areas of major susceptibility to downturn so that you can prepare contingency plans.

Depending on the structure of your business, you may find that a 1% change (upwards) in selling price or (downwards) in purchase costs has more effect on profitability than the same 1% movement in overheads. In that case, your attention is best directed to sales or purchases rather than overheads.

It is important to bear in mind that sensitivity cuts both ways. While it may not always be possible to make a upward change in an item (for example, prices) which is suggested by the analysis, you should be acutely aware of the consequences of a reversal in that, and other highly sensitive areas.

Using sensitivity analysis

Sensitivity analysis is typically used as an after-the-event check on financial projections. Investors and bankers use it to identify areas of potential weakness in your business plan -- therefore, you must perform the analysis yourself, and be able to discuss its implications, before you present your plan to them. You should include the results of your sensitivity analysis in your business plan, to show that you have done this.

Use your analysis positively by considering the results carefully for their potential to improve your plan. For example, suppose the analysis shows that purchase prices are especially sensitive (a small rise could wipe out your forecast profit), you might attempt to negotiate agreed terms for a 12 or 24-month period from start-up with your suppliers to ensure stability of prices.

In your business plan, you should always indicate (where possible) the steps that you have taken to mitigate the exposure of your business as shown by sensitivity analysis. This is important information both for you and for readers of your business plan.

TOOL 5: WHAT IF ANALYSIS

At this stage, if you have been diligent in following the **TENBizPlan** approach, you should have a plan that is thoroughly considered and analysed. Furthermore, you should have identified the areas where your business is most susceptible to downturn and should have contingency plans ready. You should now turn to What If analysis to put the final gloss on your plan.

Using What If analysis

The key items that tend to be the focus of 99% of business strategies and decisions:

- Selling prices
- Sales volumes
- Purchase prices
- Overheads
- Credit terms.

Exercise 9.12 assesses the vulnerability of your business to a combination of changes in these items. Bankers or investors reviewing your business plan will ask these questions. This is your opportunity to work out the answers – and to take corrective action, if necessary – before presenting your plan to them.

If you are using financial projection software or spreadsheets you have developed yourself, save the original files and carry out this What If analysis on copies.

Exercise 9.12: What If Exploration

What would happen to the viability of your plan if:

◊ Sales volumes dropped by 20%?
◊ Selling prices dropped by 10%?
◊ Purchase prices increased by 5%?
◊ Overheads increased by 10%?
◊ Your customers take twice as long to pay?
◊ Your suppliers insist on payment in half the time planned?

Write the results in the table below.

| | | Results | | | |
| | | **Old position** | | **New position (cumulative)** | |
	What If % change	**Net Profit for year**	**Average cash balance**	**Net Profit for year**	**Average cash balance**
Original position					
Selling prices					
Sales volume					
Purchase Price					
Overheads					
Credit Terms					

If the What If changes suggested above are not representative of the "worst case" scenario that could befall your business, change the parameters and recalculate.

In each case, consider the results of the What If analysis. Then consider the cumulative impact. Do your financial projections stand up to these changes individually, in any combination, or altogether? If not, what can you do to prevent, or reduce the impact of, these changes? How vulnerable is your business?

Include this table in your working papers. It will be useful evidence when you discuss your business plan with your financier or banker.

A reality check

Before you started this exploration process, you saved your original draft projections. Look at those projections again. Compare them to your present final projections. Where are the differences?

If you have been using the Performance Analysis Sheets (**Figure 9H**), check back on the changes you have made – if not, identify the changes by comparing the two sets of projections and their underlying input.

Make sure that, for each input in your final projections, you have evidence from your research, preferably supported by written documentation in your working papers file. If you do not have evidence, get it now. It's too easy to change your financial projections to achieve a desired result – if you cannot back up your input, your projections are meaningless.

For example, your original projections may have shown that you expected to sell 100 units of Product X at €15 each. Your final projections now show that you expect to sell 350 units of Product X at €22 each. You must be able to justify this higher level of Sales. Check now that you can.

The Funding Gap

We promised to return to this, the one blank spot on your route towards a robust and soundly-based business plan.

At this stage, you have followed a directed and systematic approach to assessing and amending your forecast financial projections. You are almost at the point where you have a robust business plan – except that you may still have a funding gap. The extent of this gap should now be very clear. Check the current position. How can it be bridged?

Unless your financial circumstances have changed since you first started to assess your forecasts, it is unlikely that you will find any comfort in either Owners' Equity or Owners' Loans. You have contributed all you have (or all you are willing to contribute – almost the same thing). You are now looking for external funding.

You should see bridging the funding gap as the final step in the process of building your financial projections. The true funding gap – the one you will look to external sources to fill – is what's left after you have explored all the options set out in this stage of finalising your financial projections.

Second, you need to be sure that your funding is appropriate to your need. Once you are sure of the size of the gap (and have tested it rigorously), you can then try different types of funding to fill it. Because the different types of funding (external equity, external loans, leases and subsidies) have different consequences from both a profit and cashflow perspective, you need to test to see which (or which combination) is best suited to your needs.

Third, once you have chosen your type of funding, you need to be able to repay it if it is a loan or lease, or justify the investment by way of increased profits if it is equity. Subsidies are often non-repayable, with a consequent beneficial effect on profits and cashflow – although they sometimes come with stringent conditions attached that can offset the benefits.

Once you are satisfied that the funding gap has been bridged, run the new forecast through the assessment process set out in this chapter. Test it thoroughly for flaws and weaknesses. When you have found and rectified them all, repeat the exercise for the other funding packages. Decide which is best and set about obtaining it.

The steps involved are:

- Review **Chapter 8** and refresh your memory about the different types of funding and their consequences on profit and cashflow
- Select types of funding to bridge your funding gap, based on their appropriateness to your needs, making sure that you have adequate funding. **Figure 8A** shows the types of funding available, and their advantages and disadvantages
- Model the different funding arrangements under consideration
- Select the most appropriate funding arrangement and seek to implement them in your financial projections, testing each funding arrangement using the tools outlined earlier in this chapter
- If a funding arrangement is not feasible, review your work and try again.

The key elements of your application for external funding (from whatever source) will be:

- The amount of funding you need
- The appropriateness of the type of funding requested
- Your ability to repay the loan or earn sufficient profits to justify an equity investment
- Security, in the case of a loan, if the business fails.

Before you submit your application, you must be sure that the amount of funding requested is the maximum needed (preferably a little more, to be on the safe side – but not too much more, so that you are not paying for funding you don't need).

REDUCING RISK

This guide sets out probably the best way of reducing the risk involved in your start-up – producing a well-thought out business plan.

The final step is to quantify the risks in your start-up. **Exercises 9.13** and **9.14** help you to do that. They show you what is at risk (your personal investment and any borrowings), how long for, and other factors that help you assess the risk.

The main risk is that things can just go wrong. You can be unlucky. You may be delayed in your planning, or your start-up, by circumstances outside your control. Identify the sources of risk, and their probability of occurrence, by completing **Exercise 9.13** and:

- The impact it will have on your business, your cashflow and your personal income

- Consider whether you can do anything to remove the risk.

EXERCISE 9.13: WHAT'S AT RISK?

What happens if:	Probability	Impact	Action to remove
◊ You get sick for a long period?			
◊ Your spouse/partner gets sick?			
◊ Your computer breaks down?			
◊ Your machinery breaks down?			
◊ Your transport breaks down?			
◊ A key supplier lets you down?			
◊ A major customer defaults on payment?			

EXERCISE 9.14: QUANTIFYING THE RISKS

E

Personal investment	€ _____
Total borrowing	€ _____
Annual cash flow	€ _____
Period personal investment is at risk	€ _____
Period borrowing is at risk	€ _____
Security given	€ _____
Time commitment over risk period	€ _____
Expected profit over risk period	€ _____
Salary required over risk period	€ _____

When you have identified the risks to which you are (or may be) exposed:

- Reconsider your business plan and look at alternatives
- Review your insurance situation (personal and business)
- Review your dependency (if any) on specific suppliers
- Review your dependency (if any) on specific customers.

First ask yourself: What is the worst that can happen?
Then prepare to accept it. Then proceed to improve on the worst.
DALE CARNEGIE

THE TENBizPlan APPROACH TO BUSINESS PLANNING

Text

In this chapter, you have created no draft text for input into your business plan document.

Evidence

File copies of all of the exercises that you have completed in **Chapter 9**, for ease of reference later.

In particular, evidence supporting changes in the input to your financial projections – for example, showing how sales can increase from 300 units monthly in the original projections to 500 units monthly in the finalised projections – will be a crucial part of your evidence supporting your business plan.

Numbers

In this chapter, you finalised your financial projections as part of the process of business planning.

Key Question

The following Key Question was posed at the start of the chapter to focus your thoughts as you read through it:

Have I the best plan possible?

In answering the Key Question, you should consider:

- Your original forecast financial projections
- Your Break-even analysis
- Your Ratio analysis
- Your Sensitivity analysis
- Your What If analysis
- Your risk reduction review
- Your final projections.

10

THE BUSINESS PLAN DOCUMENT

The Key Question for this chapter is:

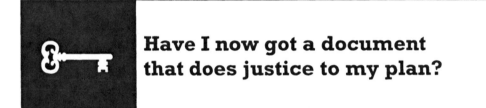

Have I now got a document that does justice to my plan?

Your business plan is almost complete – but not quite. You still need to add text and tidy up some other loose ends. You may be in a hurry to get started, now that you see the end in sight.

But don't rush just yet. Take your time through this section, which may save you from some simple, but costly, mistakes.

Output from this chapter

This chapter will show you:

- How to add the text elements to your final financial projections to form a coherent business plan
- How to combine all the elements into a document for presentation to a variety of audiences.

Your links to other chapters in this guide are now more for the purpose of refreshing your memory or checking facts and figures, rather than extending your research, since that should now be completed.

FINALISING THE TEXT

A business plan is a document that summarises these points about your business:

- Where it has come from
- Where it is now
- Where it is going in the future
- How it intends to get there
- How much money it needs to fulfil its plans
- What makes it likely to succeed
- What threats or disadvantages must be overcome on the way.

The format that uses to achieve this can be summarised as:

- **Executive Summary:** A single page that encourages further reading
- **Introduction:** Basic information about the business and the purpose of the plan
- **Promoter(s):** Who you (and your team) are and your qualifications for starting and running the business
- **Project Overview:** A description of the business, its mission statement, trends in its industry, targets, employment (actual and potential) and the legal status of the business
- **Marketing:** A summary of your marketing plan, backed up by a market overview, details of your customers, competition, products/services, price, distribution and promotion strategies and a sales forecast
- **Process & Resources:** Your products/services in more detail, how they are made/delivered, how you will make sure of quality, what staff you will need and how they will be organised
- **Finance & Funding:** A summary of your financial projections, with your funding requirement (and your own contribution) highlighted
- **Appendices:** Including financial projections – profit and loss account, balance sheet and cashflow – and any other relevant information.

This format is shown in **Appendix A**, which identifies the Exercises from which the text input should be drawn.

In **Chapters 2** through to **8**, you have already drafted and input text into the following sections of your business plan:

- Promoter(s)
- Project Overview
- Marketing
- Process.

This text may need to be revised in the light of your final financial projections, as amended in **Chapter 9**.

In addition, you have yet to write text for these sections:

- Executive Summary
- Introduction
- Finance & Funding.

However, the first step is to ensure that the text you have written so far ties in with the final financial projections – for example, that you are not saying that you expect to sell 500 units monthly when the projections show sales of 450 monthly.

Matching text and financial projections

Your starting point is **Exercise 10.1**.

EXERCISE 10.1: REVISING THE TEXT

Print out your business plan document. Then read it carefully, noting:

◊ Places where text is incomplete
◊ Places where text is missing
◊ Places where you know you have changed your financial projections in **Chapter 9**.

Where text is incomplete or missing, start writing. Go back to the appropriate chapter of **TENBizPlan**. Identify the exercise that generated the text and re-perform it. Read other parts of that chapter, as appropriate, to refresh your memory of the issues.

Where you have made changes to your financial projections in **Chapter 9,** you will have three types of changes to make in your text:

- **Changes to numbers mentioned in the text:** For example, your paragraph on Sales estimates in the "Marketing" section of your plan may read: "We expect to sell 15,000 units of Product X and 5,000 units of Product Y each month in the first year." Your final financial projections may show monthly sales of 13,500 and 5,800 units of each product. You must make sure that the text matches the numbers

- **Changes to information in the text:** For example, you may have changed the name of a product during your research and not updated your text. Do it now

- **Changes to the thrust of the text:** For example, your text may read: "Marketing expenditure on promotional activity will be highest in the initial months of trading and is expected to stabilise within the first four months." Your financial projections may show that promotional activity continues to be high relative to sales until month 8, when it begins to fall, but only slowly. Change your text to reflect this.

Use **Exercise 10.2** to help you to check that the text and financial projections match.

Exercise 10.2: Matching Text and Financial Projections

If you have made changes to the financial projections in these screens ...	Check your text here ...
Sales	Project Overview Marketing Process
Overheads	Marketing Process
Funding	Promoter(s)
Fixed Assets	Process

Adding new text

The sections that still remain to be added to your plan are:

- Executive Summary
- Introduction
- Finance & Funding.

Start with the "Introduction", where you set out the basic information that a reader will want to know about your business (see *Tailoring your business plan* later in this chapter):

- **The purpose of the plan:** Are you looking for an equity investment, a loan, or a subsidy or have you another purpose in mind?

- **Business name and contact details:** Where can the reader reach you for more information?

- **Whether the business is in operation or has yet to start:** If your business is seeking funds but has already started, you need to explain why you have gone ahead; if your business is dependent on fund-raising to start, you need to be clear about the consequences of delay

- **The business objective:** What are you aiming to achieve?

- **The product/service range:** What will you sell?

- **The promoter(s).**

Try a draft in **Exercise 10.3**.

EXERCISE 10.3: INTRODUCTION

Write your draft of the Introduction to your business plan now.

The Executive Summary:

- Persuades the reader that the idea is good, to encourage them to read on – many readers of business plans never go beyond the Executive Summary because it fails to excite them
- Summarises the company, its objectives, and why it will be successful
- Describes the products, the market, critical financial information
- Outlines what finance is required -- how much, in what form and when
- Assumes that its reader is not expert in your industry and knows nothing about your business
- Is short and easy to read.

Try a draft of your Executive Summary in **Exercise 10.4**.

Exercise 10.4: Executive Summary

Write your draft of the Executive Summary for your business plan now.

_____

Finance & Funding

A central part of the "Finance & Funding" section of your business plan is your funding request – how much money you need, in what form, when, and for what. You should explain:

- How much funding your business requires
- How much you have contributed yourself
- How much you have already secured from other sources (identify the sources)
- How much you still need to raise and what form you expect it to take (equity, debt or subsidies).

Now try a draft in **Exercise 10.5**.

_____

Exercise 10.5: Finance & Funding

Try a draft of the Finance & Funding section of your business plan now.

_____

BACKING UP YOUR PLAN WITH EVIDENCE

A key element of your business plan for anyone who reads it is the assumptions that underpin the figures. Knowing your assumptions gives the reader a basis for challenging the projections in a constructive manner.

For example, in relation to staff salaries, you might project costs of €154,000 for the first year. In arriving at this figure, based on your expected level of activity, you have assumed that:

- You will need five staff
- Two of the staff will be senior people, paid €30,000 pa each plus benefits, and incurring other costs equivalent to a further €6,000 pa each
- The other three will be paid on average €12,000 pa each, including benefits and other costs
- You will be paid €40,000, with benefits and other costs of €6,000 pa.

If you explain this, in the Employment sub-section of the "Project Overview" section, a reader of your business plan can assess whether, in their view:

- Five people (six, including you) can handle the work involved in your projected level of activity
- The balance of responsibility between the six people appears sensible
- The salary and benefits levels are reasonable, in the light of the reader's own experience and market conditions.

In your own work on the business planning process, you will have:

- Made sure that the number of staff is right (not too many, nor too few)
- Checked the planned salary and benefit levels against market surveys and other competitors.

Share the confidence that comes from thorough research with your readers.

And when they come with questions, have your answers ready in your working papers. For example, by reference to your working papers only, you should be able to show an inquiring reader:

- Your process and how you arrived at the number of jobs (**Chapter 6** and **Exercises 7.1** and **7.2**)

- How you arrived at the responsibilities of the individual jobs (Job descriptions – **Figure 7B**)
- How you arrived at the salary and benefits packages for each job (copies of salary surveys – **Exercise 7.4**).

Your working papers, into which you have been adding copies of the exercises and other information throughout your work on this programme, now comes into their own. They will give you an edge in meetings with potential investors or bankers – allowing you to provide supporting evidence for all the details in your business plan, based on your thorough research.

Your working papers also provide an essential reality check – the more your working papers can answer the questions posed in **Exercise 10.6**, which extend the Key Questions posed in each chapter, the better your chances of business success. If you cannot provide adequate evidence, you are simply "taking a chance" and must accept the statistical probability of failure.

EXERCISE 10.6: EVIDENCE & YOUR WORKING PAPERS

This is a critical "wrap-up" exercise. Readers of your business plan will ask these questions. You must have the answers — and the evidence to back them up. Do not risk presenting your business plan externally without completing this exercise first

Questions	Your answers should be in your business plan ...	... backed up by external evidence ...	... or internal evidence
Promoters Can you show that you and your colleagues are suited to this particular venture?	◊ Promoter(s)		◊ CVs ◊ Personal circumstances (Exercise 2.11) ◊ Commitment (Exercise 2.12)

Questions	Your answers should be in your business plan ...	... backed up by external evidence ...	... or internal evidence
Organisation Can you show that you have completed all the relevant legal requirements to set up your business?	◊ Project Overview, *Business status*	◊ Legal status (Exercise 4.1) ◊ Taxation (Exercise 4.3) ◊ Licensing (Exercise 4.5) ◊ Trade mark registrations and patent applications (Exercise 6.12)	
Organisation Can you show that you have an appropriate organisational structure in place to manage your business?	◊ Project Overview, *Organisation*		◊ Organisation structure (Exercise 7.1) ◊ Information systems (Exercise 6.18)
Sales Can you show where your sales will come from?	◊ Marketing, *Summary of Marketing Strategy* ◊ Marketing, *Market Overview* ◊ Marketing, Customers	◊ Market research ◊ Letters of comfort/forward orders	◊ Marketing plan (Exercise 5.48) ◊ Promotion budget (Exercise 5.47)
Sales Can you show that you will be paid as quickly as you expect?	◊ Marketing, *Price*	◊ Market research ◊ Letters of comfort/forward orders (including agreed credit terms)	◊ Credit terms (Exercise 5.32)

Questions	Your answers should be in your business plan ...	... backed up by external evidence ...	... or internal evidence
Sales Can you show that you have established the resources and activities that will be needed to generate, handle and meet your projected sales and that you have a plan to put them into place?	◊ Project Overview, *Organisation* ◊ Marketing, Summary of *Marketing Strategy* ◊ Marketing, *Place* ◊ Marketing, *Promotion* ◊ Process & Resources, *Process*	◊ Quotations for fixed assets required showing price, terms and availability ◊ Deeds or Lease to premises ◊ Evidence of compliance with planning and other legal requirements for premises ◊ External research showing availability of suitable staff	◊ Marketing Plan (Exercise 5.48) ◊ Promotion budget (Exercise 5.47) ◊ Order processing and other selling functions (Exercise 6.16) ◊ Production process (Exercise 6.5) ◊ Logistics/ Distribution (Exercise 6.8) ◊ Organisational structure (Exercise 7.1) ◊ Workload (Exercise 7.2)
Purchases Can you show that you can secure supplies when you need them and under the terms assumed?	◊ Process & Resources, *Process*	◊ Contracts or letters of comfort from suppliers specifying prices, minimum order quantities, and payment terms ◊ Supplier price lists	◊ Purchasing function (Exercise 6.2) ◊ Credit terms (Exercise 6.4)
Administration Can you show that you have a realistic plan for the administration and running of the business?	◊ Project Overview, *Organisation* ◊ Process & Resources, *Process*	◊ Quotations for services referred to in your overhead budget	◊ Administration (Exercise 6.19) ◊ Analysis of the overheads required to run the business (Exercise 6.24)

Questions	Your answers should be in your business plan ...	... backed up by external evidence ...	... or internal evidence
Funding Can you show that you have clearly calculated the funding required?	◊ Finance & Funding ◊ Financial projections		◊ Break-even analysis (Exercise 9.3) ◊ Ratio analysis (Exercises 9.4 to 9.11) ◊ Sensitivity analysis ◊ What If analysis (Exercise 9.12)
Funding Can you show that you will be able to finance your business as planned?	◊ Finance & Funding ◊ Financial projections	◊ Letters confirming external equity, loans, leases, etc, if not already paid in ◊ Valuations of any assets you are transferring to the business	◊ Financial projections ◊ "Ownership" of the financial implications of your business plan

TAILORING YOUR BUSINESS PLAN

There are a number of people who may use your business plan, and each will have their own perspective:

- **You:** To manage the business
- **Your work colleagues and/or staff:** To understand their roles in implementing it
- **Bankers:** To assess of any loan applications you make
- **Investors:** To judge the risk/return potential of your business
- **Advisers to the business:** To let them quickly "read in" to your business strategies
- **Customers or suppliers:** In certain special circumstances, you may circulate parts of the plan to important customers or suppliers, to gain their support.

As in any communication situation, the key to the style and emphasis you need is determined by:

- Why you want the person to read the document? (For example, to invest in, or loan money to, the business or for another purpose?)
- The level of detail they require to make a judgement
- The level of confidentiality needed and offered.

Always use **Exercise 10.7** before you give a copy of your business plan to a third party.

When tailoring your business plan for a particular audience, bear in mid five things:

- If you don't succeed in raising funds with your business plan, it's probably not your plan that's at fault (unless you are specifically told so) but your choice of audience
- Don't twist your plan to say what you think your reader wants to see – be true to your research
- Be objective. It is your actual performance that will be judged six, 12 or 18 months later. Plans that are not viable will be found out then, if they slip through the financier's review

- Above all, don't lie – to yourself or others
- Be patient. If your plan doesn't stack up, accept it and look for a better vehicle for the skills you have learned on this programme.

Exercise 10.7: Tailoring Your Business Plan

Who will be reading my business plan? (List organisation name, contact name and their position)

What do I want as a result of their review of my business plan?

What information does the reader need to make the decision to give me what I want?

Do I need to provide detailed information now or can I wait until a preliminary interest has been established and provide details later?

Which of the following do I need to include in the package of information?

- ◊ Covering letter?
- ◊ Summary of business plan?
- ◊ Detailed business plan?
- ◊ Financial projections?
- ◊ Analysis reports?

PRESENTING YOUR BUSINESS PLAN

If you need to raise funds, your business plan is your ticket to financing your business. It should communicate your ability to make your business a success. Therefore, when you are asked to make a presentation of your business plan, there are two critical aspects:

- The business plan itself
- You.

Of these, at this stage, the business plan is the least important. If you have worked through this guide to this point and put into practice its suggestions, you will be confident that your business plan is an accurate and well-thought out reflection of your research and your plans. If you have been asked to make a presentation on it, you know that your reader thinks the same. It's now up to you!

In presenting your business plan, you must show:

- Credibility
- Willingness to work and prepare
- Ability to sell
- A positive attitude
- Professionalism.

Remember, the only objective evidence that you can show at this stage is the thoroughness with which you have completed the business planning process.

Start your presentation with the Executive Summary from your business plan. Put it on an overhead projector slide. If it won't fit, it's too long. If you can't cut it, break it up and put it on two slides. Never use a cluttered slide. Use key words, and keep the number of words on a slide to the minimum necessary – never more than 15 or so.

Make your business idea real. Bring it to life. Show your product or a prototype. Demonstrate it. Show its features, particularly the ones that your market research has shown are important to customers. Explain why these features are important. Sell the product to your listeners.

In the early 1990s, Victor Kiam, the owner of the Remington Shaver Company, went on TV in an advertisement, saying "I bought a Remington razor. I liked it so much I bought the company". That's the effect you want to have on the audience for your business plan presentation – you want them to like the product so much that they want to buy into your company.

When you come to discuss the financial aspects of your business plan, make sure that you know every single figure, its origin, its calculation, the reason it is in the plan, the impact it has on other figures – all of this off by heart. The exploration process that you have worked in **Chapter 9** gives you an edge over most entrepreneurs in the level of detailed understanding that it has given you of your own business. Use it.

You must **BE** the business plan. If you cannot explain and defend its contents, it reflects badly on you as a potential business partner.

Prepare your presentation carefully. This is no time for a few notes scribbled out on a scrap of paper. Write out what you want to say.

Anticipate questions that you might be asked. Try and build the answers into your presentation, so that you have answered them before they can be asked.

Rehearse your presentation in front of family and friends. Ask them to be critical and to shoot as many holes in the plan as they can. Build their reactions into your presentation.

And practice, practice, practice.

If you can, visit the room in which your presentation will be made a day or so before the presentation and check (and double-check) that any equipment you need, like overhead projectors, etc., will be available.

If you are using your own technology, check, double and triple-check that it works – and bring a back-up with you anyway.

On the day, make sure you are at the appointed place in plenty of time – not too early and definitely not late.

Try to find out in advance who you will be meeting. Ask around to find out what their backgrounds are – use this information in your presentation, to tailor the presentation to them.

And then relax. It's your business. You know more about it than any investor, or banker will ever learn. You are a self-confident, capable, well-organised entrepreneur with a thoroughly-researched and well-tested business plan. Go for it!

A FINAL REALITY CHECK

Your business plan is now almost finished – except that, just like your product/service, which you researched and tested in the market – you must polish your business plan.

Perform the Reality Check in **Exercise 10.8**. Then give your plan to a few trusted friends to read through. Ask them to pick holes in it. Don't be defensive. Use their comments to improve the plan. And ALWAYS try to read your business plan from the reader's perspective.

EXERCISE 10.8: A REALITY CHECK

Before you consider your business plan complete, run these final checks:

Is the Executive Summary:
◊   Short?   ☐
◊   Relevant?   ☐
◊   To the point?   ☐
◊   Interesting?   ☐
◊   Packed with "Ooomph"?   ☐

Check the entire business plan (get help if you need it) for:
◊   **Spelling mistakes** – Use a spelling checker   ☐
◊   **Grammatical mistakes** – Use a grammar checker   ☐
◊   **Page numbering** – Are the pages all in order, with no gaps or
    duplication?   ☐
◊   **Chapter/section numbering** – Are the chapters/sections all in order,
    with no gaps or duplication?   ☐
◊   **Cross-references between sections/pages** – Are these correct? ☐
◊   **Logical structure** – Does the plan flow in a sensible order?   ☐
◊   **Jargon/use of language** – Do you introduce concepts,
    explain jargon, demystify complicated things for the reader?   ☐
◊   **Length** – Is it too long? Could you cut parts out, without damaging it?
    Could sections be moved into an Appendix?   ☐
◊   **Type size/style** – Is it easy to read? Are headings clearly identifiable? ☐
◊   **Colour** – If you are using coloured type, does it help or does it distract?
    Keep it simple.   ☐

THE TENBIZPLAN APPROACH TO BUSINESS PLANNING

Text

In this chapter, you have revised and created new text to finalise your business plan document.

Evidence

File copies of all of the exercises that you have completed in **Chapter 10**, for ease of reference later.

Numbers

In this chapter, you checked that your financial projections matched the text of your business plan.

Key Question

The following Key Question was posed at the start of the chapter to focus your thoughts as you read through it:

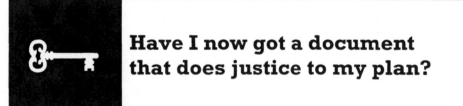

Have I now got a document that does justice to my plan?

In answering the Key Question, you should consider:

- Your financial projections
- Your business plan
- Your audience(s).

And now it's time to say "Good luck!" You have completed a rigorous and challenging programme, designed to provide you with a sound understanding of business planning and a robust business plan for your own business to prove it. Congratulations on staying the course and best wishes for success with your new business.

Stay in touch – let us know how you get on with your planning and give your feedback on **TENBizPlan** in practice through the web-site at **http://www.tenbizplan.com**.

APPENDIX A

BUSINESS PLAN

<COMPANY NAME>

<COMPANY ADDRESS, ETC>

<DATE>

Contents

EXECUTIVE SUMMARY

<Exercise 10.4, Executive Summary>

Introduction

<Exercise 10.3, Introduction>

PROMOTER(S)

Promoter(s)

<Exercise 2.13, The Promoter(s)>

PROJECT OVERVIEW

Description of business

<Exercise 3.22, Idea Definition – III>

Mission statement

<Exercise 5.16, Mission Statement>

Industry trends

<Exercise 5.10, SWOT Analysis>

Targets

<Exercise 5.14, Targets>

Organisation

<Exercise 7.1, An organisation structure for your business>

Business status

<Exercise 4.1, Legal structure>

MARKETING

Summary of marketing strategy
      <Exercise 5.48, Marketing Plan>

Market Overview
      <Exercise 5.10, SWOT Analysis>

Customers
       <Exercise 5.4, Customers>

Competitors
       <Exercise 5.9, Competitors>

Products/Services
      <Exercise 5.24, Product/Service – Summary>

Place
      <Exercise 5.30, Place – Summary>

Price
      <Exercise 5.31, Price – Summary>

Promotion

<Exercise 5.47, Promotion – Summary>

Sales forecast (including Forward orders)

<Exercise 5.49, Sales forecasts>

PROCESS

Process

<Exercise 6.5, Production process>

Quality Assurance

<Exercise 6.15, Quality>

People

<Exercise 7.2, Calculating the workload>

FINANCE & FUNDING

Summary of financial projections

Funding

<Exercise 10.5 – Finance & Funding>

Total required

Already found

Now requested

APPENDICES

Detailed projections

Other information
<Include as appropriate>

CERTIFICATION

The ICM Diploma in Entrepreneurial Business Planning

TENBizPlan is the nominated text for candidates studying for the award of the ICM Diploma in Entrepreneurial Business Planning.

ICM (The Institute of Commercial Management) is a globally-recognised UK-based educational Awarding, Assessing and Certifying Board, specialising in business and management education.

Tuition leading to ICM's examinations is provided by approved public and private sector education and training providers in more than 120 countries. More than one and a half million candidates have undertaken ICM examinations over the past 20 years.

The certification process leading to the award of the ICM Diploma in Entrepreneurial Business Planning consists of:

- Continuous assessment by the local tutor (or submission of worksheets where students follow a self-study programme)
- Multiple-choice examination to test the candidate's ability to apply the **TENBizPlan** approach to business planning, and
- A review of a business plan produced by the student.

For further information about ICM or the ICM Diploma in Entrepreneurial Business Planning, contact:

Institute of Commercial Management
PO Box 125, Christchurch, Dorset BH23 1YF
T: + 44 (0)1202 490 555 F: + 44 (0)1202 490 666
E: instcm@instcm.co.uk W: http://www.icm.ac.uk

OAK TREE PRESS

Oak Tree Press is the leading business book publisher in Ireland, with a list of over 170 titles, which provide both breadth and depth of content in the areas of social inclusion, economy, enterprise development and management.

Micro-enterprise development
Oak Tree Press has a special focus on micro-enterprise development and is increasingly a developer and publisher of enterprise training and support solutions.

It publishes a range of start-up guides:
- Successful Micro Entrepreneurship: Applying the Rules of Business
- Planning for Success: A Business Plan Workbook for Start-ups
- Starting Your Own Business: A Workbook
- Starting a Business in Ireland

as well as pre-start-up publications:
- Look Before You Leap: A Guide to Self-Employment
- Fire in the Belly: An Exploration of the Entrepreneurial Spirit

and the website, http://www.startingabusinessinireland.com.

It is currently developing a range of growth-focused publications.

In addition, Oak Tree Press has developed SPOTcheck, a web-based business assessment tool for:
- Entrepreneurs to 'rate' their businesses on a self-assessment basis
- Business advisers to structure their analysis of a client company.

SPOTcheck:

- Provides an analytical framework against which owner/managers and business advisers can make a structured assessment of a business' potential for growth
- Provides a basis for prescribing the appropriate business development interventions for the business
- Tracks progress made between two or more SPOTcheck assessments at different times
- Compares the assessment against the averages for similar types of business (benchmarking).

SPOTcheck will shortly be available on-line at www.spotcheckonline.com.

Train the Trainers/Consultancy

Oak Tree Press has worked extensively in training trainers and as consultants in developing strategic and business plans for both the private and public sector as well as social economy business planning.

Oak Tree Press has developed a methodology, *Individual Career Path Planning & Self-Employment*, for the long-term unemployed, which is used by the Local Employment Services across Ireland, and is under consideration in the UK as a methodology for training business advisers by SFEDI.

Customised Content and Solutions

Much of Oak Tree Press' enterprise training and support solutions are available for customisation to local situations and needs.

For further information, contact:

Ron Immink or Brian O'Kane
Oak Tree Press
19 Rutland Street, Cork, Ireland
T: + 353 21 431 3855 F: + 353 21 431 3496
E: info@oaktreepress.com

Printed in the United Kingdom by
Lightning Source UK Ltd., Milton Keynes
141084UK00001B/72/A

9 781860 762444